KNOWING CHRISTIANITY

THE OLD TESTAMENT

KNOWING CHRISTIANITY

A series edited by Dr. William Neil to provide for thinking laymen a solid but non-technical presentation of what the Christian religion is and what it has to say in this atomic age.

The first titles are:

THE CHRISTIAN FAITH
THE OLD TESTAMENT

KNOWING CHRISTIANITY

The
Old Testament

by

THE REV.
ROBERT DAVIDSON
M.A., B.D.
University of St. Andrews

J. B. LIPPINCOTT COMPANY
Philadelphia and New York

2.07

Copyright © 1964 by Robert Davidson

Printed in the United States of America. Library
of Congress Catalog Card Number: 64-23472

TO

ST. MARY'S COLLEGE,

UNIVERSITY OF ST. ANDREWS

ABBREVIATIONS

A.V.   Authorised Version of the Bible 1611

R.V.   Revised Version 1881

R.S.V.   Revised Standard Version 1952

A.N.E.T.   *Ancient Near Eastern Texts relating to the Old Testament,* ed. J. B. Pritchard (Princeton University Press) 1950

D.O.T.T.   *Documents from Old Testament Times,* ed. D. Winton Thomas (Thomas Nelson and Sons Ltd.) 1958

EDITOR'S PREFACE

To judge by the unending flow of religious literature from the various publishing houses there is an increasingly large demand on the part of ordinary intelligent people to know more about what Christianity has to say. This series is designed to help to meet this need and to cater for just this kind of people.

It assumes that there is a growing body of readers, both inside and outside the Church, who are prepared to give serious attention to the nature and claims of the Christian faith, and who expect to be given by theologians authoritative and up-to-date answers to the kind of questions thinking people want to ask.

More and more it becomes clear that we are unlikely to get any answers that will satisfy the deepest needs of the human spirit from any other quarter. Present-day science and philosophy give us little help on the ultimate questions of human destiny. Social, political and educational panaceas leave most of us unpersuaded. If we are not to end our quest for the truth about ourselves and the world we live in in cynicism and disillusionment where else can we turn but to religion?

Too often in the past two thousand years the worst advertisement for Christianity has been its supporters and advocates. Yet alone of all the great world religions it has shown that a faith which was oriental in origin could be transplanted into the western world and from there strike root again in the east. The present identification of Christianity in the minds of Asians and Africans with European culture and western capitalism or imperialism is a passing phase. To say that no other religion has the same potentialities as a world-wide faith for everyman is neither to denigrate the God-given truth in Buddhism, Islam and the rest, nor to say that at this stage

Christianity as generally practised and understood in the west presents much more than a caricature of its purpose.

Perhaps the best corrective to hasty judgement is to measure these two thousand years against the untold millions of years of man's development. Organised Christianity is still in its infancy, as is the mind of man as he seeks to grapple with truths that could only come to him by revelation. The half has not yet been told and the full implications for human thought and action of the coming of God in Christ have as yet been only dimly grasped by most of us.

It is as a contribution to a deeper understanding of the mystery that surrounds us that this series is offered. The early volumes deal, as is only right, with fundamental issues — the historical impact of Christianity upon mankind based on its Jewish origins and establishing itself in the wider world; the essence of the Christian faith and the character of Christian behaviour. Later volumes in the series will deal with various aspects of Christian thought and practice in relation to human life in all its variety and with its perennial problems.

The intention is to build up over the years a library which under the general title of 'Knowing Christianity' will provide for thinking laymen a solid but non-technical presentation of what the Christian religion is and what it has to say in this atomic age.

The writers invited to contribute to this series are not only experts in their own fields but are all men who are deeply concerned that the gulf should be bridged between the specialised studies of the theologian and the untheologically minded average reader who nevertheless wants to know what theology has to say. I am sure that I speak in the name of all my colleagues in this venture when I express the hope that this series will do much to bridge the gap.

WILLIAM NEIL

The University,
Nottingham

CONTENTS

		Page
Editor's Preface		7
Author's Preface		10

Chapter

I.	INTRODUCING THE OLD TESTAMENT	11
II.	GOD AND HISTORY	21
III.	THE GOD OF THE COVENANT	40
IV.	GOD AND THE COMMUNITY —THE RESPONSIBLE SOCIETY	59
V.	THE PEOPLE OF GOD —FAILURE AND CHALLENGE	81
VI.	GOD AND WORSHIP	103
VII.	GOD IN THE PSALMS	125
VIII.	GOD AND WISDOM	142
IX.	GOD AND THE TROUBLED MIND	157
X.	GOD AND MAN	186
XI.	GOD AND THE FUTURE	210
	EPILOGUE	231
	Bibliography	233
	Index	234

9

AUTHOR'S PREFACE

THIS is not an 'introduction' to the Old Testament in the accepted sense of that word. Little, perhaps too little, has been said about the problems of the date, authorship and form of the various books in the Old Testament. Rather is it an extended essay, the primary interest of which lies in that deep unity of thought concerning God and man which is to be found amid the rich diversity of the books of the Old Testament. My indebtedness to Old Testament scholars, both Protestant and Roman Catholic, will be evident to anyone acquainted with recent work in the Old Testament field. It is a pleasure, as a Protestant, to acknowledge my particular indebtedness to the masterly survey of Israel's life and culture in Père Roland de Vaux's *Ancient Israel*.

I am more immediately and personally indebted to my father-in-law, Rev. R. A. Robertson, M.A. of Nicolson Street Church, Edinburgh and to one of my students, Miss M. McCallum, M.A., both of whom read the manuscript, rid it of many errors and made numerous helpful suggestions. Miss McCallum also undertook the laborious task of compiling the Indices. My wife, Elizabeth, somehow found the time and the patience to do the task for which she alone is competent, the converting of my erratic handwriting into typescript. The editor of the series, Dr. William Neil, first suggested that I should contribute this volume and has throughout given me the benefit of his helpful criticism and advice.

The dedication is an acknowledgement of the debt I owe to the College in which, as a student, my interest in the Old Testament was first kindled, and within the fellowship of whose staff and students I am now privileged to teach.

R.D.

Chapter One

INTRODUCING THE OLD TESTAMENT

"READING the Old Testament is like eating a large crab; it turns out to be mostly shell with very little meat in it."[1] Many people today would agree with this remark of a Chinese pastor. Is it worth running the risk of spiritual indigestion for the sake of that "very little meat", particularly if that meat can be found elsewhere in a more readily palatable form?

Why should we concern ourselves with long outdated pictures of the universe and how it came into being (e.g., Gen. 1), when modern scientific research is revealing to us a universe breathtaking in its immensity and complexity? Why should we pretend to find God in stories of primitive savagery and violence repellent to the moral sensitivity of a modern humanist (e.g. Judges 20; Josh. 10; 1 Sam. 15) when a verdict has already been given against such stories in the Bible itself by One who said "God is love" (John 3.16)? Why in the age of space research and nuclear strategy should we interest ourselves in a book which is concerned with the fortunes of a small, politically insignificant nation in the Ancient Near East? Why, indeed, should we want to know the Old Testament unless we have a scholarly axe to grind or are touched by a certain brand of religious fanaticism?

It is well to be reminded that bewilderment about the Old Testament and resistance to it are nothing new. In the second century A.D. a Christian heretic called Marcion was convinced that the God of the Old Testament was not the God of Jesus. It is not without significance, however, that having decided to discard the Old Testament, he found the New Testament as accepted by the Church something of a problem. Of the

[1] Quoted by G. E. Phillips, *The Old Testament in the World Church*, p. 22.

11

Gospels, he concluded that only the Gospel of Luke, and that in a carefully edited form, was free from the taint of Old Testament heresy. For the rest, only a few of Paul's letters won their way into Marcion's New Testament. In this respect, Marcion was more honest than some of his latter day followers in the Church. He knew that the New Testament, as it stands, cannot be separated from the Old Testament.

Some fifty years earlier than Marcion, when the Jewish communities in the Graeco-Roman world were the object of a good deal of suspicion and misunderstanding, a Jewish writer, Flavius Josephus, endeavoured to dispel prejudice by giving an account of the beliefs and practices of the Jewish community and of the book upon which its life was built. While admitting that the Jews can hardly compare with the Greeks in the rich diversity of their literature, Josephus claims that the Jews have nothing of which to be ashamed. "For we do not possess one thousand books inconsistent with one another and self-contradictory, but only twenty-two books, rightly accredited, which contain the records of all time."[1]

This statement of Josephus may well serve us as a convenient general introduction to the Old Testament since it focuses attention upon two things which we must never forget in any fruitful approach to the Old Testament.

1. The Old Testament is not a book; it is a collection of books, indeed a library of books in which we shall find examples of the many-sided literary output of a people.

Here is *history*, e.g., Genesis 12 ff., Exodus, Joshua, Judges, Samuel, Kings, Ezra, Nehemiah, Chronicles, history written, as we shall see, from a peculiar standpoint; none the less these books contain the records of a nation's historical pilgrimage. While we may not be as certain as Josephus that there are no inconsistencies or self-contradictions in such books, they do enable us to write with a fair degree of confidence the history of the Hebrew people in Old Testament times.

[1] Josephus, *Against Apion*, I.8.

12

Here is *poetry*; traditional ballads preserving the memory of notable tribal victories, e.g., the Song of Deborah (Judges 5); elegiac poetry witnessing to both personal (2 Sam. 1.17-27) and national (Lamentations) grief and tragedy; a collection of love lyrics of unsurpassed emotional intensity (Song of Songs); a profound dramatic poem wrestling with the mystery of seemingly undeserved suffering in God's world (Job).

Here is the crystallised *folk wisdom* of a nation; the keen observations on life and human conduct of pious sages and troubled sceptics (Proverbs and Ecclesiastes).

Here are *short stories* (Ruth, Jonah, Esther).

Here is a *tract for the times,* the manifesto of a resistance movement which, in an age of persecution, produced many a martyr for the Jewish faith (Daniel).

Here are the *oracles of the prophets*, a series of books to which it is difficult to find any real parallel in literature (Isaiah, Jeremiah, Ezekiel and the twelve shorter prophetic books).

The Old Testament is the literary legacy of a people, richly varied and worthy of our attention in its own right as literature. We may seek to know the Old Testament solely as literature preserving for us an episode of human culture which, on any reckoning, has exercised a creative influence on all subsequent history.[1]

2. The Old Testament as we possess it, however, is a carefully selected library of books, and the principle of selection was not mere literary excellence but the fact that, in the words of Josephus, these books were "rightly accredited" or as one manuscript tradition says "rightly accredited as divine". The literary output of the Hebrew people in Old Testament times may have been much more extensive than we imagine. The Old Testament itself provides us with ample evidence for the existence of books now irretrievably lost—a collection of Hebrew lyric poems entitled 'The Book of Yashar' (2 Sam. 1.18); another collection of poems entitled 'Laments' (2

[1] cf. the stimulating approach to the Old Testament on this level by W. A. Irwin in *The Old Testament, Keystone of Human Culture.*

Chron. 35.25) and the various historical sources cited by the editors of the Book of Kings (cf. 2 Kings 14.28; 15.11, etc.). From this literature of a people the books which now stand in the Old Testament were preserved and cherished because it was believed that they witnessed to the dealings of God with the Hebrew people. The Old Testament is a Canon of Sacred Scriptures, a collection of writings now regarded as normative for faith and conduct by both Jews and Christians.

We are still far from certain as to the details of how this Canon of Sacred Scripture came into being, but at least we may note several significant signposts on the way to our present Old Testament.

According to the narrative in 2 Kings 22, while certain necessary repair work was being carried out in the temple at Jerusalem, there was discovered "the book of the law". The year is 621 B.C. This "book of the law", which on good grounds we may equate with the bulk of our present Book of Deuteronomy, was regarded by its discoverers as authoritative since it was made the basis of a national reformation which had the backing both of the king and the religious authorities. "It is written" has become the court of appeal in matters of faith. A decisive step has been taken along the path which leads to the Bible.

The next signpost again points us to the city of Jerusalem, but some two hundred years later and in very different conditions. We stand now on the other side of one of the great watersheds in Hebrew life and faith, the exile in Babylon. During that exile, many of the religious leaders of the community, notably the priests, pondering upon the meaning of the decline and fall of the Hebrew nation, collected and gave new shape to the nation's traditions. Once the opportunity to return to Jerusalem came, those who were courageous enough to face the challenge and hazards of reconstruction found themselves confronted with many grave difficulties. When Ezra 'the priest, the scribe' came from Babylon to Jerusalem, probably in the year 397 B.C., he found a community whose morale was at a low ebb. Summoning a public meeting in the square before the Water Gate, Ezra, according to the narrative in Neh. 8, mounted a wooden pulpit and read to the people out of "the book of the law of Moses which the LORD had given to Israel" (Neh. 8.1). What exactly this book was is difficult to determine, but it may not have been very different from the Pentateuch, the five books which stand at the head of our Old Testament, Genesis, Exodus, Leviticus, Numbers and Deuteronomy, that part of the Old Testament which was to be henceforth supremely authoritative for the Jewish people.

There is a further point of interest in the narrative of Neh. 8 for the story of the growth of the Old Testament. When Ezra read from what must have been a scroll written in Hebrew, certain Levites

> "helped the people to understand the law . . . they read from the book, from the law of God and interpreted it; they gave the meaning so that the people understood what was being read" (8.7-8).

The book was being read by Ezra in a language which many of them no longer understood, Aramaic having replaced Hebrew as the everyday language in Palestine. This rendering of the Old Testament into the vernacular of the day was the origin of the various early translations of the Old Testament, 'Targums' as they are called from an Aramaic word meaning 'to translate'. Aramaic Targums arose to meet the needs not only of Palestinian Jews, but of eastern Jewish communities such as that in Babylon. The most famous of all such Targums, however, is the Septuagint, the 'Seventy', so-called because, according to tradition, it was the work of seventy, or to be more precise, seventy-two Jewish scholars. This Greek translation, or rather, series of translations was produced from the second century B.C. onwards to meet the needs of Greek-speaking Jews in Egypt. It was to achieve lasting fame as the Bible of the Greek-speaking Christian church. Because it became the possession of the Christian church and some of its readings were used somewhat rashly by Christians in controversy with Jews, the Septuagint was disowned by the Jews who in the course of the second century A.D. produced their own more exact and literal translations of the Hebrew Old Testament.

In the prologue to the Book of Ecclesiasticus or the Wisdom of Ben Sirach, one of the books now found in the Apocrypha, Ben Sirach's grandson writing about 130 B.C. tells how his worthy ancestor applied himself diligently to "the reading of the law and the prophets and the other books of our fathers". This is our earliest evidence for what was to become the classical threefold division of the Old Testament in Jewish tradition, a division which explains the order of the books in the Hebrew Old Testament.

(a) *The Law*—the first five books of the Old Testament, Genesis to Deuteronomy. 'Law' is a very inadequate translation of the Hebrew word *Torah*. 'Revelation' is perhaps nearer the mark, for Genesis to Deuteronomy contain not only 'law' in the sense of rules or commandments, but also stories of the origin of the universe and man, and the traditional account of the early history of the Hebrew people before the time of their settlement in Canaan, their 'land of promise'. *Torah* means all the knowledge of God, his purposes and his instruction which came to Israel, according to tradition, through the dynamic, prophetic leadership of Moses. For the Jew, this Torah is the supreme rule of faith, all else in the Old Testament is but commentary upon it. A reading from Torah is obligatory at every service in the synagogue.

Tradition made Moses the author of Torah, but scholarship has long been dissatisfied with this view. Much of the material within Torah probably circulated for centuries in Israel on the lips of tribal bards and elders before ever it was written down. Moreover, there are many indications that Torah as we know it has been gradually built up from different sources, four at least, according to the documentary theory which in its classical form we owe to the great nineteenth century German Old Testament scholar, J. Wellhausen. The earliest

16

of these sources, probably tenth century B.C. is known as the 'J' source from the fact that it consistently uses the name YHWH (JHWH)[1] for God and probably emanates from the southern kingdom of Judah. Perhaps a century later there came from the northern kingdom of Israel or Ephraim the 'E' source using the name *'elohim* for God. These northern 'E' and southern 'J' traditions were probably dovetailed together some time after the fall of the northern kingdom in 721 B.C. The third source, 'D', most of our present book of Deuteronomy, was the basis of the religious reformation of 621 B.C. Finally the different sources were edited and set within the framework of a post-exilic (*circa* fifth century B.C.) priestly account of the traditions of Israel, i.e., 'P'.[2] Even if this documentary theory should stand the test of time—and it is under fire, though as yet inconclusive fire from many quarters—it is wise to remember that the dates assigned to the different sources tell us very little about the antiquity of the material in these sources. Even if 'P' is a post-exilic compilation of priestly traditions, these traditions preserve much very old material, some of it, especially in cultic matters, demonstrably older than some of the material in the 'J' source. Perhaps the sources are best described as the work of "selective artists who, each in his own time and situation, set down the living tradition as they experience it, and as it interprets the situation they face".[3]

[1] YHWH, R.V. and R.S.V. 'the LORD', is now usually written Yahweh which probably is as near as we can get to the original pronunciation. A.V. Jehovah is a curious word, not in common use until the 16th century A.D., a mixture of the consonants of the word YHWH and the vowels of the Hebrew *'adonai* lord or master. Through excessive reverence for the mysterious divine name YHWH, Jews from the time of the exile always said *'adonai*, lord, where the Old Testament text read YHWH. For convenience, we shall retain the R.S.V. rendering 'the LORD' in quotations from the Old Testament.

[2] For an analysis of the different sources and a judicious survey of the problems raised by this approach to Torah, cf. G. W. Anderson, *A Critical Introduction to the Old Testament*, pp. 23 ff.

[3] J. C. Rylaarsdam in *Interpreter's Bible*, Vol. I, p. 853.

(b) *The Prophets.* This section of the Old Testament is divided traditionally into two parts.

(i) *The former prophets,* i.e., the books of Joshua, Judges, Samuel and Kings, books which seem superficially to be merely historical narratives. Jewish tradition, however, with a deeper insight, knew that in these books we are confronted with an interpretation of Israel's history to which we may most fitly apply the title 'prophetic'.

(ii) *The latter prophets,* i.e., the three major prophetic books, Isaiah, Ezekiel and Jeremiah, and the scroll containing the twelve minor or shorter prophetic books, Hosea, Joel, Amos, Obadiah, Jonah, Micah, Nahum, Habakkuk, Zephaniah, Haggai, Zechariah, Malachi. Essentially these prophetic books were considered to provide a commentary on and an interpretation of Torah. The prophets were not professional writers. The books attributed to them consist in the main of collections of brief dramatic utterances, 'oracles', supplemented by a certain amount of biographical or autobiographical information. The earliest collection is that attributed to Amos *circa* 750 B.C. Such oracles were probably preserved at first in the memory of groups of disciples who would not hesitate to adapt their master's words to the circumstances of their own day. It is often difficult to decide whether we are dealing with the words of the prophet whose name appears in the title of a book, or with the teaching of his followers. Each book, however, does preserve a prophetic tradition which stems ultimately from a creative prophetic personality.[1]

(c) *The Writings.* The books in this third section of the Hebrew Old Testament, which never achieved in Jewish circles the measure of authority granted to Torah or even the commentary on Torah provided by the prophets, were called simply the 'Writings', or to give them their more familiar Greek title, the *Hagiographa*, the sacred writings. The Writings are a very varied collection of books, Psalms, Proverbs, Job,

[1] cf. G. W. Anderson *op. cit.,* pp. 97 ff.

the five *Megilloth* or festival scrolls—so called because the five books in this scroll are associated with five of the great occasions in the Jewish religious year, Ruth with the harvest festival of Weeks or Ingathering, Song of Songs with Passover, Ecclesiastes with the Feast of Tabernacles, Lamentations with the annual commemoration of the destruction of Jerusalem, Esther with the feast of Purim—Daniel, Ezra, Nehemiah and Chronicles.

When Jerusalem was sacked and pillaged by the Roman legions in A.D. 70 the Jewish state ceased to exist—only in our own day have we witnessed its reconstitution. The future of the Jewish people, lacking any national homeland, lay in their religion and in the book which enshrined it. It now became vitally important, particularly in view of the emergence of a powerful heretical Jewish sect, Christianity, that the foundation documents of the Jewish faith should be clearly defined. Towards the end of the first century A.D. a council of Jewish rabbis met at the small Palestinian resort of Jamnia. This council can hardly be said to have decided which books were to be regarded as canonical. In most cases tradition had already given its verdict. There could be no dispute concerning Torah and the Prophets. Misgivings were however still felt in certain circles about some of the Writings, in particular Ecclesiastes, Song of Songs and Esther. The rabbis, however, considered Ecclesiastes, Song of Songs and Esther as acceptable and worthy of inclusion among the sacred writings and the Hebrew canon of the Old Testament was finally fixed.

Outside Palestine, among the Jewish communities scattered throughout the Graeco-Roman world and particularly in Egypt, there seems to have been a much less stringent attitude to what was acceptable as sacred scripture. The Septuagint contains many books not found in the Hebrew Old Testament —further historical material, 1 Esdras, 1-iv Maccabees; additions to certain Hebrew books, e.g., to Jeremiah there is attached Baruch and the Epistle of Jeremiah, to Daniel the stories of Susannah and Bel and the Dragon; short stories such as Judith and Tobit; two books belonging to the wisdom tradition, Ecclesiasticus and the Wisdom of Solomon; and a collection of eighteen psalms known as the Psalms of Solomon. Since the Reformation, the Protestant churches have in the main adhered to the Palestinian Hebrew canon of the Old Testament, while the Roman Catholic church has continued to accept the wider canon of the Old Testament as it is to be found in the Septuagint tradition.

If we are to know the Old Testament aright, we must take with equal seriousness both the fact that it is the literature of a people and the fact that it is a canon of sacred scripture. It is one of the merits of modern biblical scholarship that it does enable us to handle the Old Testament as the literature of a people, to ask concerning each and every book in it the kind of question that we are entitled to ask of any book. What kind of book is this? Is it poetry or prose, history or a novel? Is Genesis I to be approached as a scientific or pseudo-scientific document, or is it a hymn? Is Daniel an example of sixth century B.C. crystal gazing in which by some supernatural vision a man saw foreshadowed the events of the twentieth or twenty-first century after Christ, or is it an underground manifesto written in the blood of the martyrs of the second century B.C. with a message in the first instance for that and for every age of persecution? Such questions are important and the way in which we answer them will control our understanding of the Old Testament. They are however, only so many steps on the way to our asking the ultimately important question. What has the Old Testament, in all the rich diversity of its books, to say to us about the meaning of life, about God and man? In the Old Testament we are faced with a particular witness to God and his relationship to the world, with a faith which challenges and offends, answers certain questions and leads us to the point of asking others. The Old Testament is worth knowing only if this witness and this faith have continuing relevance for our life.

Chapter Two

GOD AND HISTORY

THE Hebrews made their entry upon the stage of the Ancient Near East at a comparatively late date. Mesopotamia had already witnessed the rise and fall of many city states remarkable both for their political institutions and for their advanced culture; in Egypt, the pyramids had for centuries been weathered by the wind and sand of the desert; in Palestine itself there had been settled community life in and around Jericho for over four thousand years before Old Testament history begins. Stories which for centuries were part of the living tradition of the people before ever they were put into writing, tell how Abraham, the pilgrim father of the Hebrew race, migrated with his family westwards from Mesopotamia to the highlands of Canaan some time in the first half of the second millennium B.C. Famine drove the descendants of Abraham to seek the hospitality of Egypt, until hospitality turned into enslavement. Early in the thirteenth century B.C. the Hebrew slaves made good their escape into the desert under the dynamic leadership of Moses. There in the desert a decisive religious experience and years of hardship moulded them into a community disciplined enough to win and to retain a foothold in Canaan. For a time they were content to form, with related groups, a loose-knit tribal federation, acknowledging a common religious loyalty, acting together in the hour of crisis, but without any permanent central political authority. Sustained pressure, however, from intruders into the Ancient Near East, the Philistines, who seem to have come across the Mediterranean from somewhere north of the Balkans, forced the Hebrew tribes to seek a more stable and effective political organisation.[1] By popular consent Saul became the first king of the Hebrews. David, his successor (1000-961 B.C.) finally crushed the Philistine threat, gave his kingdom a new capital city at Jerusalem, and made the Hebrews a power to be reckoned with among the states of the Ancient Near East. His son Solomon (961-922 B.C.) by skilful diplomacy and vigorous commercial enterprise enriched his kingdom, but through his extravagant tastes, heavy taxation and a policy of forced labour, alienated the affections of his people. On his death, the kingdom split into two, the northern kingdom of Israel (or Ephraim) and the southern kingdom of Judah. The northern kingdom, standing astride one of the main trade routes of the Ancient Near East, was inevitably deeply involved in the power politics of the day. Like many another small state, Israel was swept away by the ruthless imperialism of Assyria in 721 B.C. The southern kingdom of Judah, little more than a mountain fastness centring upon Jerusalem, survived by dint of neutrality and subservience until 586 B.C. when the Babylonian armies destroyed Jerusalem. When Babylon in turn fell to Cyrus (539 B.C.) exiled Jews were permitted to return to Jerusalem to rebuild their ruined homeland. During the fifth and fourth centuries B.C. reconstruction, both physical and spiritual, proceeded under the benevolent eye of the Persian authorities.

When Alexander the Great struck east in 334 B.C., he came not solely as a military genius but as an apostle of the Greek way of life. That the Greeks had much that was attractive to offer the Jews soon became apparent but when an attempt was made in the interests of cultural and religious uniformity to proscribe the Jewish faith, Judah was soon in open revolt. Under the leadership of the Maccabees, the Jews won a century of independence (164-63 B.C.), an ill-starred century besmirched by the folly of ambitious and unscrupulous Jewish

[1] These Philistines, who bequeathed to the country its name, Palestine, were strongly established in city states on the coastal plain of Canaan by the early twelfth century B.C. after abortive attempts to gain a footing in Egypt.

monarchs. In 63 B.C. Rome intervened to turn a domestic quarrel to her own advantage. There followed a period of ever increasing resentment against Rome culminating in the Jewish war of A.D. 66-70 which, apart from an abortive uprising in the thirties of the second century, effectively sealed the political fate of the Jewish nation.

This could well be the story of many another small nation — the struggle for national unity and independence, the brief period of political greatness, the bitter discovery that in the long run such a nation was but an insignificant pawn in the game of international power politics. It could be, but is it?

Among the peoples of the Ancient Near East, the Hebrews had a unique sense of history. Egyptian Pharaohs carefully recorded their successful campaigns and victories. There are lists of kings and expedition records from Assyrian and Babylonian sources. Nothing, however, remotely resembles what we find in Genesis 12 ff to 2 Kings, a continuous historical narrative unfolding the fortunes of a people from its beginning in Abraham to the hour of national crisis, the fall of Jerusalem in 586 B.C., a period of over a thousand years. This change from chronicling the names of kings and preserving records of the personal egotism of monarchs to the writing of history can only take place where there is a conviction that running through events and linking them meaningfully to one another there is some ultimate purpose. The brief sketch which we have given of Hebrew history is false precisely because it has omitted the one thing that led to the writing of that history, the belief that all events were God-centred, and that everything that happened in the life of the Hebrew people was a revelation of the character and purposes of God. We may best see what this means by taking a series of samples from different periods of Old Testament history.

1. Hebrew tradition (e.g., Gen. 11.28, 31; 15.7; Neh. 9.7) traced the coming of their pilgrim father Abraham from Mesopotamia. If this reflects a genuine historical tradition, we

naturally want to ask many questions. Why did Abraham and his family move west to Canaan? What political, social or economic factors prompted their migration? Were they driven from their homes by invasion or land-hunger, or was Abraham perhaps the victim of a wanderlust? But consider the way in which a Hebrew writer of the time of David or Solomon reports the incident:

> Now the LORD said to Abram, "Go from your country and your kindred and your father's house to the land that I will show you. And I will make of you a great nation, and I will bless you, and make your name great, so that you will be a blessing. I will bless those who bless you, and him who curses you I will curse; and by you all the families of the earth will bless themselves." So Abram went as the LORD had told him. (Gen. 12.1-4a.)

Here is an interpretation of events in terms of God. The initiative comes from God. He 'calls' Abraham; he calls him with a purpose, the creation of a great nation whose destiny is linked to that of 'all the families of the earth'.

2. There is little doubt that the pivotal event in all Hebrew history was the escape of certain Hebrews, under the leadership of Moses, from enslavement in Egypt. Not only is the event recorded at length in Exodus 1-15, but it is the theme of early Hebrew confessions of faith and liturgies.[1] When a Hebrew dedicated the first fruits of harvest to God at a temple, he accompanied his act with the following confession of faith:

> "The Egyptians treated us harshly, and afflicted us, and laid upon us hard bondage. Then we cried to the LORD the God of our fathers, and the LORD heard our voice, and saw our affliction, our toil and our oppression; and the LORD brought us out of Egypt with a mighty hand and an outstretched arm, with great terror, with signs and wonders" (Deut. 26.6-8; cf. Joshua 24.5-7).

Prophets and Psalmists recall this event:

[1] It is indeed probable that the narrative of Ex. 1-15 took shape as the liturgy for the feast of the Passover.

"Also I brought you up out of the land of Egypt" (Amos 2.10).

"When Israel was a child, I loved him,
and out of Egypt I called my son" (Hos. 11.1).

(cf. Mic. 6.4; Jer. 2.2-7; Ezek. 20.5-6; Ps. 66.6; 78.18-53; 136.10-11).

At the head of that summary of rules for life under the kingship of God which we call the Ten Commandments, there stands this declaration,

"I am the LORD your God, who brought you out of the land of Egypt, out of the house of bondage" (Exod. 20.2; Deut. 5.6).

This was not a world-shaking event by our normal standards of judgement. Even if the Egyptians had been given to recording national setbacks—which they were not—they would hardly have done more than note the regrettable departure of a source of cheap slave labour. It is clear, however, that the Old Testament does not speak of this incident as a 'departure' or even as an escape story. To the Old Testament it is an event in which *God delivered* these slaves, setting them free to become a nation, to become his people. It is a mighty act of God. Why is it so described in the Old Testament? Is it because the event in itself was so 'supernatural' that no other interpretation was possible? A quick reading of the Exodus narrative with its stories of 'signs' worked by Moses in Pharaoh's presence, the ten plagues, the pillar of cloud by day and fire by night, the Hebrews crossing the sea dry shod while the pursuing Egyptian chariotry are drowned, may suggest this. We must remember, however, that the story as it comes to us in Exodus 1-15 is the story as it has been told and retold for centuries by believing people. It would hardly be surprising if the miraculous element in it had been heightened. Furthermore, it is a story which has circulated among the Hebrews in several different versions, elements from 'J', 'E' and 'P' being dovetailed together in the narrative as we know it. Of the ten plagues, not all of which appear in any one version, nine are closely linked to seasonal conditions in the Nile valley, though the same can hardly be said for the tenth plague which finally drove Pharaoh to release the slaves.

> At midnight the LORD smote all the first-born in the land of Egypt, from the first-born of Pharaoh who sat on his throne to the first-born of the captive who was in the dungeon, and all the first-born of the cattle (Exod. 12.29).

Likewise the crossing of the Reed or Papyrus Sea described in Exod. 14.21-29 has been given a 'natural' interpretation in terms of wind, tide and sand.[1] We may never be certain as to some of the details of this event. It is not only *what* happened that is important, but the *interpretation* of what happened, and the interpretation is rooted in a personal encounter between Moses and God. According to the narrative, Moses, a Hebrew child brought up in the Egyptian court, was forced as a young man to flee to Midian because of his impulsive murder of an Egyptian slave master. There in the desert of Midian his curiosity was roused by a bush which seemed to be aflame, yet was not burned. When God spoke to Moses out of the bush, commanding him to be the agent of his people's deliverance from enslavement, Moses searched for excuses to absolve himself from a responsibility he did not wish to face. Among his excuses is this:

> "If I come to the people of Israel and say to them, 'The God of your fathers has sent me to you,' and they ask me, 'What is his name?' what shall I say to them?" God said to Moses, "I AM WHO I AM." And he said, "Say this to the people of Israel, 'I AM has sent me to you'." God also said to Moses, "Say this to the people of Israel, 'The LORD, the God of your fathers, the God of Abraham, the God of Isaac, and the God of Jacob has sent me to you'." (Exod. 3.13b-15).

To understand this passage aright, we must realise the significance of a name to Ancient Near Eastern society. To be able to name someone is to know the character of that person, and to have power over him for good or ill. To ask the name of God is equivalent to asking to be let into the

[1] e.g. W. J. Phythian-Adams, *The Call of Israel*, pp. 160 ff.

26

secret of his character and power. The answer Moses received was intended to give an explanation of the personal name YHWH by which God was known to the Hebrews. The origin and precise meaning of this name are still in dispute. This passage links it with the Hebrew verb 'to be' or 'to become'. It could thus mean 'He who is' or 'He causes to be' or 'He will be'. Instead of being given a character sketch of God, Moses is given a promise, 'I am who I am' or 'I will be who I will be', i.e., I am the God who is and who will be active in whatever situations you are called to face. On the basis of this experience, Moses interpreted to the people the events of the exodus from Egypt as the mighty act of God. This is the pattern throughout the Old Testament. Events are interpreted through the eyes of what we may call prophetic faith. The events themselves may be dramatic, mysterious or very ordinary, but all are seen in the context of belief in a God who is active in and through history.

3. Judges to 2 Kings provides us with a continuous narrative of the history of the Hebrews from the time of their settlement in Canaan till the overthrow in 586 B.C. of the last surviving remnant of the once proud empire of David and Solomon. This historical narrative comes to us from the hands of editors steeped in the same faith by which Moses interpreted to his people the Exodus story. To be more precise, we call this history Deuteronomic, since at many points it clearly reveals the language and the outlook of the book of Deuteronomy. Let us look at two examples of the handling of history by these editors.

(a) The period described in the book of Judges is a confused period in Hebrew history. The Hebrews having gained a foothold in Canaan were hard pressed to maintain their position. Various tribal groups settled in different parts of the country, adapting themselves to the life of the native Canaanite population whose culture and religion was very different from their own. There was little sense of unity among the tribes. The difficulty of communications encouraged the 'parish pump' mentality. Only a common crisis drew the tribes together. Look, however, at the general framework within which the Judges' narrative places the events of this period.

> And the people of Israel did what was evil in the sight of the LORD, forgetting the LORD their God, and serving the Baals and Asheroth (i.e., the gods and goddesses of the Canaanites). Therefore the anger of the LORD was kindled against Israel (Judges 3.7-8a).

There follows a period of oppression by marauding invaders from the desert.

> But when the people of Israel cried to the LORD, the LORD raised up a deliverer for the people of Israel, who delivered them (Judges 3.9a).

Invasion is not merely the influx of hungry nomads from the desert, but the judgement of God against a people who had wavered in their religious loyalty. The man who eventually repels the oppressors is not merely a gifted leader thrown up in the hour of crisis, but a 'deliverer' sent by God to his repentant people. History is the arena of God's activity, not merely the interplay of economic and political forces.

> (b). But the people who followed Omri overcame the people who followed Tibni the son of Ginath; so Tibni died and Omri became king. In the thirty-first year of Asa king of Judah, Omri began to reign over Israel, and reigned for twelve years; six years he reigned in Tirzah. He bought the hill of Samaria from Shemer for two talents of silver; and he fortified the hill, and called the name of the city which he built, Samaria, after the name of Shemer, the owner of the hill. Omri did what was evil in the sight of the LORD, and did more evil than all who were before him. For he walked in all the way of Jereboam, the son of Nebat, and in the sins which he made Israel to sin, provoking the LORD, the God of Israel, to anger by their idols. Now the rest of the acts of Omri which he did, and the might that he showed, are they not written in the Book of the Chronicles of the Kings of Israel? (1 Kings 16.22-27).

Thus in six short verses, the narrative in 1 Kings describes the reign in Israel of Omri. Yet Omri was in political and military terms one of the most important kings of Israel in the ninth century B.C. Not only did he found a new capital, as the Kings' narrative reports, but he struck terror into the hearts of surrounding peoples. A Moabite inscription admits

> Omri, king of Israel, he oppressed Moab many days . . . And Omri had taken possession of the land of Medeba and (Israel) dwelt in it in his days, and half the days of his son, forty years.[1]

Long after Omri's day, Israel still appears in Assyrian records as 'the house of Omri'.[2] The verdict which the Kings' narrative makes on Omri is not political or military but theological. It views Omri solely in the light of what it conceives the purposes of God to be. Omri is thus the ruler of a schismatic, heretical kingdom, and therefore may be, as are all the rulers of the northern kingdom, dismissed with the crushing words, he "did what was evil in the sight of the LORD" (1 Kings 16.25). This verdict would hardly satisfy a modern historian, but it is a verdict consistent with the whole Old Testament approach to history. For the same reason, to Omri's son Ahab, in many respects a weakling compared with his father, the book of Kings devotes six chapters (1 Kings 17-22), because in the reign of Ahab and particularly in his conflict with the prophet Elijah, issue was joined over some of the most important factors in God's relationship to Israel and the Israelite royal family.[3]

4. Central to the witness of the prophets, collections of whose oracles began with those of Amos in the mid eighth century B.C., is the conviction that Yahweh, the God of Israel, is the "living God" who does both good and ill, who holds

[1] D.O.T.T. p. 196.
[2] A.N.E.T. pp. 281 ff.
[3] cf. pp. 74 f.

the destiny of men and nations in the hollow of his hands (cf. Jer. 10.1-10). The Old Testament prophet is not a religious crystal gazer. The message on his lips is "Thus saith the LORD". He is a man standing under divine compulsion with a word to speak from God to the situation of his own day. To be sure, he will speak of the future, but only of the future as determined by the purposes of God and the people's present response to these purposes. He ever challenges the people, in the light of a God-filled past, to face the challenge of a God-filled present and to re-order their life in face of God's insistent demands.

The spectre which haunted the council chambers of the small states of the Ancient Near East during the ninth and increasingly during the eighth century B.C. was that of Assyria, one of the most ruthlessly efficient totalitarian regimes the world has known. Desperately, states such as Israel and Judah sought by means of politically expedient alliances to obtain some kind of balance of power. But the writing was on the wall. Israel perished in 721 B.C. and other communities, including Judah, were forced to pay tribute to their Assyrian overlords. On the death of Sargon II of Assyria in 705 B.C. many of the small states in Syria and Palestine, including Judah under King Hezekiah, rose in revolt to bid for their independence. In the campaign of 701 B.C., Sennacherib, Sargon's successor, effectively dealt with most of the states in revolt, besieging though failing to capture Jerusalem, and forcing Hezekiah into submission before events in Babylon compelled him to return home. In this critical hour influential voices were raised in the court at Jerusalem in favour of seeking to guarantee Judah's future by an Egyptian alliance. It was a moment when men were convinced of only one thing, that God was on the side of the big battalions. Not so the prophet Isaiah; he resolutely opposed the pro-Egyptian lobby. He staked his faith on the conviction that the outcome of events lay, not with the Assyrians nor with the Egyptians, but with God.

"Woe to those who go down to Egypt for help
and rely on horses,
who trust in chariots because they are many;
and in horsemen because they are very strong,
but do not look to the Holy One of Israel
or consult the LORD!
And yet he is wise and brings disaster,
he does not call back his words,
but will arise against the house of the evil-doers,
and against the helpers of those who work iniquity.
The Egyptians are men, and not God;
and their horses are flesh, and not spirit.
When the LORD stretches out his hand,
the helper will stumble, and he who is helped will fall,
and they will all perish together" (Isa. 31.1-3; cf. 30.1-5).

Notice the contrast in the last verse. The Egyptians are *men*, not God; their horses *flesh*, symbol of frailty and transience not *spirit*, not the creative dynamic power of God who shapes all life. 2 Kings 19 and the parallel narrative in Isaiah 37 recount what happened. Jerusalem at the eleventh hour was saved from a powerful Assyrian investing force. Herodotus, the Greek historian, says that the Assyrian army was overrun by a plague of mice. Perhaps bubonic plague broke out. The Old Testament simply declares that

the angel of the LORD went forth, and slew a hundred and eighty-five thousand in the camp of the Assyrians (2 Kings 19.35; Isa. 37.36).

The faith of one generation may so easily become in different circumstances the heresy of a later age. The incident just discussed sowed in people's minds the dangerous doctrine that Jerusalem would serenely ride the storms of history, her safety guaranteed by Yahweh. One hundred years later, when Babylon had succeeded Assyria as the mistress of the Ancient Near East, Jerusalem, a city at once spiritually arrogant and morally corrupt, comforted herself with the conviction that as long as Yahweh dwelt in her midst in his temple no disaster could befall her. Realistic politicians sought to put teeth into this doctrine by negotiating for an Egyptian expeditionary force. Jeremiah, the prophet of this age of national breakdown, was equally convinced of the presence of Yahweh in Jerusalem, but to him it was a dangerous presence. The people made the mistake of believing that God existed to serve the nation; Jeremiah knew that the nation existed to serve the purposes of God. From the outset of his career he was convinced that God was on the *qui vive*, "watching over his word to perform it" (Jer. 1.12), and that word could only be a destructive word to a corrupt nation. When the Babylonian (Chaldean) army had momentarily withdrawn from besieging Jerusalem to settle scores with the Egyptians, Jeremiah had this to say to the pathetic vacillating monarch who presided over the ruins of his people:

> "Thus says the LORD, Do not deceive yourselves, saying, 'The Chaldeans will surely stay away from us,' for they will not stay away. For even if you should defeat the whole army of Chaldeans who are fighting against you, and there remained of them only wounded men, every man in his tent, they would rise up and burn this city with fire" (Jer. 37.9-10).

This is hardly a realistic picture. It is not intended to be. Jeremiah is convinced that only through the destruction of Jerusalem can God's purposes be fulfilled. Since God is in control, "watching over his word to perform it", the fate of the city is sealed. The same conviction that God was active in and through contemporary events led Isaiah to declare that Jerusalem would survive, and Jeremiah to the conviction that Jerusalem must be destroyed.

5. From historians and prophets we turn to the witness of a poet, to a much misunderstood book, Lamentations. The five poems which make up Lamentations all describe the response of faith in the catastrophic event of 586 B.C. In typical dirge and lament style, the poet sounds every note on the keyboard of grief. The city is sacked (1.4; 2.8); worship has ceased, the temple is a charred ruin (2.6-7); hunger stalks the streets, family life has been rudely disrupted (1.11; 2.11-12; 4.4,

9-10). Well over a thousand years earlier a similar disaster
had struck the flourishing Sumerian city of Ur. It is commemorated in the 'Lament over the Destruction of Ur'.[1]
More than time however separates the two poems. We see
this clearly when we ask how each poem deals with the
inevitable question, "Why did disaster strike?" The background to the Ur lament is polytheistic. The patron goddess
of Ur is Ningal. She is not responsible for the tragedy. Along
with other gods and goddesses who deserted their temples,
she fled the city in the hour of disaster. The destruction of
Ur had been decreed by two of the most powerful gods in the
Sumerian pantheon, Anu and Enlil. The Ur lament presents
us with the picture of the patron goddess appealing in vain
against the destruction of her own city to two other gods
who, for reasons best known to themselves, have decreed its
destruction. What of Lamentations?

> Zion stretches out her hands,
> but there is none to comfort her;
> the LORD has commanded against Jacob
> that his neighbours should be his foes (1.17).

In picture upon picture in 2.1-8 the truth is hammered home
that it is Yahweh who has decreed the fate of his own city.
This is "the day of his anger" (v. 1); he has become "like
an enemy" to his own people (v. 5). Lamentations has broken
completely with the concept of God as the private patron
saint of the community which worships him. If Yahweh had
been only this to the Hebrews, he would have been buried in
the debris of Jerusalem, forgotten like Ningal of Ur, or
Chemosh the god of Moab, until some archaeologist discovered
a poem or an inscription containing his name. But to the poet
of Lamentations and to the prophetic faith which he reflects,
Yahweh is the Lord of all history. Even tragedy is the
expression of his will. His people can walk in confidence into
the darkness, because it is his darkness and whatever else
they find, they shall find him there.

[1] Text in A.N.E.T., pp. 455 ff.

6. Nowhere does this faith in God as the controller of all events, the supreme actor on the stage of human history, shine more brilliantly than in the work of the unknown poet prophet who penned Isaiah 40-55. He speaks to his fellow Jews exiled in Babylon. Living conditions for them were not unduly harsh, but spiritually the community was at a low ebb. Surrounded by the splendours of imperial Babylon, confronted by the impressive ceremonial of Babylonian religious ritual, many were tempted to say, "Our God has forgotten us; he is no longer interested in us. Either that or he is powerless" (cf. 40.27-28). Not so, says Second Isaiah,

> "Behold, the LORD GOD comes with might,
>   and his arm rules for him" (40.10).

> "All the nations are as nothing before him,
>   they are accounted by him as less
>   than nothing and emptiness" (40.17).

> He "brings princes to nought,
>   and makes the rulers of the earth as nothing" (40.23).

Great events were shaking the Babylonian empire to its very foundations as Second Isaiah wrote. Cyrus the Persian was cracking open the empire on its eastern frontiers. To many it must have seemed as if one imperialism was about to be replaced by another. But this was not the whole truth as seen through the eyes of the prophet.

> "Who stirred up one from the east
>   whom victory meets at every step?
>   He gives up nations before him,
>   so that he tramples kings under foot;
>   he makes them like dust with his sword,
>   like driven stubble with his bow.
>   He pursues them and passes on safely,
>   by paths his feet have not trod.
>   Who has performed and done this,
>   calling the generations from the beginning?
>   I, the LORD, the first,
>   and with the last; I am He" (41.2-4; cf. 41.25 ff.).

34

Yahweh is the instigator of these events, and in events yet to come the motivating and directing power is Yahweh's. Cyrus may be a pagan militarist, but the ultimate judgement upon him is that he is Yahweh's 'anointed' opening doors for the Jewish people (45.1).

"He is my shepherd,
and he shall fulfil all my purpose" (44.28).

It is from this standpoint that the prophet conceives his brilliant satire on paganism with its numerous costly idols upon which craftsmen have lavished their skill and devotion. It is not that he objects to the representation of God in any form, though as a good Jew he certainly would so object. His criticism is much more fundamental. Such idols in his eyes are mere blocks of wood, metal or stone, utterly powerless, incapable even of movement, exercising no control whatever over the events of the day (cf. 40.18-20; 41.21-24; 44.9-20). This satire reaches a magnificent climax in 46.1-4, where he depicts the gods of Babylon, Bel and Nebo, as being carted unceremoniously out of the falling city by their refugee worshippers, "burdens on weary beasts". In contrast, Yahweh is the God who throughout history has carried and will carry his people.

We shall never come to grips with the thought of the Old Testament unless we realise that the Hebrews came to know God in and through the infinitely varied pattern of events which were their national history, in and through victory and defeat, tragedy and national renewal. Other faiths may be content to sit lightly to human history, to offer their devotees an escape from the challenge and mystery in events into some timeless reality. Not so the Old Testament. It takes history seriously as the place where men meet God, as the arena in which God's purposes are being worked out even when the precise outline of these purposes is far from clear. It can no more give up history than it can give up God.

This attitude to history is a declaration of faith, something

35

which, by its very nature, can neither be proved nor disproved by logical demonstration. Certainly it cannot be proved, as has sometimes been rashly claimed, by archaeology. W. Keller, for example, speaks of the contribution of archaeology to biblical studies in the following terms:

"In view of the overwhelming mass of authentic and well-attested evidence now available, as I thought of the sceptical criticism which, from the eighteenth century onwards, would fain have demolished the Bible altogether, there kept hammering on my brain this one sentence, 'The Bible is right after all.' "[1]

But what do we mean by saying 'The Bible is right after all'—right in what sense? Archaeology has an important contribution to make to our study of the Bible, but we must see that contribution in its proper perspective. Let us take two examples.

(a) Towards the end of the nineteenth century, the general attitude towards the patriarchal narratives in Genesis was one of extreme scepticism. Abraham was regarded as "a free creation of conscious art"[2]; that is to say, the product of later Hebrew imagination, projecting into the remote past an ideal ancestor for the Hebrew people. This attitude was possible not only because the stories concerning Abraham had been written down at a much later date than the events they claimed to describe, but also because the history of the Ancient Near East in the second millennium B.C. was virtually a blank. Today the climate of opinion has changed. Most scholars would claim that in the patriarchal narratives we are in touch with a genuine historical tradition, however suspicious we may be of some of the detail. Partly this is a result of a new understanding of the factors which shaped Old Testament literature, in particular the part played by oral tradition in

[1] *The Bible as History*, English translation by W. Neil, Introduction.

[2] J. Wellhausen, *Prolegomenon to the History of Israel*, p. 320 (English translation).

36

conserving information, but to a large extent it is the result of the light thrown on the political, religious and social history of the period by recent discoveries. To mention only the most significant of them, from Asia Minor have come the Cappadocian tablets (nineteenth century B.C.) written in old Assyrian and shedding light on vigorous Assyrian business enterprises and trade links in this period. From the eighteenth century B.C. come the Mari texts with their evidence of a powerful Amorite city state in North Mesopotamia in the general region from which Abraham moved west to Canaan. A Hurrian community at Nuzi in Mesopotamia has bequeathed us tablets of the fifteenth century B.C., family documents, business transactions, records of court proceedings, which contain some remarkable parallels to patriarchal customs. From Egypt have come the Tell el Amarna letters witnessing to the instability and political confusion in Egyptian-dominated Canaan of the fourteenth century B.C. In documents from many quarters including Tell el Amarna, there appear from 2000 B.C. onwards, the mysterious 'Habiru', a restless unsettled class of people whose name is linked etymologically with that of the Hebrews in the Old Testament. Not only can we now begin to write the history of the Ancient Near East in the second millennium B.C., but we can see how the narratives concerning Abraham, Isaac and Jacob fit into the general tribal movement and social milieu of this period, and *of no other*. The record is therefore not merely the prefabrication of later generations. Thus far archaeology can help us. It cannot be too strongly emphasised, however, that all this does not prove or disprove that Abraham left Mesopotamia in response to a call from God, and in the hope that from him would come a nation which would forward God's purposes in the world.

(b) When the Hebrews under Joshua invaded Canaan from across the Jordan, the first major obstacle in their path was the strongly fortified city of Jericho. According to the narrative in Joshua, the Hebrews at the command of Yahweh marched round the city walls for seven days, the priests blowing trumpets and carrying with them the ark of the covenant, symbol of Yahweh's presence in the midst of his people. On the seventh day the walls of Jericho mysteriously fell down, the Hebrews clambered into the now defenceless city, slew its inhabitants and razed it to the ground. The site of Jericho has been extensively excavated. According to the excavation reports of 1930, Jericho at the time of the Hebrew invasion had two rings of defensive walls, an outer one six feet thick and an inner one twelve feet thick. Everywhere on the ruins of these walls "traces of intense fire were plain to see, including reddened masses of brick, cracked stones, charred timber and ashes".[1] The date suggested by the evidence pointed to *circa* 1400 B.C. according to Garstang; others have disputed this verdict. The temptation to assume that this evidence proved the truth of the narrative in Joshua 6 was strong. Even if this archaeological evidence had stood the test of time, however, it would have proved nothing more than the fact that *circa* 1400 B.C. Jericho was violently destroyed and razed to the ground. It could not have proved that this happened in the miraculous way suggested in the Old Testament narrative. In point of fact, more recent excavations at Jericho have led to a drastic re-interpretation of the evidence. The walls which Garstang believed to belong to the time of Joshua are of much earlier date. As far as we know "the excavation of Jericho . . . has thrown no light on the walls of Jericho of which the destruction is so vividly described in the Book of Joshua".[2] This no more disproves the biblical story than the previous dating of the archaeological evidence proved it.

Archaeology can be of considerable assistance to us in reconstructing the background to Old Testament history and thought: what it cannot do is to prove that particular interpretation of history to which every Old Testament historical

[1] J. Garstang, *Joshua Judges*, p. 145.
[2] K. Kenyon, *Digging up Jericho*, p. 262 (1957).

writer and prophet bears witness. We no longer believe that the study of history is a purely neutral discipline concerned with the collection of 'facts' —whatever they may be—from the past. All historical writing which has any claim to greatness implies both a selection of the material at the historian's disposal and an interpretative standpoint. We may have a Marxist interpretation of history in which economic determinism provides the clue to the meaning of events, or at the opposite extreme a Churchillian view of history in which the controlling factor is the influence of great men. We may have a humanist interpretation or a biblical interpretation. "Our final interpretation of history is the most sovereign decision we can take and it is clear that every one of us, standing alone in the universe, has to take it for himself. It is our decision about religion, about our total attitude to things, about the way we will appropriate life. And it is inseparable from our decision about the role we are going to play ourselves in that very drama of history".[1]

The Old Testament challenges us to see this drama as God's drama and to play our role in the light of the continuing pressure of the purposes of God in all events, the God who has made himself known in that part of the drama which is the history of the Hebrews.

[1] H. Butterfield, *Christianity and History*, p. 25.

Chapter Three

THE GOD OF THE COVENANT

IT was the glory of Athenian democracy, said Pericles, to be the "educator of Greece".[1] Most peoples who have left their mark on history have coined a phrase which aptly expresses much that is distinctive in their life and their sense of mission. For the Hebrews this phrase was "the people of God". This did not mean that, with spiritual arrogance, they claimed to be a supremely religious or devout nation. It declared their faith that through no merit of their own, they stood in a particular relationship to the living God, a relationship which is expressed in the word 'covenant' (berith). A covenant is an agreement entered into by two parties, whether individuals or communities, an agreement implying for both parties rights and responsibilities. One of the clearest examples of such a covenant is in the narrative of Gen. 31.43 ff. The background to it is the tale of mutual trickery and deceit between Jacob and Laban which culminated in Jacob's hurried flight from his father-in-law's household. When Laban eventually overtakes Jacob, instead of resorting to action which might have involved shedding the blood of his own kith and kin, he says:

"Come now, let us make a covenant, you and I; and let it be a witness between you and me" (Gen. 31.44).

A cairn of stones is erected to mark the spot where the covenant is solemnised, and the contracting parties share a sacrificial meal, a sign of their new brotherhood. Any violation of the covenant will be avenged by the gods who have witnessed it. Very similar is the story of the covenant between Jonathan and David which bound them together in a loyalty and friend-

[1] Thucydides, Bk. II, xli.

40

ship that only death could break (1 Sam. 18.3). Old Testament writers take this familiar idea of a covenant and use it to express their understanding of the life of the Hebrew people in relationship to God.

In the earliest source in the book of Genesis, the 'J' source, Yahweh at a moment of crisis in Abraham's life makes a covenant with him (15.2 ff). The story describes a rite which may explain the technical expression in Hebrew for making a covenant, i.e., 'to cut a covenant'. Certain sacrificial animals are taken and cut in half, the parties to the covenant passing through between the severed portions. If Jer. 34.18 ff and parallels in other cultures preserve the original meaning of this act, then the severing of the victims was a symbolic act through which the parties pledged their faith to one another in some such words as, "May God do likewise to me if I break this covenant". Certain significant features in the Genesis story however must be noted. The covenant begins with a declaration as to who God is and what he has done.

"I am the LORD who brought you from Ur of the Chaldeans, to give you this land to possess" (v. 7).

Nor does Abraham himself pass through between the severed victims, only "a smoking fire pot and a flaming torch" (v. 17) symbols of the presence of God, cf. the pillar of cloud and fire in the Exodus story, Exod. 3.2; 13.21; 19.9. In other words, this is not a treaty concluded on equal terms between God and Abraham. The initiative throughout comes from God. It is rooted in his character. In a sense the covenant may be described as God's gift to Abraham.

The priestly tradition ('P') in Genesis 17 similarly has an account of a covenant made by God with Abraham. No description is given of the ritual involved, but the meaning of the covenant is underlined and, in contrast to chapter 15, emphasis is laid upon the obligations which rest upon Abraham and his descendants as a result of the covenant (17.9 ff.). It is still however God's covenant. "I will make my covenant between me and you" (17.2, cf. v. 7). The importance of the covenant idea for the Old Testament is stressed in this narrative by the fact that a rite, widely practised in the Ancient Near East and in primitive societies throughout the world, and usually regarded as a rite of initiation into manhood or marriage, the rite of circumcision, becomes among the Hebrews the sign of the covenant (17.11), the visible mark in the flesh of every male Hebrew of the relationship which God had established with his people.

It is when we come to the Exodus narrative, however, that the idea of the covenant finds its fullest expression in the Old Testament. Once out of Egypt, the tribes under the leadership of Moses wander for a while in the desert until they come to Mount Sinai—or Horeb according to certain Old Testament sources—there to meet God in a moment of mystery and wonder.

> On the morning of the third day there were thunders and lightnings, and a thick cloud upon the mountain, and a very loud trumpet blast, so that all the people who were in the camp trembled. Then Moses brought the people out of the camp to meet God; and they took their stand at the foot of the mountain. And Mount Sinai was wrapped in smoke, because the LORD descended upon it in fire; and the smoke of it went up like the smoke of a kiln, and the whole mountain quaked greatly (Exod. 19.16-18).

Much concerning this incident is uncertain. The site of the mountain is still in dispute. Tradition places it in the south of the Sinaitic peninsula. But the significance of this event for the future history of the Hebrews can hardly be overestimated. Here refugee slaves were faced with their destiny as "the people of God".

The charter, as it were, of this covenant is to be found in the tradition of the Ten Words, preserved in slightly different forms in Exod. 20.2-17 and Deut. 5.6-21. The difference in the two versions centres mainly upon the reason given for certain of the injunctions; contrast the reason given for the

celebration of the Sabbath in Exod. 20.8 with that given in
Deut. 5.12. Both versions may be commentary expansions of
an originally shorter form:

I am Yahweh your God who brought you out of the land of
Egypt, out of the house of bondage.
1. You shall have no other gods before me.
2. You shall not make yourself a graven image.
3. You shall not take the name of Yahweh, your God, in vain.
4. Remember the Sabbath to keep it holy.
5. Honour your father and your mother.
6. You shall not kill.
7. You shall not commit adultery.
8. You shall not steal.
9. You shall not bear false witness against your neighbour.
10. You shall not covet your neighbour's house.

Recent research has suggested that the closest parallels to this
covenant and its charter are to be found, not in the Jacob-
Laban type of covenant, but in the formal treaties drawn up
between the Great King and his vassal states within the Hittite
Empire round about the Mosaic period.[1] Such treaties usually
began with a prologue containing the name and titles of the
Emperor and a reminder of his benevolence to his subjects.
Thereafter the obligations incumbent upon the Emperor's
loyal vassals were listed. They included no dealings with the
Emperor's enemies, good relationships with other vassal
states, prompt payment of annual tribute, acceptance of
imperial policy and the provision of contingents to serve in
the imperial army. Such a treaty was deposited for safety in
some local shrine and publicly read to the people from time
to time, as a reminder of their obligations. In structure, the
charter of the Mount Sinai covenant is remarkably similar. It
begins with a preamble declaring who God is and what he has
done for his people. It prohibits his subject people from
entering into relationship with other gods. It lays specific
obligations upon them. Not only so, but Hebrew tradition

[1] G. E. Mendenhall, *Law and Covenant in Israel and in the Ancient Near East*
(The Biblical Colloquium, Pittsburgh, 1955).

declares that the stone tablets on which the charter was inscribed were carried by the Hebrews during their wanderings in the wilderness in a wooden receptacle called the 'ark of the covenant' under priestly supervision (cf. Deut. 10.1-5). There is, moreover, evidence that the public recital of this charter or appropriate expansions of it was made the basis of a periodic renewal of the nation's loyalty to Yahweh (cf. Deut. 5.2-3; 29.10 ff.). Since much later Hebrew religious history is an attempt to work out the implications of this covenant, to interpret and reinterpret it in the light of changing circumstances, let us look more closely at the covenant charter.

1. The initiative of Yahweh

"I am the LORD your God, who brought you out of the land of Egypt, out of the house of bondage" (Exod. 20.2; Deut. 5.6).

The covenant at Mount Sinai is the declaration of the kingship of Yahweh over his people, but it is the kingship of a liberator. In Old Testament tradition the story of the Exodus and the story of the covenant at Mount Sinai lie side by side, the one inevitably following and being dependent on the other. It is because Yahweh has delivered the people out of enslavement that he now claims their allegiance. As in the Genesis account of the covenant with Abraham, the initiative is Yahweh's. In the words of Moses to the people during the ceremony which ratified the covenant, this is "the covenant which the LORD has made with you" (Exod. 24.8). The wonder of deliverance by God is stamped upon the faith of the Old Testament. The background against which the covenant at Mount Sinai is ratified is this sense of a mighty act of Yahweh so dramatically enshrined in the triumph song in which Miriam, the sister of Moses, commemorated the Exodus experience.

"Sing to the LORD, for he has triumphed gloriously;
the horse and his rider he has thrown into the sea"
(Exod. 15.21)

To put it in other terms, the Hebrews did not choose to be the people of God, they were chosen by God. The great reality undergirding all Hebrew faith is not their grasp of God but God's grasp of them. To this truth they were repeatedly recalled by prophets and psalmists, priests and poets. The prophet Ezekiel, for example, speaks of the beginnings of the Hebrew nation as the story of an unwanted baby, exposed in the desert to die, a baby gathered up in the loving compassion of God.

"Thus says the LORD God to Jerusalem: Your origin and your birth are of the land of the Canaanites; your father was an Amorite, and your mother a Hittite. And as for your birth, on the day you were born your navel string was not cut, nor were you washed with water to cleanse you, nor rubbed with salt, nor swathed with bands. No eye pitied you, to do any of these things to you out of compassion for you; but you were cast out on the open field, for you were abhorred, on the day that you were born. And when I passed by you, and saw you weltering in your blood, I said to you in your blood, 'Live, and grow up like a plant of the field' " (Ezek. 16.3-7a).

It is in the Book of Deuteronomy, a meditation upon the meaning of the covenant in the form of a Mosaic sermon, that we find the most profound attempt to grapple with the mystery of God's gracious approach to his people.

"For ask now of the days that are past, which were before you, since the day that God created man upon the earth, and ask from one end of heaven to the other, whether such a great thing as this has ever happened or was ever heard of. Did any people ever hear the voice of a god speaking out of the midst of the fire as you have heard, and still live? Or has any god ever attempted to go and take a nation for himself from the midst of another nation, by trials, by signs, by wonders, and by war, by a mighty hand and an outstretched arm, and by great terrors, according to all the LORD your God did for you in Egypt before your eyes?" (Deut. 4.32-34, cf. 6.21 ff.).

Yahweh has taken Israel to belong to himself, "the people of his own possession" (Deut. 4.20); a community which is holy to Yahweh, that is to say, set apart, separated from other people to belong to Yahweh; a people "for his own possession" — one Hebrew word lies behind this phrase 'for his own possession', a word which always denotes something of value to its owner, something personally selected (Deut. 14.2, cf. 7.6; 26.18; Exod. 19.5). But Deuteronomy is not content merely to state the fact of Yahweh's choice of Israel, it goes on to ask 'Why should this be?' What led Yahweh to deliver this group of slaves and enter into covenant relationship with them? The answer Deuteronomy gives to this question is a surprising one for anybody who would dismiss the God of the Old Testament as a somewhat capricious and bloodthirsty tyrant. It is to be found in one word 'love', a love which Deuteronomy usually traces back to God's dealings with the pilgrim father of the Hebrew people (cf. Deut. 4.37; 10.14-15). The fullest statement of the theme is to be found in Deut. 7.7-8:

"It was not because you were more in number than any other people that the LORD set his love upon you and chose you, for you were the fewest of all peoples; but it is because the LORD loves you, and is keeping the oath which he swore to your fathers, that the LORD has brought you out with a mighty hand, and redeemed you from the house of bondage, from the hand of Pharaoh king of Egypt".

We must beware of importing into this word 'love' the lush sentimentality which threatens to debase it in modern currency, but it is the word used in the Old Testament for the attitude of father to son, husband to wife. There is in it something of the spontaneous self-giving which lies at the heart of all true love, whether human or divine. The Old Testament is so often dismissed, even in Christian circles, as outmoded legalism that it is important to recognise that this outgoing love of God is the rock upon which the faith of the Old Testament is built.[1] In the fullest sense of the word, the Old Testament is a Gospel, the proclamation of good news,

[1] cf. G. A. F. Knight, *Law and Grace.*

46

the good news of God's saving initiative and concern demonstrated in the history of his people.

2. The exclusiveness of Yahweh

"You shall have no other gods before me" (Exod. 20.3;
Deut. 5.7), a statement which may mean either you shall have
no other gods *in preference to me* or *in addition to me* (lit., over
or upon my face). In themselves, these words do not necessarily deny the existence of other gods. Indeed, in settings
which are polytheistic, similar statements are made about one
of the gods whose writ is regarded as supreme. It is said of
the Babylonian god Marduk, "Thine appointment has no
equal, thine authority is absolute", words immediately preceded and followed by the statement that Marduk has been
"enrolled within the number of the great gods".[1]

In the story of the covenant, however, with its declaration
of the kingship of Yahweh over his people, it means something
more. It commits the Hebrews to the exclusive worship of
a God who has demonstrated his power over the forces of
nature (the plagues, the crossing of the Reed Sea) and of
history (the defeat of the might of Pharaoh and the Egyptian
armies, and by implication, the gods of Egypt). It has indeed
been seriously argued within recent years that Moses was a
monotheist.[2] This is perhaps to put the issue in the wrong
way. The Hebrews, at the time of the Exodus and the Mount
Sinai covenant, were hardly interested in the speculative
religio-philosophical question as to whether there be one or
many gods. They were confronted with the challenge that, as
far as they were concerned, there was to be henceforth only
one God, Yahweh. Are we dealing then merely with 'henotheism', the worship by one tribe or nation of one god as its
tribal or national god without any resistance to the fact that
other people worship other gods, Yahweh being the god of

[1] *Creation Epic* IV, 113-5, D.O.T.T., p. 8.
[2] W. F. Albright, *From Stone Age to Christianity*, p. 207.

the Hebrews in much the same sense as Chemosh was the tribal god of Moab? The Moabite stone (*circa* 830 B.C.), describing from a Moabite point of view relations between Moab and Israel, underlines the element of truth in this view.[1] Disaster befalling the Moabites is attributed to the anger of Chemosh, victory to his saving power. Conquered cities are consecrated to Chemosh, the entire population being sacrificed to the god—the so-called *herem* or ban. Such ideas are easily paralleled in the Old Testament, cf. 1 Sam. 15 where Samuel castigates King Saul for failing to apply the 'ban' ruthlessly to the Amalekites. It may be that for long enough many Hebrews were little more than 'henotheists', but this comparison with Moabite belief in Chemosh must be modified in the light of two factors.

In the first place we know nothing of the history of the relationship between Chemosh and Moab: Chemosh is just one among many of the tribal gods of the Ancient Near East, of interest to scholars, but otherwise, for centuries a forgotten deity. We can, on the contrary, trace the history of the relationship between Yahweh and the Hebrews from its beginnings in the Exodus story to the point some seven hundred years later when, with the very future of the Hebrew people in jeopardy, a prophet can say of Yahweh

> "Turn to me and be saved,
> all the ends of the earth!
> For I am God, and there is no other" (Isa. 45.22).

In the second place, the relationship between Yahweh and Israel was never merely that of a tribal god considered to be the natural 'father' of his tribe. This relationship had a historical beginning in a series of events in which Yahweh by his mighty act claimed this people as his own. This claim carried with it a positive overtone of exclusiveness which is most clearly stated in an early code of law found in Exodus 34:

[1] For the text of the Moabite stone, cf. D.O.T.T., pp. 195-198.

"You shall worship no other god, for the LORD whose name is Jealous, is a jealous God" (Exod. 34.14, cf. Josh. 24.19-20).

The word translated 'jealous' indicates, when applied to Yahweh, the intense zeal of exclusive love bent on maintaining an exclusive claim.

One strand in the religious history of the Old Testament centres upon the struggle to maintain that exclusive claim. It was a struggle between the many, who were all too ready to take the path of religious compromise, and the few, men of prophetic stature like Moses, who witnessed to the jealousy of Yahweh.

(a) The first crisis in the people's religious loyalty came with the settlement in Canaan. In Canaan the Hebrews found the native population practising a religion ideally suited to the life of the Canaanite peasant farmer. Until the thirties of this century, our knowledge of Canaanite religion was fragmentary and uncertain, derived in the main from references in the Old Testament to Baal and to certain religious practices regarded with abhorrence by Hebrew orthodoxy. The discovery of texts, dated *circa* 1400 B.C. from the site of Ugarit on the Syrian coast have helped to clarify the picture. In these texts we find a typical pantheon of gods, its senior member being *El*, "the Father of men". The most active god in this North Canaanite pantheon, however, is *Ba'al*, personification of the life-giving, beneficent forces in nature, the fertilising rain locked in conflict, in certain of the Ugaritic myths, with *Moth*, death, the power of sterility. The myths tell how Baal dies at the hands of Moth, only to be resuscitated through the vigorous activity of his sister, the virgin *'Anath*, the most active goddess in the pantheon. Among other goddesses there is *'Athirath* who appears in the Old Testament as Asherah, a word translated by the A.V. as 'grove', but now known to be some form of representation of the goddess Athirat (cf. Deut. 16.21; Judges 6.26; 1 Kings 15.13; 2 Kings 17.16; 21.3, etc.). This religion is intimately related to the rhythm of the seasons upon which the farmer depends. He seeks to guarantee to himself a good harvest by participating in the correct fertility ritual.[1] The dilemma of the Hebrew settlers in Canaan is obvious. They had to become peasant farmers. Must they not at the same time participate in a religion which ensured the peasant farmer a fair reward for his labours? Many Hebrews did so participate. Hebrew religion bears the marks of a twofold attempt to come to a working agreement between Yahweh and the gods of Canaan.

(i) Why should the Hebrews not retain Yahweh as the national god of the Hebrew community, their help and stay in times of national crisis, and at the same time pay homage to the gods who are concerned with giving fertility to the soil? After all, Yahweh had demonstrated his power in Egypt by defeating his people's enemies, and through long years of wandering in the desert, but there was no guarantee that he was a farmer's god. This is the pattern of Hebrew life in the early days of the settlement in Canaan as it is recorded for us by the prophetic historians who edited the early traditions of this period now to be found in the Book of Judges. Under normal conditions, the Hebrews "forsook the LORD, and served the Baals and the Ashtaroth" (Judges 2.13)—the plural forms denote different manifestations of Baal and Athirat. In the hour of crisis tribal groups, under the leadership of a gifted judge or deliverer, rally to the banner of Yahweh. Witness the Song of Deborah (Judges 5), one of the earliest and most dramatic Hebrew ballads describing how the fiery cross of Yahweh summoned the tribes to do battle against a North Canaanite alliance. Although the editors of Judges have set all the stories of early Hebrew heroes within the framework of the stereotyped formula, apostasy to Canaanite gods followed by a rallying to Yahweh in the hour of crisis, there is no reason to doubt that the formula is rooted in reality. Such departmentalism in religion has always appealed to men.

[1] For the nature of such rituals and their challenge to Hebrew faith, cf. Chapter Four, pp. 75 ff.

Much later, at a time when the religion of the northern kingdom of Israel was deeply corroded by Canaanite ideas and practices, the prophet Hosea complains in the name of Yahweh:

> "And she (i.e. Israel) did not know
> that it was I who gave her
> the grain, the wine and the oil,
> and who lavished upon her silver
> and gold which they used for Baal" (Hos. 2.8).

(ii) More subtly and dangerously, it was always possible to transfer to Yahweh the character and functions of Baal, and thus to continue the worship of Baal under another name. This process was helped by the fact that during the settlement the Hebrews took over sites, such as Shiloh and Shechem, which had long been centres of Canaanite worship. A change of name given to a god, and many religious practices hallowed by the centuries could continue virtually unchanged. Alongside an altar to Yahweh there would stand an Asherah (Deut. 16.21). This confronted Hebrew faith with a serious challenge, since whatever Yahweh was, he was not merely a god of nature.

If this view had prevailed, there is no reason why Yahweh should not have been assigned a place alongside other gods in a Canaanite-Hebrew pantheon. Indeed that is what we find in certain Aramaic documents of the fifth century B.C. from a Jewish mercenary garrison in Egypt. We do not know for certain when this Jewish outpost was established at Elephantine on the southern borders of Egypt, but its religious outlook probably reflects much that passed for popular religion in pre-exilic Israel. The colony had a temple to Yahu, a variant form of the name Yahweh, but it also paid homage to several other gods with distinctly Canaanite names—Ishum-bethel, Anat-bethel, Herem-bethel—and most significant of all a goddess called Anat-Yahu which by analogy can only mean Anat the female consort of Yahu. Yahweh was well on the way to having many divine relatives and no vital religious future.[1]

In the light of the baneful influence that Canaanite religion exercised over the Hebrews, Old Testament writers thunder against Canaanite religion and its symbols. In particular, the Book of Deuteronomy demands the complete eradication of the native Canaanite population and all its ways (Deut. 7.1-5; 20.10-18). This, however, is a theory which was hardly put into practice, a case of being wise after the event. The future of Yahwism lay not with the extermination of those who thought otherwise, but with the witness of a faithful minority who shunned compromise and continually troubled the Hebrew conscience. On another level it lay with a theology which would work out the true relationship between Yahweh and all created things. This is precisely what is given to us in Genesis 1, a chapter which, in its present form, may come from an exilic priestly source, but the structure of which was probably hammered out in conflict with Baalism. It asserts the exclusive claim of the God of the Hebrews over all creation. Other cosmologies, stories of the creating and ordering of the universe, which we find in the Ancient Near East are polytheistic. In the Babylonian creation epic, for example, the universe is created as the result of a conflict between Marduk, the patron god of Babylon, and Tiamat, the goddess of the waters of chaos. Instead of many gods and goddesses, Gen. 1 states,

"In the beginning God . . ."; instead of a titanic struggle between gods and goddesses, there is the brief, power-charged word, "God said" (1, 3, 6, 9, 11, 14, 20, 26) . . . "and it was so" (1, 7, 9, 11, 13, 24). More importantly in the light of the Canaanite background, the God of Genesis 1 is not one of the forces of nature, such as the power of fertility. He is not to be equated with anything in the realm of nature. He is transcendent, standing over against the world, source of all life within it, and yet sharply distinguished from the world.

[1] cf. D.O.T.T., pp. 256 ff. A.N.E.T., p. 491. E. G. H. Kraeling, *The Brooklyn Museum Aramaic Papyri.*

It was only by some such doctrine of creation which would effectively relate God to the world, to the seasons and the crops, yet at the same time avoid any thought of the deification of Nature, that Hebrew faith could effectively answer the challenge which the settlement in Canaan brought to the exclusiveness of Yahweh.

(b) A somewhat different threat to the exclusive claim of Yahweh to his people's loyalty arose from another sphere, politics. There was no clear cut distinction between religion and politics in the Ancient Near East. Political subjection involved paying some degree of homage to the gods of the conquerors; political alliances meant granting recognition in some form or other to the gods of the allies. Ahab, King of Israel (869-850 B.C.) set the seal on friendly relations with his northern Phoenician neighbours by marrying a Phoenician princess, "Jezebel, the daughter of Ethbaal, King of the Sidonians" (1 Kings 16.31, cf. 1 Kings 11.1-8 and the religious provision which Solomon made for his foreign wives). This meant the establishment in Israel of the worship of the Phoenician god Baal Melqart and his appropriate female consort, Asherah. Under the patronage of the royal family, this religion took a firm grip in Israel, loyalists to Yahweh being persecuted. Four hundred and fifty prophets of Baal and four hundred prophets of Asherah were centred on the court. This is the background to the dramatic story of the conflict on Mount Carmel between the prophets of Baal and Elijah the champion of Yahweh (1 Kings 18.20 ff.). The issue at stake is summarised in the challenging words of Elijah to the people:

"How long will you go limping with two different opinions? If the LORD is God, follow him; but if Baal, then follow him" (1 Kings 18.21).

It cannot be in Israel Baal Melqart *and* Yahweh; it must be *either* Baal Melqart *or* Yahweh. Yahweh brooks no rival in his people's affections. The Mount Carmel incident culminated in the people declaring anew their faith in the words, "Yahweh he is God, Yahweh he is God". That did not mean that the issue was closed once and for all. When over a hundred years later, Ahaz (735-715 B.C.) sought safety for the southern kingdom of Judah by coming to terms with the Assyrians, he is said to have imported into the temple of Yahweh at Jerusalem a copy of an altar he saw in Damascus, no doubt an altar of Assyrian design at which Assyrian gods were worshipped (2 Kings 16.10 ff.). This is one reason why the prophet Isaiah countered Ahaz' pro-Assyrian policy with a policy of political neutrality and trust in Yahweh alone (cf. pp. 30 ff.). Similarly Manasseh (687-642 B.C.) succeeded in keeping Judah at peace by faithfully licking the boots of his Assyrian overlords, but at a price, the price of allowing in Jerusalem the worship of the stars and the planets "the host of heaven", a reflection of contemporary Assyrian religious practice (2 Kings 21.1 ff.). In the case both of Ahaz and Manasseh, the Old Testament claims that they also encouraged the worship of native Canaanite gods and goddesses, Baal and Asherah. Once the policy of exclusive loyalty to Yahweh was broken, there was no reason why as comprehensive a religious insurance policy as possible should not be contracted.

The opposite side of the coin may be seen in the religious reformation carried out under King Josiah in 621 B.C. This reformation involved the liquidation of all foreign and Canaanite cults, and as a means to this end the purified worship of Yahweh was henceforth to be centralised in the Jerusalem temple. This was not merely a religious act. It carried with it a declaration of rebellion by Josiah against his Assyrian overlord, and Josiah died fighting for national political and religious freedom against the Egyptian allies of Assyria (2 Kings 23.29 which must be read as in R.S.V. "Pharaoh Neco, king of Egypt, went up *to* (i.e., to assist) the King of Assyria . . ." and not as in the older English versions, "*against* the king of Assyria").

Against all such forms of religious compromise there were

those among the Hebrews who, from the covenant at Mount Sinai onwards, stood for the exclusiveness of Yahweh. "You shall have no other gods before me". They are the spiritual forefathers of the three great monotheistic faiths of the modern world, Judaism, Christianity and Islam.

3. The mystery of Yahweh

"You shall not make yourself a graven image" (cf. Exod. 20.4; Deut. 5.8; 4.15 ff.).

We may gaze at the gods and goddesses of the Ancient Near East on many a tableau and statuette—Asiatic war gods such as Rephesh, kilted with shield and spear in left hand, axe in right hand; El seated upon a throne receiving an offering from some devotee; the storm god standing astride a bull; numerous figurines of the fertility goddess; Marduk of Babylon with his ornate conical crown; the deities of Egypt sometimes represented in animal form, Anubis sitting as a jackal on top of a funerary chest, Horus the hawk, the goddess Isis protectively spreading her wings around Osiris.[1] No tableau or figurine, however, exists to allow us to gaze on Yahweh, the God of Israel. Yet the pressure to produce some such tangible and visible representation of Yahweh to stand alongside images of Baal and Athirat must have been great from the time of the settlement in Canaan onwards. We do find in narratives from the early settlement period references to small cult objects, such as the ephod (Judges 8.27; 17.5), the teraphim (Judges 18.14 ff.) and the graven image owned by Micah (Judges 17.3). This no more argues against the Mosaic origin of the prohibition on images than the fact that many Hebrews succumbed to the lure of Baalism argues against the fact that from the Sinai covenant onwards there was an element of exclusiveness in Yahwism.

The narrative of 1 Kings 12 tells us how, after the break up of the empire of David and Solomon into the rival kingdoms of Israel and Judah, Jeroboam, the instigator of the revolt of

[1] J. B. Pritchard, *The Ancient Near East in Pictures*.

the northern tribes and the first king of northern Israel, sought to wean his people's religious loyalty from Jerusalem and its temple by giving royal patronage to two northern shrines, one at Bethel, the other at Dan, in each of which he placed a calf of gold.

"You have gone up to Jerusalem long enough. Behold your gods, O Israel, who brought you up out of the land of Egypt" (1 Kings 12.28, cf. Exod. 32).

In the eyes of the Deuteronomic historian this was a heinous sin, but it is doubtful whether it was ever intended as a deliberate violation of the law against graven images. A bull calf is a fit symbol for a fertility god; Baal is sometimes depicted as standing upon such a calf. Jeroboam's calves may therefore have been intended merely as the pedestals upon which Yahweh stood invisible.

Why this prohibition against any attempt to represent Yahweh through 'graven image' or likeness? The only specific reason given in the Old Testament for this prohibition is to be found in Deut. 4.15 ff.:

"Since you saw no form on the day that the LORD spoke to you at Horeb out of the midst of the fire, beware lest you act corruptly by making a graven image for yourselves, in the form of any figure" (cf. Exod. 20.21-23).

What they did see, according to Exod. 19.16, was thunder and lightning, a mountain girt with smoke and flame, an awesome mysterious sight such as is often found in the Old Testament in association with Yahweh's coming to his people —the burning bush that was not consumed (Exod. 3.2-3); the pillar of cloud by day and fire by night (Exod. 13.21 ff.); a temple filled with smoke and through the swirling smoke the glimpse of a throne surrounded by seraphim (Isa. 6.1-4); a flashing storm cloud out of which emerge four bizarre creatures bearing a throne-chariot across the sky (Ezek. 1). Such is what Ezekiel, in a terse yet curiously vague phrase, describes as "the likeness of the glory of Yahweh" (Ezek.

1.28), the word glory (*kabhodh,* literally weight) being a technical term in the religious language of the Old Testament to describe the self-manifestation of God.

But it was not only the mysterious awesomeness of Yahweh which was incapable of being expressed in terms of any man-made image or likeness. A static image was a wholly inadequate symbol of a god in whose very name, Yahweh, was written something of the restless, dynamic, creative energy which shapes all creation and all history. It is in the light of this that we find Second Isaiah "pushing Mosaic religion to a magnificent conclusion",[1] in his opening words of reassurance to his exiled despondent fellow countrymen. All creation is Yahweh's. He controls all events. The greatest imperial powers are as nothing before him, "nothing and emptiness" (Isa. 40.12 ff.; 21 ff.).

> "To whom then will you liken God,
>   or what likeness compare with him?
>   The idol! a workman casts it,
>   and a goldsmith overlays it with gold,
>   and casts for it silver chains.
>   He who is impoverished chooses for an offering
>   wood that will not rot;
>   he seeks out a skilful craftsman
>   to set up an image that will not move" (40. 18-20).

4. The dread of Yahweh

"You shall not take the name of Yahweh your God in vain" (Exod. 20.7; Deut. 5.11).

This does not mean that the Hebrews were forbidden to take oaths which involved invoking the name of Yahweh. It does mean that they had to take with the utmost seriousness what was involved in using the name of Yahweh. His name, his character, was not one with which they could trifle. When they took oaths in the name of Yahweh it had to be in full consciousness of what they were doing and without any trace of equivocation or falsehood (cf. Lev. 19.12). It would be

[1] J. Muilenburg in *The Interpreter's Bible, ad loc.*

wrong, however, to think that this prohibition applies only to the narrow field of the taking of oaths. It was intended to embrace the whole of life. One of the best commentaries on this is to be found in Joshua 24. The occasion is a tribal gathering at Shechem at which the covenant bond between Yahweh and the people is renewed. It may contain the memory of an occasion when Hebrew kinsmen who had never been enslaved in Egypt and had not experienced the Exodus and the meeting with Yahweh at Sinai, were received into the people of Yahweh and taught the presuppositions and obligations of the covenant. The narrative begins, (vv. 1-13) with what is really an expansion of "I am Yahweh your God who brought you out of the land of Egypt", that is to say with a recital of the mighty acts of Yahweh, beginning with the migration of the Hebrew pilgrim fathers up to the time of the settlement in Canaan. In the light of this, Joshua summons the people to renew their allegiance to Yahweh and to Yahweh alone (vv. 14-15). The people respond "we also will serve the LORD, for he is our God" (v. 18b). Joshua thereupon reminds them that this is not a declaration which can be made lightly; it is a decision fraught with future good or ill.

> But Joshua said to the people, "You cannot serve the LORD; for he is a holy God; he is a jealous God; he will not forgive your transgressions or your sins. If you forsake the LORD and serve foreign gods, then he will turn and do you harm, and consume you, after having done you good." And the people said to Joshua, "Nay; but we will serve the LORD." Then Joshua said to the people, "You are witnesses against yourselves that you have chosen the LORD, to serve him!" And they said "We are witnesses." (vv. 19-22).

It will be the task of the next chapter to trace something of the seriousness of this decision in terms of daily conduct, and the meaning of community life within the people of God.

Chapter Four

GOD AND THE COMMUNITY—THE
RESPONSIBLE SOCIETY

1. The prologue and the first three statements in the charter of the covenant sketch the character and claims of Yahweh; the remainder of the charter is concerned with the meaning of life together under the kingship of Yahweh. This is true even of the command to "remember the Sabbath day to keep it holy" (Exod. 20.8) which particularly in its Deuteronomic form (Deut. 5.12 ff.) takes on a strongly ethical and humanitarian motive in its concern that there should be an opportunity for rest even for the servants with the household.[1] The remaining statements are signposts for the right ordering of any healthy society, inculcating respect for parents, safeguarding the sanctity of life, marriage, property, and banning perjury and covetousness.

For centuries, when the Old Testament was virtually the only document which had survived from the Ancient Near East, such commandments and the expansion and restatement of them which we find in various law codes in the Old Testament, were regarded as the earliest steps in man's moral pilgrimage. They enshrined basic moral principles, first revealed to the Hebrews and binding upon all men ever since. Today, our approach must be rather different. The Old Testament is no longer our only, nor by any means our earliest witness to moral standards and the laws by which men sought to order society in the Ancient Near East. From Mesopotamia have come the Sumerian law code of Lipit Ishtar (19th cent. B.C.), the Akkadian Laws of Eshnunna of roughly similar date,

[1] For a further discussion of Sabbath in the context of worship, cf. Chapter Six, pp. 122 ff.

the Babylonian Code of Hammurabi (18th cent. B.C.), and Assyrian laws transcribed in the twelfth century B.C. but probably centuries older; from Asia Minor have come tablets of the laws of the Hittite Empire, in their present form fourteenth century B.C. but reflecting much older social customs. In addition to such formal codes of law, there are numerous legal documents from Egypt and Mesopotamia, concerned with the administration of the law, with property, taxation, loans, divorce, slavery. All of this reflects social customs and moral standards centuries before the Hebrews were conscious of their destiny as the people of Yahweh.[1] The Hebrews were not the pioneers of morality.

Jeremiah gives us a slashing indictment of an irresponsible monarch whose conduct he sets in sharp contrast to the ideal of kingship exemplified in his father Josiah.

> "Did not your father eat and drink
> and do justice and righteousness?
> Then it was well with him.
> He judged the cause of the poor and needy;
> then it was well.
> Is not this to know me?
> says the LORD" (Jer. 22.15-16).

Over a thousand years before the time of Jeremiah, however, the prologue to the Code of Hammurabi sketched a similar ideal.

> "Anu and Enlil named me
> to promote the welfare of the peoples,
> Hammurabi, the devout god-fearing prince,
> to cause justice to prevail in the land,
> to destroy the wicked and the evil
> that the strong might not oppress the weak
> to rise like the sun over the black-headed people
> and to light up the land."[2]

And in the Ugaritic material (*circa* 1400 B.C.) a son accuses

---

[1] cf. A.N.E.T., pp. 159-226.
[2] Prologue 1, A.N.E.T., p. 164, cf. Epilogue A.N.E.T., p. 177.

his ailing father of failing to fulfil his kingly functions in the following words:

> "By slow degrees thou art growing old
> And in the tomb thou wilt abide.
> Thou hast let thy hand fall into error.
> Thou dost not judge the case of the widow,
> Nor decide the suit of the oppressed."[1]

When we examine the law codes of the Old Testament and of the Ancient Near East we find that often they handle similar, typical situations. Take for example the Code of Hammurabi and one of the earliest Hebrew law codes, the Book of the Covenant (Exod. 20.22-23.33). Both codes deal with debt slavery.

Hammurabi	*Book of the Covenant*
"If a debt renders a citizen distrainable, and he has sold for money his wife, or son, or daughter, or if anyone is sold for service in lieu of debt, they shall work for three years in the house of their purchaser or their distrainer. In the fourth year they shall attain their freedom" (117).	"When you buy a Hebrew slave, he shall serve six years, and in the seventh he shall go out free, for nothing" (Exod. 21.2).

Both deal with various types of assault laying down the *lex talionis* for injuries inflicted against a free born citizen, and a lesser penalty in the case of slaves and serfs.

Hammurabi	*Book of the Covenant*
"If a citizen has destroyed the eye of one of citizen status, they shall destroy his eye. If he has broken the bone of a citizen, his bone shall they break. If he has destroyed the eye of a slave of a citizen, or	"If any harm follows, then you shall give life for life, eye for eye, tooth for tooth, hand for hand, foot for foot, burn for burn, wound for wound, stripe for stripe. When a man strikes the eye of

[1] D.O.T.T., p. 121.

has broken the bone of a serf, he shall pay half of his market value" (196-197 and 199).

his slave, male or female, and destroys it, he shall let the slave go free for the eye's sake. If he knocks out the tooth of his slave, male or female, he shall let the slave go free for the tooth's sake" (Exod. 21. 23-27).

Both deal with the case of a goring ox, and draw a distinction between the penalty in the case of a first offence and in the case when the owner of the ox knows that his animal has a tendency to gore.

Hammurabi

"If an ox has gored a citizen, while going along the road, and has occasioned his death, there shall be no penalty attached to this case.
If the offending ox belonged to a citizen who has been notified by the authorities of its propensity to gore, and he has not removed its horns, or has not tethered the ox, and that ox gored a man of citizen status, occasioning his death, he shall pay a half-mina of silver. If he was the serf of a citizen, he shall pay a third of a mina of silver" (250-252).[1]

Book of the Covenant

"When an ox gores a man or woman to death, the ox shall be stoned, and its flesh shall not be eaten; but the owner of the ox shall be clear. But if the ox has been accustomed to gore in the past, and its owner has been warned but has not kept it in, and it kills a man or a woman, the ox shall be stoned, and its owner also shall be put to death. If a ransom is laid on him, then he shall give for the redemption of his life whatever is laid upon him. If it gores a man's son or daughter, he shall be dealt with according to this same rule. If the ox gores a slave, male or female, the owner shall give to their master thirty shekels of silver, and the ox shall be stoned" (Exod. 21.28-32).

The similarities are all the more interesting when we realize that the two codes deal with very different social conditions,

[1] Quotations from D.O.T.T. pp. 30-35.

Hammurabi legislating for a complex life of an empire with important commercial centres, the Book of the Covenant stemming from an early stage of the Hebrew settlement in Canaan and dealing with a fairly simple agricultural community. It would be difficult to prove any direct link between the two codes, since there are equally striking differences both in spirit and in emphasis. Both probably reflect to some extent long accepted social practices in the Ancient Near East.

In both the Code of Hammurabi and the Book of the Covenant we are dealing with laws couched in the typical case formula of many law codes, a general statement introduced by a word meaning 'in the case that' (if or when), and within this general statement provision being made for certain specific cases. Thus Exod. 21.2 states the general formula concerning debt slavery, vv. 3-6 dealing in turn with specific instances, that is to say, what is to be done if the debt slave is (a) single or married before he comes into slavery (v. 3); (b) given a wife by his master after he enters his service (v. 4); (c) unwilling to leave his master at the end of the prescribed period of service (vv. 5-6).

Moreover, it was generally believed throughout the Ancient Near East that law was given to men by the gods. The stele on which is inscribed the Code of Hammurabi is topped by a relief showing Hammurabi receiving his laws from Shamash, the Babylonian sun god, and god of justice. The Epilogue to the Code itself declares:

> "I Hammurabi am the king of justice
> to whom Shamash committed law."[1]

There is therefore nothing unusual in the form of most of the laws of the Old Testament, nor in the fact that they are claimed to be of divine origin. Wherein does their distinctiveness, if any, belong? Two points are worth noting.

(a) While it is true that most Hebrew law employs the case

[1] A.N.E.T., p. 178b.

63

formula common to Ancient Near East legislations, not all of it appears in this form. The charter of the covenant, for example, is not in this form, but in what is called the apodictic form, the direct address, "You shall not" or "You shall". This form appears in all Hebrew law codes. In the Book of the Covenant we find:

"You shall not permit a sorceress to live" (Exod. 22.18).
"You shall not wrong a stranger or oppress him" (Exod. 22.21).
"You shall not afflict any widow or orphan" (Exod. 22.22).
(Cf. 22.28, 29, 31: 23.1, 2, 6, 9.)

It is true that in a few cases in the Code of Hammurabi and in later Assyrian laws, the normal case formula is replaced by direct statements, e.g.,

"Female slaves must not veil themselves, and he who has seen a female slave veiled must arrest her (and) bring her to the palace tribunal."[1]

But none of these laws uses the direct address in the second person singular or plural. The only instances outside Israel where this 'You shall' or 'You shall not' form occurs are significantly in treaty documents, particularly Hittite treaty documents which, as we have already seen, provide us with the closest parallels to the charter of the covenant of the Old Testament.[2] From the time of the Exodus and the covenant at Mount Sinai onwards, the Hebrew people thought of themselves not merely as a nation in a social or political sense, but as the people of Yahweh, a community standing responsibly under the kingship of Yahweh. Certain of their basic moral standards they traced back to a moment of personal encounter with Yahweh, such standards being binding because they were the expression of the moral kingly rule of Yahweh over his people. Yahweh was therefore involved in the way his people acted towards one another and in a far more direct and personal way than is implied in the bare assertion that law

[1] *Middle Assyrian Laws*, Tablet A.40 x. A.N.E.T., p. 183 where further examples e.g., Hammurabi 36.38-40 are cited.
[2] cf. R. de Vaux, *Ancient Israel*, p. 147

comes to men from the gods. This becomes immediately evident when we consider the second factor.

(b) The Code of Hammurabi is set within the framework of a Prologue and Epilogue which stress the divine origin of the laws and claim that divine punishment will overtake any violation of the law. Within the code itself, however, there is no mention of Shamash or of any other god. The code is purely a corpus of customary civil law without any religious orientation or emphasis. Within the Old Testament law codes however, we do find a distinctive religious emphasis, which will become clear if we look at the various forms of legislation safeguarding the position of the 'stranger' or resident alien with the Hebrew community.

> "You shall not wrong a stranger or oppress him, for you were strangers in the land of Egypt" (Exod. 22.21, cf. 23.9).

> "When a stranger sojourns with you in your land, you shall not do him wrong. The stranger who sojourns with you shall be to you as the native among you, and you shall love him as yourself; for you were strangers in the land of Egypt: I am the LORD your God" (Lev. 19.33-34, cf. Deut. 10.9).

Notice how in each case there is a reference to the Hebrews' own experience of being 'strangers' in Egypt. Not only so, but the Leviticus passage culminates in the words, "I am Yahweh your God", a phrase which inevitably recalls the Exodus experience, "I am Yahweh your God who brought you out of the land of Egypt". The implication of such legislation is that, because Yahweh had shown his compassion to the people when they were strangers, so must they show a like compassion to the strangers in their midst. "As Yahweh . . . so shall you" becomes one of the most important moral directives in the Old Testament. The known character of God is to be reflected in the conduct of his people. The Law of Holiness (Lev. 17-26) takes its name from the fact that the key phrase round which its teaching is built is "You shall be holy for I the LORD your God am holy" (19.2; 20.7; 21.8).

In the Book of Deuteronomy the reiterated call is to "love Yahweh your God" (6.5; 10.12; 11.1, 13, 22; 19.9;) precisely because Israel owes her very existence to the fact that Yahweh had set his love upon her (7.7-8). As Yahweh had loved, so must his people. When Deuteronomy deals with regulations governing the release of a debtor slave in the seventh year, it has this to say:

> "And when you let him go free from you, you shall not let him go empty-handed; you shall furnish him liberally out of your flock, out of your threshing floor, and out of your wine press; as the LORD your God has blessed you, you shall give to him. You shall remember that you were a slave in the land of Egypt, and the LORD your God redeemed you; therefore I command you this day" (Deut. 15.13-15).

Notice the reason given for release. As Yahweh had redeemed his people, securing their release from enslavement in Egypt, so must they be prepared to release their enslaved brother. Nor must the slave be sent out empty-handed "as the LORD your God has blessed you, you shall give to him". In as much as Yahweh's blessing consisted in his giving of the good things of life, this is equivalent to saying, "as Yahweh has given, so must you give".

2. The charter of the covenant at Mount Sinai shows us the Hebrews as the people of Yahweh committed to ordering their life in the light of, and in response to, the continuing activity of Yahweh, the God who had delivered them out of enslavement in Egypt. If the commandments contained in the charter of the covenant provided them with certain basic directives for living, they were never regarded as a final or complete declaration of Yahweh's will. That will needed ever to be interpreted afresh against the background of changing social and political factors. We can trace several such reinterpretations within the Old Testament.

The earliest is probably the *Book of the Covenant* (Exod. 20.22-23.33), a code which already presupposes in certain of its provisions that the Hebrews are leading a settled agricultural life in Canaan. As it stands before us it is a curious mixture of laws of different types and probably of different origin. There are the characteristic case laws introduced by 'when' (*ki*) or 'if' (*'im*) (21.1-11; 21.18-22.8; 22.10-16, 25-27; 23.4-5). There are apodictic laws, 'You shall not', 'You shall' (20.23-24; 22.18, 21-22; 22.28-23.3; 23.6-19). There are laws stated in a terse rhythmic formula beginning with a participle in Hebrew and dealing always with capital offences, e.g., He who mortally smites a man shall be put to death (21.12, 15-17; 22.19-20). The contents of the code are equally varied. Among the subjects for which it legislates are debt slavery (21.1-11), assault (21.12-27), the dangerous ox (21.28-36), theft (22.1-3), property offences (22.5-6), breach of trust (22.7-15), sexual offences (22.16-19), the treatment of strangers, widows, orphans and the poor (22.21-27, cf. 23.9), perversion of justice (23.1-3, 6-8), and various religious matters ranging from the correct specifications for an altar (20.24-26) to the celebration of Sabbath and the most important festivals of the religious year (23.12-16). In the varied formulation of its laws, the varied comprehensiveness of its material and the distinctive religious emphasis to which it witnesses (see above), the Book of the Covenant is typical of other and later law codes in the Old Testament.

The Deuteronomic Code[1] formed the basis of the religious reformation in Judah under King Josiah in the year 621 B.C., but it undoubtedly contains much older material, probably originating in priestly circles in the northern kingdom of Israel. This code consists of a series of sermonic variations of the law, rather than of formal legislation. It stems from the crisis in the people's loyalty to Yahweh occasioned by the settlement in Canaan and the influence of Canaanite religious and social practices. It is characterised by:

[1] Its precise extent is debated—certainly it contained Deuteronomy 12-26, but possibly more of the material within our present Book of Deuteronomy.

(a) The stress which it lays upon the issues at stake in the people's attitude to the law of Yahweh. The whole well-being of the community depends upon its keeping the provisions of the law.

> "Be careful to heed all these words which I command you, that it may go well with you and with your children after you for ever, when you do what is good and right in the sight of the LORD your God" (12.28).

Chapters 27 and 28 contain a series of blessings and curses directly related to the people's response to Yahweh's instructions.

> "And if you obey the voice of the LORD your God, being careful to do all his commandments which I command you this day, the LORD your God will set you high above all the nations of the earth. And all these blessings shall come upon you and overtake you, if you obey the voice of the LORD your God" (28.1-2).

> "But if you will not obey the voice of the LORD your God or be careful to do all his commandments and his statutes which I command you this day, then all these curses shall come upon you and overtake you" (28.15; cf. 11.13-17, 26-28).

(b) Much of its legislation is marked by a strongly humanitarian emphasis. Anything which threatens to undermine the people's single-hearted loyalty to Yahweh is to be mercilessly crushed (12.2-3; cf. 13.6-18; 17.2-7; 18.9-14), but in other respects Deuteronomy develops and extends the note of compassion which is evident in the Book of the Covenant in its concern for the stranger, the widow, the orphan and the poor. Provision is made for a place of refuge for the unintentional homicide (19.4-10); certain categories of men including newly-weds and cowards are to be excused from service in the forces (20.1-8; cf. 24.5)[1]; the feelings of a debtor are to be respected (24.10-11; cf. 15.12-15); servants are to be given their rights (24.14-15); the alien, the orphan and the

[1] Some of the provisions in this section may derive ultimately from primitive tabu, but they have been humanised in Deuteronomy.

68

widow are not only to be protected by the law, but provided for (24.17-22).

The Law of Holiness (Lev. 17-26) is a compilation of priestly directives of varied date and character, but probably edited sometime early in the sixth century B.C. Much of it, like other priestly instruction in Exodus, Leviticus, Numbers and Ezekiel, is concerned with regulations for worship, different types of sacrifice, the duties of the priesthood, the great occasions of the religious year (cf. 17; 19.1-7; 21.1-24.9), but it also deals at length with sexual offences (18; 19.20-22; 20.10-21) and with the needs of the resident alien and the poor (19.9-10, 33; 23.22). It further seeks to safeguard the rights of one's fellow-citizens in the community, including the deaf and the blind, its teaching culminating in the injunction:

> "You shall not hate your brother in your heart, but you shall reason with your neighbour, lest you bear sin because of him. You shall not take vengeance or bear any grudge against the sons of your own people, but you shall love your neighbour as yourself: I am the LORD" (19.17-18).

Even if the 'neighbour' here mentioned is confined to a fellow Hebrew and possibly the resident alien, it remains a praiseworthy and exacting demand. It is typical of this code that many of its injunctions end with the words, "I am Yahweh", or "I am Yahweh your God",[1] thus stressing the fundamental and continuing religious experience in the light of which the life of society had to be organised.

3. It must not be assumed from all this that the Old Testament presents us with the picture of a people fired with enthusiasm for keeping the instructions of Yahweh; far from it. Whatever the critical problems raised by the narrative of Exodus 32, it is symbolic of a continuing tension within the Old Testament that, while Moses in his lonely vigil on Mount Sinai is receiving

[1] cf. 18.5, 30; 19.4, 10, 11, 14, 16, 18, 25, 28, 30, 31, 32, 34, 37; 22.3, 30, 33; 23; 22, 43.

the charter of the covenant, the stone tablets "written with the finger of God" (Exod. 31.18), the people, impatient with Moses' long absence, take their golden ear-rings, make a molten calf and sacrifice to it to the accompaniment of the ritual chant.

"These are your gods, O Israel, who brought you up out of the land of Egypt" (Exod. 32.4, 8).

Moses in this narrative, interceding with Yahweh on behalf of the people (32.11-14), smashing in righteous indignation the stone tablets on which are inscribed the laws (32.15-20), challenging the people in the words, "Who is on the LORD's side?" (32.25-27), is the prototype of a succession of Old Testament prophets. Representing the people in prayer, facing them with the stern consequences of disobedience, challenging them to repent, to turn in their tracks, the great prophetic figures in the Old Testament bear witness to the moral kingship of Yahweh over his people. Often in revolt against society as they saw it, they were no mere revolutionaries; nor were they iconoclasts though they fearlessly carried protest to its logical conclusion. They were in the best sense of the word traditionalists who sought to interpret to successive generations the meaning of their responsibility as the people of Yahweh. Such men were drawn from all walks of life. Amos was a hill shepherd (Amos 1.1; 7.14); Isaiah of Jerusalem was probably a courtier (Isa. 36 ff.); Jeremiah came from a priestly family (Jer. 1.1); Micah was in all likelihood a peasant farmer. They did not belong to any professional religious caste, though later prophets were conscious of standing in a goodly tradition (Jer. 7.25; 25.4; 29.19; 35.15)[1]. Indeed they were often bitterly critical of the official representatives of religion, the priests in particular coming under the lash of their invective. Traditionally the priest was not merely a cultic official who performed the correct sacrificial ritual. He

[1] For the relationship between such prophets and the 'sons of the prophets', the members of the official prophetic guilds, cf. pp. 84 ff.

was the guardian and interpreter of *Torah,* Yahweh's instructions to his people. Versions of *Torah* would be kept in the local sanctuaries, and it was the function of the priest to instruct the people in the known demands of Yahweh. It is precisely because they have failed to do this that Jeremiah bitterly criticises them.

> "The priests did not say, 'Where is the LORD?'
> Those who handle the law did not know me" (Jer. 2.8).

Elsewhere he accuses the priests of being more interested in lining their own pockets than in confronting the people with the disturbing challenge of Yahweh's requirements (Jer. 6.13; 8.10). Often in conflict with the establishment (cf. Amos 7.10; Jer. 20.1-6; 38), the prophet took his stand upon a self-authenticating religious experience in which Yahweh laid hand upon him, and summoned him to be his spokesman.

> "The LORD took me from following the flock" (Amos 7.15).

> "Now the word of the LORD came to me saying,
> 'Before I formed you in the womb I knew you,
> and before you were born I consecrated you;
> I appointed you a prophet to the nations' " (Jer. 1.4-5).

> "And I heard the voice of the LORD saying, 'Whom shall I send,
> and who will go for us?' Then I said, 'Here I am! Send me' "
> (Isa. 6.8).

This religious encounter is as varied as the men who experienced it, but from it there emerges a man overwhelmed with the sense of divine compulsion, certain that Yahweh has spoken to him a word of immediate moral relevance to the day. He stands before his people as the herald of the kingship of Yahweh. "Thus saith Yahweh" is the burden of his message. In a sense they are men on the defensive, admittedly a very belligerent defensive, seeking to check every threat to the rule of Yahweh over his people.

The forces which threatened to blind the people to their moral responsibilities as the people of Yahweh were doubtless as infinitely varied as the motives of the human heart, but two factors in the political, social and religious background to Hebrew life in Canaan call for comment.

(a) There was a threat to the moral kingship of Yahweh from the advent of human kingship in Israel. When the Hebrews invaded Canaan, and for many years thereafter, they formed a loose-knit tribal federation or amphictyony, held together by a common religious loyalty which was periodically renewed and strengthened by a tribal gathering at some central shrine. For the rest, it was left to the hour of crisis to produce a gifted leader able to rally the people to common action against an invader (cf. Joshua-Judges). Severe and sustained pressure from the Philistine city states of the coastal plain proved the political and military inadequacy of this system. There was need for a permanent central authority with power to act decisively in the name of all the tribes. What more natural than that the Hebrews should adopt from neighbouring Canaanite city states an institution which had a long history in the Ancient Near East, Kingship. To adopt is easy, but to integrate what has been adopted into the life of the community may raise difficult questions. The coming of kingship faced the Hebrews with certain problems. What kind of kingship was this to be? In particular, what was to be the relationship between the king who occupied the throne and Yahweh who, from Mount Sinai onwards, had been enthroned over the life of his people? These issues are fought out in the historical narratives in the Old Testament in the relationship between king and prophet.

In the various traditions which have been handed down, Samuel is a curiously complex figure. He is a 'seer', one with the gift of supernatural sight, the person to whom you would go to discover the whereabouts of lost asses (1 Sam. 9). He is a priest, brought up in the temple at Shiloh (1 Sam. 2-4), present at great sacrificial occasions (1 Sam. 9.13 ff.), fulfilling the traditional priestly functions of administering Yahweh's Torah to the people (1 Sam. 12.1-5, cf. 15-17). Above all he is a prophet—a note, in the narrative which describes Samuel as a seer, indicates how the figure of Samuel cuts across all neat classifications by declaring

> "Formerly in Israel, when a man went to inquire of God, he said, 'Come, let us go to the seer'; for he who is now called a prophet was formerly called a seer" (1 Sam. 9.9).

A commanding figure among the Hebrews, he takes the initiative, according to one strand in the tradition, in having Saul elected as first king in Israel (1 Sam. 9.1-10.16). Another strand in the tradition significantly suggests that Samuel only grudgingly acquiesced in the popular desire for a king, and not before declaring that it was tantamount to rebellion against Yahweh (cf. 1 Sam. 12, in particular v. 17). What is certain is that, once Saul was established as king, there was friction between him and Samuel. This was no merely personal vendetta. Greater issues were at stake. Trouble came to a head after Saul's victory over the Amalekites. According to accepted custom, the defeated enemy was placed under the 'ban' (ḥerem), that is to say the entire community and its possessions were destroyed in what was virtually an act of sacrifice to the god who had given his people victory (cf. Joshua 6.17; Deut. 20.16-18, and the Moabite stone). Saul, well aware of this, chose to keep for himself certain of the spoils of victory, including Agag, King of the Amalekites. When challenged by Samuel, he put forward the lame excuse that he was reserving Agag and the best of his flock for a special sacrifice to Yahweh. Samuel will have none of it. Unerringly, he goes to the heart of the matter.

> "Has the LORD as great delight in burnt offerings and sacrifices,
>   as in obeying the voice of the LORD?
> Behold, to obey is better than sacrifice,
>   and to hearken than the fat of rams.
> For rebellion is as the sin of divination,
>   and stubbornness is as iniquity and idolatry.
> Because you have rejected the word of the LORD,
>   he has also rejected you from being king" (1 Sam. 15.22-23).

We must not allow humanitarian instincts to run away with us in interpreting this story. We may find the whole concept of ḥerem morally indefensible, but the crucial issue in the story centres upon one word 'obedience', the obedience of a king. Is a Hebrew king to be allowed to play fast and loose with Yahweh-sanctioned customs, just because he is the king, or is he, like any other Hebrew, under the ultimate kingship of Yahweh and thus bound to obey the law of Yahweh? Whatever the symbolism intended by a king such as Hammurabi receiving the law from Shamash the god of justice, the king in the Ancient Near East tended to be an absolute monarch whose every word and act was law. It could not be so among the Hebrews. They acknowledged only one absolute monarch, Yahweh. The prophetic heralds never allowed the ruling monarch among the Hebrews to forget this truth. Even David, who came to represent the ideal of Hebrew kingship, learned this lesson the hard way. When through the abuse of power he liquidated one of his own loyal mercenaries, Uriah the Hittite, in order to gratify his lust for Uriah's wife Bathsheba, he was called to account by the voice of prophetic challenge. In that exquisite parable of the poor shepherd, whose one ewe lamb became the victim of a rich man's rapacity (2 Sam. 12.1-4), David is made by Nathan the prophet to see his own act for what it is, ruthless murder and theft in violation of the law of Yahweh. Would any oriental monarch outside Israel have seen it in this light, or at the word of a commoner have confessed, "I have sinned against the LORD" (2 Sam. 12.13)? The issues are sharply focused in the relationship between the prophet Elijah on the one hand and King Ahab and his foreign Queen Jezebel on the other (1 Kings 21). Jezebel, brought up in court circles which accepted that the king's word was law, could not understand why Ahab hesitated to confiscate a peasant's small-holding to make way for the enlargement of the palace vegetable garden. Ahab, though sulking, was sufficient of the Hebrew to know that Naboth could not legally be forced to part with his plot. The land was not his to alienate; it was family property, held in trust from Yahweh to be handed down to succeeding generations. Jezebel mocks Ahab's scruples and behind a façade of legality has Naboth liquidated. On the way to take possession of the fruits of his wife's ruthless employment of royal power, Ahab is confronted by Elijah.

"Ahab said to Elijah, 'Have you found me, O my enemy?' He answered, 'I have found you, because you have sold yourself to do what is evil in the sight of the LORD" (1 Kings 21.20).

There follows a word of stern judgement upon the entire royal house.

The words of Andrew Melville to James VI of Scotland are worth recalling. "There are two kings and two kingdoms in Scotland. There is Christ Jesus the King and his Kingdom the Kirk whose subject King James the Sixth is, and of whose kingdom not a king, nor a lord, nor a head but a member".[1] While the Old Testament prophets would hardly have accepted the sixteenth century Scottish doctrine of the two kingdoms, the kirk and the state, they were insistent that there were two kings, only one of whom, Yahweh, could claim absolute power. As far as Yahweh and his kingly decrees were concerned, the man who sat upon the throne in Jerusalem or in Samaria was but a member of the covenant community, as bound by the charter of the covenant, and the laws which developed from it, as the poorest peasant in the land.

(b) An even more serious threat to the moral kingship of Yahweh came from religion. We have already looked briefly at the type of religion which the Hebrews encountered when they settled in Canaan.[2] Essentially it was a religion designed to enable men to control and to fit themselves into the environment in which they lived. Its chief gods and goddesses were representations of nature in its various aspects, fertility and drought, life and death. It was concerned to ensure man's physical survival and the material well being of society. It was

[1] *Autobiography and Diary of James Melville*, edited by Pitcairn for the Woodrow Society, p. 370.   [2] cf. pp. 49 ff.

not concerned with the quality of a man's life; it made no searching moral demands. Provided the correct ritual were performed at the appropriate occasion in the year, provided suitable sacrifices were offered, then a god such as Baal could be relied upon to bless his people and ensure the fertility of their fields for the coming year. It was such a religion masquerading as the true worship of Yahweh that the prophets vigorously denounced. They did not speak to a godless community whose churches were sparsely attended. They spoke to a people who were only too religious, who flocked to temples whose services satisfied their deep emotional needs and dulled their conscience.

In the northern kingdom of Israel in Amos' day (*circa* 750 B.C.), in an age of increasing prosperity and national self-confidence, community life left much to be desired. The poor were trodden underfoot (Amos 2.6; 5.10-11; 8.4) while the social *élite* wallowed in the lap of luxury (4.1; 6.4-6). Sharp business practices were only too common (8.4-6). Bribery perverted the course of justice (5.12). Religion flourished. Temples such as Bethel and Gilgal were on festive occasions thronged with worshippers, ostentatiously proclaiming their piety. Pilgrimages to Beersheba, a traditional holy site in the far south, were popular. Amos, in a few pungent phrases, gives us his verdict on this religion. Perhaps echoing a pilgrim cry, he says:

"Come to Bethel, and transgress;
    to Gilgal, and multiply transgression" (4.4).

"I hate, I despise your feasts,
    and I take no delight in your solemn assemblies.
Even though you offer me your burnt offerings and
    cereal offerings,
I will not accept them,
and the peace offerings of your fatted beasts
I will not look upon.
Take away from me the noise of your songs;
    to the melody of your harps I will not listen"
                        (5.21-23, cf. 5.4-5).

Such a religion going hand in hand with social corruption and callous indifference to the needs of men is an open affront to the moral kingship of Yahweh. Slightly later, Hosea draws much the same picture of Israelite life, a community deeply, almost superstitiously religious (cf. Hos. 4.11-13), but a community in which

> "There is no faithfulness or kindness,
> and no knowledge of God in the land;
> there is swearing, lying, killing, stealing and
> committing adultery;
> they break all bounds and murder follows murder"
>
> (4.1b-2).

Isaiah and Micah provide us with similar evidence for the state of Judean society towards the close of the eighth century B.C.—murder and robbery, drunken debauchery, bribery and shameless exploitation of the poor, the orphan and the widow (Isa. 1.2-15, 21-23; 3.13-18; 5.8-12; Mic. 2.1-2; 3.1-3).

Not only was this a religion without any moral or social relevance but in certain important respects it actively encouraged immorality. No great imagination is needed to see the link between the fertility of the soil and the fertility of the human race. Central to the fertility cult ritual there is frequently dramatised sexual intercourse between the god and goddess of fertility, such intercourse stimulating and releasing the fertilising power in nature. Among the personnel of the temples were women described literally as 'holy women' (qedheshoth), women "in the service of the gods"; this is the basic religious meaning of holy (q-d-sh) and it does not necessarily carry with it any moral connotation. It was considered an act of piety for worshippers to have intercourse with such 'holy women', temple prostitutes, probably in the belief that through a process of sympathetic magic such sexual activity would help the gods and goddesses of fertility to fulfil their function. There is little point, says Hosea, in talking about the standards of chastity incumbent upon women,

77

"for the men themselves go aside with harlots,
and sacrifice with cult prostitutes" (Hos. 4.14b).

To the prophets this is not an act of religious significance but
sheer immorality and offence against the moral holiness of
Yahweh (Amos 2.7).

Against such a religion with its social irrelevance and its
practice of cult prostitution, the prophets made a repeated
plea for 'righteousness' and 'justice' within society as alone
being consistent with the acceptance of the kingship of Yahweh
over the nation's life. Amos caps his indictment of the
ritual of his day with the words:

"But let justice roll down like waters,
and righteousness like an ever-flowing stream"
(Amos 5.24, cf. 5.7, 15; Isa. 1.27, 5.14; Mic. 3.1, 6.8).

These two words, justice (*mishpat*) and righteousness (*sedhaqa*)
echo in one form or another across the teaching of all the great
prophetic figures in the Old Testament. This does not mean
that the prophets of the eighth century B.C. onwards suddenly
gave a new moral content to the religion of the Hebrews. In
themselves the words are curiously ambiguous in content.
Taken together and read in the light of the religious pilgrimage
of the Hebrew people, they point us to that correct ordering
of society which is alone consistent with the claim to be the
people of Yahweh. Whatever the root meaning of the words —
and in the case of *sedhaqa* this is far from certain—both words
have about them in the Old Testament a certain legal flavour.
Mishpat is, strictly speaking, the decision of a *shophet* or judge,
the verdict given in some particular case, a verdict which
aims at giving the parties involved what is their due. Inevitably
such 'decisions' (*mishpatim*) were taken in the light of what
was traditionally accepted as right within the community.
Mishpat, therefore, came to mean on the one hand traditional
practice, custom, habit (cf. 2 Kings 17.33) and on the other,
what is right. The Book of the Covenant is introduced in
Exod. 21.2 with the words, "Now these are the *mishpatim*

which you shall set before them" that is to say, here are the ordinances or judgements by which the life of society must be ordered. When two parties are in dispute, the effect of the judge's decision is to make one party to the case 'in the right', the other 'in the wrong'. This being 'in the right' is one of the earliest meanings of the word *ṣedhaqa* and its corresponding adjective *ṣaddiq*. In the Ugaritic texts, for example, the word is used to describe a legitimate wife.[1] In the Tell el Amarna correspondence a Canaanite vassal king protests that, whatever others may have insinuated, he is 'in the right', innocent, above the board in all his dealings with his Egyptian over-lord.[2] In the early narrative in Genesis 38 Sheikh Judah acknowledges that in the light of accepted social custom his daughter-in-law Tamar is more 'in the right' than he, though he had just convicted her of adultery. 'Sacrifices of righteous-ness' (A.V.) in the Old Testament mean sacrifices offered to God in accordance with correct ritual practice and conditions as laid down in the law (Deut. 33.19; Ps. 4.5); while 'balances of righteousness' (Lv. 19. 36) mean scales which weigh and measure according to the right standards laid down by the community. The prophetic demand for righteousness is there-fore a demand that the community should be 'in the right' with Yahweh and in prophetic eyes there is only one way so to be 'in the right'. The demand for 'justice' and 'righteousness' within the community is a call for a single-hearted loyalty to Yahweh which will express itself in a society whose life is ordered in the light of Yahweh's law.

This goal of a society responsible because it lives in response to the gracious initiative of Yahweh is nowhere more clearly stated than in Deut. 6.4-5, a passage which has become the central creed of Judaism throughout the ages.

"Hear, O Israel: the LORD our God is one LORD; and you shall love the LORD your God with all your heart, and with all your soul, and with all your might."

[1] J. Gray, *The Legacy of Canaan*, pp. 94 ff.
[2] D.O.T.T., p. 39; A.N.E.T., p. 488.

"The LORD our God is one LORD" is a somewhat enigmatic phrase, four words in Hebrew capable of several different interpretations. In context, the emphasis is probably on the fact that Yahweh is the only God, the sole object of Israel's devotion. There is nothing enigmatic, however, about the words which follow. They claim unreservedly for Yahweh the mind and the will (the heart being for the Hebrews the centre not of the emotions but of the will and the intellect), and the whole life ('soul' being the vital life-principle in man). In accordance with the instructions in vv. 6-9, this passage and others which refer to the same custom in Torah[1] are placed inside a small container called *mezuzah* and fastened to the doorposts of every Jewish home, as well as being worn as frontlets attached to forehead and arm by adult male Jews at certain services in the synagogue. That home life and business, worship and recreation should reflect the moral kingship of Yahweh is the obedience to which the Hebrews were committed by becoming the people of Yahweh at Mount Sinai.

[1] Exod. 13.1-10, 11-16; Deut. 11.13-21.

Chapter Five

THE PEOPLE OF GOD—FAILURE
AND CHALLENGE

ALTHOUGH Athens saw herself in Pericles' words as the "educator of Greece", none the less during the prolonged war with Sparta which sapped much of the vitality from Athens, many unedifying things were done in the name of Athenian democracy. The more conscious a people may be of its peculiar destiny, the more it is tempted to sacrifice others to that destiny. We are only too painfully aware of what the twentieth century has sacrificed upon the altar of the 'Herrenvolk', white supremacy and Communism. Not only so, but ideals which were once ennobling may become debased and distorted beyond all recognition. The history of the Hebrew people provides many an illustration. "I am Yahweh your God, you are my people"—this, the basic covenant relationship, was capable of being misinterpreted. The events of Hebrew history made it almost inevitable that it should be so. The Exodus had dramatically demonstrated Yahweh's concern for his people. He had delivered them; he had routed their enemies. The settlement in Canaan taught the same lesson. Such literature as has survived from this period breathes the spirit of an intense religious nationalism or at least a spirit which could degenerate into such a religious nationalism. One of the earliest surviving fragments of Hebrew literature, the Song of Deborah in Judges 5 has been well described as "a spontaneous outburst of the heart of man who, having taken part in a mighty historical event, is now impelled to master it in rhythmical form, to grasp, to express, to transmit it".[1] The theme of the song is Yahweh and Israel, in particular the

[1] M. Buber, *The Prophetic Faith*, p. 8.

81

victorious exploits (literally 'righteousness') of Yahweh against a Canaanite alliance in a battle fought "at Taanach, by the waters of Megiddo" (Judges 5.19). The poem is utterly religious from beginning to end, pulsating with the conviction that the Hebrews are not merely a nation, or a motley collection of tribes, but the people of Yahweh. By dramatic contrast and conscious repetition the poet catches the mood of religious fervour and exaltation. The opening stanza, praising Yahweh for his people's willingness to offer themselves for battle (v. 2) is echoed in v. 9 after a description of the circumstances which made united action imperative. The poet's song in v. 3 is echoed by rich, poor and travellers at the wells chanting the "triumphs of the LORD" (vv. 10-11). The coming of Yahweh, God of Sinai from his southern abode in violent thunderstorm (vv. 4-5) finds its response in the description of the battle.

> From heaven fought the stars,
> from their courses they fought against Sisera.
> The torrent Kishon swept them away,
> the onrushing torrent, the torrent Kishon (vv. 20-21).

The tramp of marching feet (11b, 13), the pounding of horses' hooves (v. 22) contrasts with the treacherous inactivity of the tribes which refused to rally to the fiery cross of Yahweh (vv. 15b-17, 23), the traitors who

> came not to the help of the LORD,
> to the help of the LORD against the mighty (v. 23).

Nothing more truly demonstrates the poet's genius than the two contrasting pictures which end the poem. Jael, wife of Heber the Kenite, savagely strikes down Sisera the Canaanite commander who, exhausted by his flight from the battlefield, had sought the hospitality of her tent. Sisera's mother and her attendants meanwhile anxiously await his triumphant homecoming. He is longer than expected. He must be distributing the booty, and claiming for himself the rich spoils of victory. Into their wishful thinking breaks the poet's cry,

"So perish all thine enemies, o LORD!
But thy friends be like the sun as he rises in his might" (v. 31).

Yahweh was god of the Hebrew battle line. Into battle the people carried with them the ark of the covenant. According to Deuteronomic tradition (Deut. 10.1-5) this box of acacia wood contained the tablets on which were inscribed the charter of the covenant. The other name by which it is known in the Old Testament, 'the ark of the testimony' (Exod. 26.33; 40.21) may similarly point to its connection with the charter of the covenant, Yahweh's testimony to his people. But the ark was more than a suitable container for the tablets of the law, it was regarded in a very real sense as being the presence of Yahweh among his people. According to Numbers 10.35, Moses greeted the setting forth of the ark from the Hebrew encampment with the words,

"Arise, o LORD, and let thy enemies be scattered, and let them that hate thee flee before thee."

When the ark came to rest he said, "Return o LORD, to the ten thousand thousands of Israel" (v. 36).

Many of the historical narratives dealing with the settlement in Canaan and the early days of the monarchy make it clear that the ark was regarded both by the Hebrews and their enemies as the visible sign of the presence of Yahweh with his people (1 Sam. 4-6; 2 Sam. 6). The Philistines greet the arrival of the ark in the Hebrew camp thus,

"The gods have come into the camp . . . Woe to us! Who can deliver us from the power of these mighty gods?" (1 Sam. 4.7a, 8b).

The waters of the Jordan part before the ark to allow the people of Yahweh to cross dry shod (Joshua 3-4). The same ark, carried ceremoniously round the walls of the Canaanite bastion, Jericho, ensures its mysterious capture and destruction (Joshua 6). "So perish all thine enemies, o LORD".

Unfortunately it is but a short step from this faith to the assumption that Yahweh is merely the private patron saint of the Hebrews and that the enemies of the Hebrews must necessarily be the enemies of Yahweh. This assumption seems to have been encouraged by certain religious groups within the nation, notably the 'sons of the prophets', the prophetic guilds.[1] These sons of the prophets seem to have been attached to local shrines, and probably had an important part to play in fostering religious enthusiasm at the sanctuaries. In many respects they were the Hebrew counterparts of the prophets of Baal with whom Elijah clashed at Mount Carmel (1 Kings 18). Two things are clear about them. Firstly, like the prophets of Baal, they were subject to that highly abnormal type of religious conduct, still associated with certain revivalist movements, to which we give the name ecstasy. Sometimes such behaviour seems to have seized them involuntarily; at other times it was deliberately induced by certain well known techniques such as music and rhythmic dancing. Whatever the reason for such conduct, it transformed them into ecstatics, they became 'other than themselves', caught up in what was regarded as a type of union with the god. In Hebrew religious terminology, such conduct was said to be the result of the Spirit of Yahweh coming upon them (1 Sam. 10.9-13; 19.20-24). Secondly, if such prophets were enthusiasts, they were very much enthusiasts for Yahweh and his people. They seem to have been commonly consulted by Israelite kings on matters of policy, and invariably they adopted a highly patriotic line, either because they were dependent on royal patronage, or because they genuinely saw no possible clash between the interests of Yahweh and the interests of Israel. It is unfortunate that the same word prophet (*nabhi'*) does duty in the Old Testament for the members of such prophetic guilds and men of the stamp of Elijah, Amos, Isaiah and

[1] In Hebrew idiom, 'son of' means one belonging to a certain category. Thus *baqar* is a collective noun meaning a herd of cattle or oxen; a single ox or heifer is *ben baqar*, literally 'son of the herd', a member of the herd.

Jeremiah. True, they have certain things in common. The great prophetic figures were subject to ecstatic experiences. One of them, Elisha, seems to have been the grand master of a prophetic brotherhood centred upon Bethel and Jericho (2 Kings 2; 6.1-7). But the men who formed the goodly tradition of 'his servants, the prophets', far from being unquestioning patriots were moral realists who took seriously not only the privileges but the responsibilities of being the people of Yahweh, and the ominous consequences of failing to live up to these responsibilities. The parting of the ways is clearly seen in the story of Micaiah, son of Imlah, and the four hundred prophets in 1 Kings 22. The setting is a campaign proposed by Ahab, king of Israel, and his son-in-law Jehoshaphat, king of Judah to enforce their rights under a peace treaty (*circa* 849 B.C.). Jehoshaphat wished to ensure that the campaign had Yahweh's blessing.

> And Jehoshaphat said to the king of Israel, "Inquire first for the word of the LORD." Then the king of Israel gathered the prophets together, about four hundred men, and said to them, "Shall I go to battle against Ramoth-gilead, or shall I forbear?" And they said, "Go up; for the LORD will give it into the hand of the king" (1 Kings 22.5-6).

The master of the prophetic guild sealed this favourable response by an act of prophetic symbolism, making iron horns and declaring, "With these you shall push the Syrians until they are destroyed" (v. 11). Jehoshaphat is not wholly convinced; he wishes a second opinion. After some preliminary hedging, it comes from Micaiah, son of Imlah, whom Ahab describes as a man who "never prophesies good concerning me, but evil" (v. 8). Micaiah recounts a vision set in the heavenly court, with Yahweh deliberately sending a 'lying spirit' to the prophets to lure Ahab to his doom. In spite of abuse from the other prophets, and arrest, Micaiah insists "If you return in peace, the LORD has not spoken by me" (v. 28). The joint campaign ends in disaster and in the death of Ahab. Micaiah had taken issue with what was certainly a wide-spread belief in his day, that Yahweh could be relied upon to bless all the activities of his people.

Almost one hundred years later, Amos returns to the attack. Much of the teaching of Amos is intelligible only when placed against the background of a religious attitude which can only be regarded as a complete distortion of the covenant. Nowhere is this more evident than in what he has to say about one of the popular religious slogans of the age, "the day of the LORD".

> "Woe to you who desire the day of the LORD!
> Why would you have the day of the LORD?
> It is darkness, and not light;
> as if a man fled from a lion,
> and a bear met him;
> or went into the house and leaned with his hand against the wall,
> and a serpent bit him.
> Is not the day of the LORD darkness, and not light,
> and gloom with no brightness in it?" (Amos 5.18-20).

The origin of this belief in the day of Yahweh is much disputed. It is perhaps unnecessary to look further than the essentially historical character of Hebrew faith. In Joshua 10.12 a Hebrew victory is described as being "the day when the LORD gave the Amorites over to the men of Israel". If Yahweh thus routed his people's enemies, could he not be relied upon to do so again on some future day? Certainly in Israel in Amos' time, there were many who, blind to social decay and corruption, looked forward with eager expectancy to a day when Yahweh would triumphantly vindicate his people, liquidate all their enemies and fulfil their every desire by inaugurating an era of peace and prosperity. A good time was coming. Yahweh could be trusted to see to it, a day of light, of brightness, of joy and happiness for his people. Amos shares the conviction that Yahweh is the God of Israel. He believes firmly in the 'gospel' in the Old Testament. Yahweh had brought his people out of the enslavement in Egypt; he had been with them during their wilderness wanderings; he had paved the way for their entry into Canaan (Amos 2.9-10).

86

He is the God of the covenant, but that does not, for Amos, convert him into the private patron saint of Israel, nor does it mean that he exists solely to satisfy the desires and whims of his people. Such fond illusions Amos combats in two ways.

1. Yahweh may be the God of Israel, but he is not merely the God of Israel. The destiny of all men and all nations is within his control. He brought the Hebrews out of enslavement in Egypt; yes indeed, but he was also responsible for the coming of the Philistines from their Aegean homeland and the Aramaean movement from Mesopotamia. He is concerned with the Ethiopians as well as with Israel (9.7). The frontal attack on a purely nationalistic portrait of Yahweh is brilliantly illustrated in the sermon which forms the first major part of the book of Amos, 1.3-2.4. One by one, Amos arraigns the nations surrounding Israel before the bar of Yahweh's judgement in a series of oracles, each conforming to a set pattern.

(a) The introductory pronouncement, "Thus saith Yahweh".

(b) An indictment formula, "For three transgressions of X and for four". This is a common usage in the Old Testament and elsewhere in Ancient Near Eastern literature whereby one number capped by the following number in a series is used to indicate an unspecified number;[1] 'for transgression upon transgression'; and the word used for transgression means literally 'rebellion'. The nations are in revolt against the moral kingship of Yahweh.

(c) The threat of punishment indicated in a phrase which in its very vagueness is doubly ominous. "I will not turn it back". What is 'it'? Yahweh's anger or his judgement or punishment? We do not know. But something highly unpleasant is on the way.

[1] cf. Job 5.19; Prov. 30.15 ff. and A.N.E.T., pp. 132, 146 for Ugaritic examples.

(d) A brief description of the particular crime or crimes committed is capped by the picture of coming disaster engulfing the community. The crimes specified—wartime atrocities (1. 8, 13), forcible deportation of population (1. 6), ruthless disregard of treaty obligations (1. 9), uncontrolled aggressiveness (1. 10), an act of calculated impiety (2.2)—read like a catalogue of the war crimes of the twentieth century.

No doubt Amos' audience initially enjoyed this diatribe against peoples with whom the Hebrews were often in open conflict. But Amos is no nationalistic prophet. In 2.1-3 for instance, the Moabites are accused of a crime committed, not against Israel, but against the Edomites, one of Israel's most implacable enemies. It is the universal moral sovereignty of Yahweh which Amos stresses. Yahweh is too great to be confined within the nationalistic straitjacket that his people would impose upon him.

2. Amos directly attacks the current Israelite view of the covenant between Yahweh and his people.

> "Hear this word that the LORD has spoken against you, O people of Israel, against the whole family which I brought up out of the land of Egypt:
> You only have I known
> of all the families of the earth" (3.1-2a).

"Therefore I will protect and prosper you" is the conclusion that many an Israelite would have appended to this statement. No, says Amos,

> "therefore I will punish you
> for all your iniquities" (3.2b).

Here we must return for a moment to the opening sermon. It is constructed with rare psychological insight. As Amos condemns in turn the surrounding nations—Aramaeans (1.3-5), Philistines (1.6-8), Edomites (1.11-12), Ammonites

(1.13-15), Moabites (2.1-3) and even Judah (2.4-5)[1]—his audience is increasingly convinced that here is a man after their own heart. But the shattering climax of the sermon is still to come.

> Thus says the LORD:
> "For three transgressions of Israel,
> and for four, I will not revoke the punishment" (2.6).

This is the main burden of Amos' message, a scathing indictment of Israel for failing to fulfil her obligations under the covenant. Because Israel is the people of Yahweh, the greater her responsibility, the more severe the judgement upon her. Repeated warnings have failed to bring Israel to her senses (4.6-11); only one thing remains. "Prepare to meet your God, O Israel" (4.12b). Amos leaves the people in no doubt that such a meeting will be painful. He pronounces a funeral dirge over Israel (5.1-3). He summons her enemies to witness her just destruction (3.9-11). He talks of the coming 'day' of bitter mourning, futile repentance and utter desolation (8.9-14). The 'end' has come for Israel (8.1-3). There is no possibility of escape from the judgement of Yahweh (2.13-16; 9.1-4).

All the pre-exilic prophets are heralds of the doom of Israel and Judah just because they are heralds of the moral kingship of Yahweh. All agree with the verdict upon Israel implicit in one of Amos' visions.

> "He showed me: behold, the LORD was standing beside a wall built with a plumb line, with a plumb line in his hand. And the LORD said to me, 'Amos, what do you see?' And I said, 'A plumb line.' Then the LORD said, 'Behold, I am setting a plumb line in the midst of my people Israel: I will never again pass by them'." (7.7-8).

Set the plumb line of Yahweh's judgement against Israel and it is immediately evident that Israel is off the straight. She

[1] I see no reason to doubt the substantial authenticity of the oracle against Judah. Amos came from Judah. To have omitted an attack on Judah would have destroyed the moral objectivity for which he stood.

must be pulled down before there can be any rebuilding. To Hosea, Israel is a wife shamelessly unfaithful to her divine husband (Hos. 2). To Isaiah of Jerusalem, Judah is a vineyard which, in spite of attentive care lavished by its owner, has produced a harvest of bitter wild grapes instead of choice fruit. There is only one thing to be done. Pull down the protecting hedge and walls; let cattle trample it underfoot, thorns and thistles choke it (Isa. 5.1-7). So much for the community from which Yahweh

"looked for justice
but behold, bloodshed;
for righteousness,
but behold, a cry!" (Isa. 5.7).

The illusion of Yahweh's unconditional protection of his people was not easily destroyed. It lingered in Jerusalem until the eleventh hour. It confronted the prophet Jeremiah with one of his greatest difficulties. Early in Jeremiah's prophetic career, Judah experienced a radical religious reformation. At the instigation of reforming priests and prophets, and on the basis of the Deuteronomic scroll of the law discovered while repairs were being undertaken in the Jerusalem temple, King Josiah closed the local country shrines which had become festering sores of superstition and Canaanite religious practices, centralised worship in the Temple at Jerusalem and led his people in a renewal of their covenant obligations to Yahweh (2 Kings 22-23). Jeremiah's attitude to the reform movement is not wholly clear, but it is likely that at first he gave it his support. Jeremiah 11.1-8 may contain the record of Jeremiah's public advocacy of the reformation. This would also account for the bitter hatred he aroused in the hearts of his own kith and kin in Anathoth (11.18-23). We can well imagine what they thought of this local upstart supporting a movement which intended to close the local shrine. Whatever his original attitude, Jeremiah was to be disillusioned. Nothing is more deadly to a nation's spiritual welfare than a reformation which is not quite radical enough. Certain abuses were eliminated, but a new and dangerous heresy took their place. The one certain result of the reformation was to enhance the prestige of the temple at Jerusalem. It was the sole legitimate place for worship, the very abode of Yahweh himself. So long as the temple stood, the nation would serenely ride the storms of history. Yahweh was in their midst. "The temple of Yahweh" became a talisman, guaranteeing the safety of the city.

> "Do not trust in these deceptive words: 'This is the temple of the LORD, the temple of the LORD, the temple of the LORD'" (7.4).

is Jeremiah's comment. While other prophets encourage the mood of easy optimism by promising that no evil will befall the city (23.16-17), Jeremiah warns:

> "They have healed the wound of my people lightly, saying, 'Peace, peace,' when there is no peace" (8.11, cf. 28).

> "Is not my word like fire, says the LORD, and like a hammer which breaks the rock in pieces?" (23.29).

Fire and hammer, agents of destruction, this was the true prophetic message to a people heedless of its covenant obligations to Yahweh. This was Israel's failure which sealed her doom.

The destruction of Jerusalem by the Babylonians in 586 B.C., the sack of city and temple, vindicated the prophetic message, buried an illusion and made possible a new understanding of what it meant for Israel to be the people of Yahweh. This new understanding, born out of the travail of tragedy and exile, stems primarily from the unknown author of Isaiah 40-55, Second Isaiah, and in particular from the enigmatic figure of the Servant of Yahweh who appears in four songs embedded within his work, 42.1-4(or 9); 49.1-6; 50.4-9; 52.13-53.12. Although attempts have been made to isolate these songs from their context in Second Isaiah and to attribute them to another author, this approach is not convincing. Who was this Servant of Yahweh? No question in Old Testament scholarship has produced such endless and in certain respects such barren controversy.[1] Almost every figure of note in the Old Testament from Moses to Jeremiah, even the author of the songs himself, has been cast in this role. The traditional Jewish view is still the most convincing. The Servant is Israel the nation. Outside the songs there is no doubt that Israel is described by Second Isaiah as the Servant of Yahweh (41.8, 9; 44.12, 21; 45.4; 48.20). Even if, in certain passages, we must narrow this definition to a group within Israel or even to one prophetic figure—49.5 where the Servant has a mission to Israel is the strongest argument for this—such a group or even individual is still intended to portray Israel and all that Israel truly represents in the purposes of Yahweh.[2]

But what is the destiny of Israel, the Servant of Yahweh? There are those who see in the figure of the Servant one of the clearest statements in the Old Testament of the missionary outreach of Israel. The shackles of a narrowly nationalistic spirit are broken asunder. The Servant is to be "the prophet and missionary of true religion".[3] This view has not gone unchallenged. ". . . Essentially nationalistic in spirit . . . responsible for the narrow and exclusive views of post-exilic days . . . concerned with the restoration and exaltation of Israel . . . any place the nations have in the new order is entirely and debasingly subservient"—such is another verdict.[4] This is not merely an example of the perversity of scholarly

[1] For a survey of theories, cf. C. R. North, *The Suffering Servant in Deutero Isaiah*.

[2] cf. J. Muilenburg in *The Interpreter's Bible*, Vol. 5, pp. 406 ff.

H. W. Robinson, 'The Cross of the Servant' in *The Cross in the Old Testament*.

[3] H. W. Robinson, *op. cit.*, p. 88, cf. H. H. Rowley, *The Missionary Message of the Old Testament*.

[4] N. H. Snaith in *Studies in Old Testament Prophecy*, ed. H. H. Rowley, pp. 187 ff.

discussion. There is a certain ambiguity about some of the key phrases which describe the Servant and his mission, an ambiguity which takes us very near the heart of the Old Testament teaching about the people of Yahweh in relation to the rest of the world. The phrases in question are those which speak about the Servant as

    (a) bringing forth 'justice (*mishpaṭ*) to the nations' (42.1, 3, 4),

    (b) being 'a light to the nations' (42.6; 49.6),

    (c) being 'a covenant of the people' (42.6; 49.8).

(a) *Mishpaṭ*, as we have seen,[1] means the decision or judgement of a judge. In any case of dispute it is therefore a decision against one party and in favour of another party. "Justice to the nations" could therefore mean *either* that Israel is to be the executor of justice against the nations, that is, the heathen are to be punished for their harsh treatment of Yahweh's people, *or* it could mean that Israel is to embody Yahweh's decision in favour of the nations, that is, Israel is to be the means whereby true religion will come to all people.

(b) Similarly when the Servant is described as "a light to the nations", this may mean *either* a light seen by all peoples in the sense that all nations are to see the great things which Yahweh is about to do for his own people, *or* it may mean that Israel is to be the light and salvation of all mankind.

(c) If we think of the Servant as a group within Israel then the phrase "a covenant of the people" may mean that this group, loyal to Yahweh, is to be the means of renewing the covenant bond between Yahweh and Israel *or* if we start from the thought of the covenant as the expression of Yahweh's gracious purposes, then we may think of Israel the Servant as the embodiment of Yahweh's gracious purposes for all mankind, the means whereby the covenant faith is to be universalised. On the one view, Second Isaiah becomes a prophet whose thought is turned inwards to Israel and to what Yahweh

[1] cf. p. 78.

is going to do to vindicate his people in the eyes of the world; on the other, we have a prophet whose vision radiates outwards from Israel to embrace the whole world within the gracious purposes of Yahweh. In point of fact each interpretation stresses one side of the truth; both need to be held together if we are fully to understand Israel's mission in the world.

We are dealing here with a paradox, in the sense in which D. M. Baillie defined paradox as an inevitable part of all religious thinking, the price we have to pay for trying to describe the living God in the third person. He uses the illustration of our attempts to draw a map of the world on a flat surface. Just because the earth is spherical the attempt is bound to lead to distortion. Atlases present us with two such maps, the one depicting two hemispheres, the other Mercator's projection. "Each is a map of the whole world and they contradict each other at every point. Yet they are both needed and, taken together, they correct each other . . . So it is with the paradoxes of faith. There should always be a tension between the opposite sides of our paradoxes, driving us back to our source in our actual religious experience".[1]

There is such a paradox in Israel's thinking about herself in relationship to God and to the rest of the world, and it is a paradox which goes far back into Israel's religious experience. In the story of the call of Abraham as recorded in the 'J' strand in Genesis, there is found a theme which runs right through the stories of the pilgrim forefathers of the Hebrew race, that of the blessing given to Abraham by God.

Now the LORD said to Abram, "Go from your country and your kindred and your father's house to the land that I will show you. And I will make of you a great nation, and I will bless you, and make your name great, so that you will be a blessing. I will bless those who bless you, and him who curses you I will curse; and by you all the families of the earth will bless themselves" (Gen. 12.1-3; cf. 22.17; 26.4; 28.14).

[1] D. M. Baillie, *God was in Christ*, pp. 109 ff.

There is in this blessing a strong element of religious nationalism. Abraham's descendants are destined to be a great nation,
with a great reputation. The fate of other peoples is linked to
their treatment of the Hebrews. But there is something more.
". . . by you all the families of the earth will bless themselves". This statement must be interpreted in the light of
the use of the similar part of the Hebrew verb to bless (*b-r-k*)
in Genesis 48.20 where it is translated:

> "By you Israel will *pronounce blessings*, saying,
>   'God make you as Ephraim and as Manasseh.' "

That is to say, other nations are depicted as invoking a blessing
upon themselves in words such as, "God make us as Abraham
and his descendants". What God does in and for Israel is
regarded as being the desire of all nations. Israel's greatness
is to be the magnet drawing others to share in the blessing
she has received from God.

Turn now to an oracle which was obviously part of the
common stock of prophetic teaching in the eighth century
B.C. since it is preserved, with minor variations, in both
Isaiah and Micah.

> It shall come to pass in the latter days
> that the mountain of the house of the LORD
> shall be established as the highest of the mountains,
> and shall be raised above the hills;
> and all the nations shall flow to it,
> and many peoples shall come, and say:
>   "Come, let us go up to the mountain of the LORD,
>   to the house of the God of Jacob;
>   that he may teach us his ways
>   and that we may walk in his paths."
> For out of Zion shall go forth the law,
> and the word of the LORD from Jerusalem.
>   (Isa. 2.2-3; Mic. 4.1-2).

There is the same twin emphasis. Jerusalem, and in particular
the temple of Yahweh in Jerusalem, is to be raised to the
utmost prominence. But this is not an end in itself; it is rather

a means whereby Yahweh's instruction and Yahweh's message are to come to all the nations. A national faith is to be glorified, but not as a contribution to religious nationalism. Israel and the distinctive faith to which she bears witness are offered to all the world.

In the light of this, let us look again at the message of Second Isaiah. From the opening words of hope, "Comfort, comfort my people, says your God" (Isa. 40.1) to the closing oracle of promise, "You shall go out in joy and be led forth in peace" (Isa. 55.12) the prophet is concerned with Israel, and with the mighty act through which Yahweh is going to renew the life of his people, delivering them from captivity in Babylon (Isa. 41.14; 43.14; 44.6; 47.1 ff.; 49.5 ff.). There is to be a new Exodus, celebrated in a new song of triumph (Isa. 42.10-13; 43.16-21). This renewal of Israel is linked in the prophet's mind with the career of Cyrus, the new star upon the political horizon of the East (Isa 44.28; 45.1). But it is no mere political renewal which the prophet proclaims. Indeed it may be claimed that, given the fact that political restoration is now fast becoming possible, the prophet's purpose is to prepare his people to welcome it as the pledge of a greater restoration which will renew their understanding of their unique place in Yahweh's purposes for the world. Even the suffering and national humiliation they have endured must be offered to God in this faith (Isa. 52.13 ff.). Israel's restoration is to be Yahweh's invitation to the other nations.

> "Turn to me and be saved,
>   all the ends of the earth!
>   For I am God, and there is no other" (Isa. 45.22).

> "Behold, you shall call nations that you know not,
>   and nations that knew you not shall run to you,
>   because of the LORD your God, and of the Holy One of Israel,
>   for he has glorified you" (Isa. 55.5).

For Second Isaiah, therefore, it is the renewal of the covenant bond with Israel which is to be the means of grace for others; it is Yahweh's exaltation of Israel which is to extend his truth to all nations; it is the far-seen triumph of Yahweh which is to be the light drawing others to the true faith. To paraphrase D. M. Baillie's illustration, Second Isaiah gives us two maps of Israel in the purposes of Yahweh, one drawn on a nationalistic, the other on a universalistic scale "and they contradict each other to some extent at every point. Yet both are needed and, taken together, they correct each other". [1]

One of the basic problems of post-exilic Judaism was whether these two maps could be fruitfully held together. At times the nationalistic image tended to exclude the wider vision.

Slightly earlier than Second Isaiah, Ezekiel spoke to the people from the same general background of national catastrophe and exile. With all the realism of the pre-exilic prophets, he is convinced that there is justice in Yahweh's harsh dealings with his people. But national disaster and the withdrawal of Yahweh's presence from Jerusalem cannot be the final word. Chapter 34 opens with a scathing indictment of the 'shepherds of Israel', the kings of pre-exilic Israel and Judah ('shepherd' is a common title for the ruling monarch in the Ancient Near East cf. 1 Kings 22.17; Mic. 5.5; Jer. 10.21). Their irresponsible and callous rule is at an end; henceforth Yahweh will be the true king of his people.

> "I myself will be the shepherd of my sheep, and I will make them lie down, says the LORD God. I will seek the lost, and I will bring back the strayed, and I will bind up the crippled, and I will strengthen the weak, and the fat and the strong I will watch over; I will feed them in justice." (Ezek. 34.15-16).

But Ezekiel is not only a prophet, certain of God's future for his people, he is also a priest. In the magnificent vision of restoration which closes his book (40-48), he describes in loving detail the reconstructed temple. Yahweh is present again in the midst of his people. It is the vision of a man for

[1] D. M. Baillie, *op. cit.* For a fuller discussion cf. *Scottish Journal of Theology* Vol. 16 No. 2 pp. 166 ff.

whom worship must have been an ever enriching experience. The lesson of the past must be learned. Never again must Yahweh's judgement befall the community. Among the steps taken to guard the purity of the restored community is this,

"No foreigner, uncircumcised in heart and flesh, of all the foreigners who are among the people of Israel, shall enter my sanctuary" (Ezek. 44.9).

There is some evidence that in pre-exilic Israel foreign slaves were employed for certain menial duties in the temple precincts. Never again, says Ezekiel; this is an insult to Yahweh, a profanation of his temple, a violation of his covenant (Ezek. 44.6-8). Although this is merely an attempt to lay down regulations for the ordering of the life of the temple, it reveals a temper of racial exclusiveness and antipathy to foreigners which, claiming the sanction of religion, was to have unfortunate results. It was only too readily assumed that loyalty to Yahweh demanded a separation from everything and everyone non-Jewish.

When settlers from Samaria, pleading a common interest in the worship of Yahweh, offered to help the returned Jewish exiles to rebuild Jerusalem and the temple, their offer was spurned (Ezra 4.1-3). Both Nehemiah (Neh.13.23-27) and Ezra (Ezra 10) took drastic steps to ensure the racial and religious purity of the post exilic community by forbidding intermarriage with foreign women. Indeed such marriages were a threat to Jewish faith but, in the action that was taken against them, there was inherent the danger of fostering an attitude of exclusiveness which would blind the people of Yahweh to their responsibilities to the world. The danger was particularly real when the Jews were suffering at the hands of their non-Jewish neighbours. The Edomites, for example, took advantage of the fall of Jerusalem in 586 B.C. to settle old scores. Jewish response is seen in the virulent invective against the Edomites in the book of Obadiah. Psalm 137 begins with an exiled Jew movingly recalling the unforgettable joys of worship in Jerusalem; it ends on a note of vindictive fury.

> "Remember, O LORD, against the Edomites
>   the day of Jerusalem,
> how they said, 'Rase it, rase it!
>   Down to its foundations!'
> O daughter of Babylon, you devastator!
>   Happy shall he be who requites you
>   with what you have done to us!
>   Happy shall he be who takes your little ones
>   and dashes them against the rock!'' (Ps. 137.7-9).

The most marked example of this in the Old Testament is the book of Esther, fiction but very revealing fiction, claiming to tell of the origin of Purim, one of the most popular festivals of the Jewish religious year. It tells the story of how Esther, Jewish empress of Persia and her uncle Mordecai thwarted a plot to annihilate the Jewish communities in Persia. But the story is not content to describe how providentially the Jews escaped from the plots of their enemies. Instead of being massacred, the Jews massacre, slaying over 75,000 of their enemies. Throughout the story the name of God is never mentioned. The moral of the story, "Hurrah for the Jews, death to their enemies" is scarcely an adequate commentary on the call of Israel to be "a light to the nations".

The universalistic strand in Second Isaiah's vision, however, was never wholly lost. If Esther is fiction, enshrining a spirit of racial arrogance and hostility towards non-Jews, two other examples of Old Testament fiction point in a different direction. Nehemiah cursed and berated certain of his fellow Jews who had married Moabite women; the book of Ruth tells with disarming simplicity the story of such a Moabite girl. Not only does Ruth the Moabitess sustain her Jewish mother-in-law, with a steadfast loyalty and love, not only is she prepared to acknowledge the God of Israel (Ruth 1.16-17), but she becomes the wife of a respectable Jewish farmer and the great grandmother of good King David. It is difficult to be certain about the date of the book of Ruth. It was probably not written in conscious opposition to the exclusive policy of Nehemiah and Ezra since it is utterly devoid of the spirit of religious polemic. The point of the story, however, can hardly be missed. If Moabite blood flowed in the veins of David, kingly hero of Jewish tradition, can the Jewish attitude towards Moabites and other foreigners be hostilely negative? Does not the example of Ruth show that Israel must be prepared to make the revelation, received from Yahweh, available to all, irrespective of race? The story never doubts that Israel's faith is the true faith, Israel's God the only true God, but this faith and this God may be shared by others.

The book of Jonah goes further. Any attempt to read Jonah as historical fact reveals a lamentable failure to appreciate the fondness of the eastern mind for clothing truth in story form, as well as distracting attention from the central challenge of this missionary tract. The prophet Jonah, so the story goes, was once given a strange and unwelcome commission by God.

> "Arise, go to Nineveh, that great city, and cry against it; for their wickedness has come up before me" (1.2).

Nineveh, pagan capital of that scourge of Israel, the Assyrian Empire, was hardly the place to which any self-respecting Jew would willingly go. Jonah tries to run off to the opposite end of the world, to Tarshish in distant Spain, only to find that there was no escape from the insistent demand of God. After a series of strange adventures Jonah is back where he started, listening again to the word of God.

> "Arise, go to Nineveh, that great city, and proclaim to it the message that I tell you" (3.2).

So Jonah went to Nineveh in high dudgeon, but no doubt comforting himself with the thought that the message he had for Nineveh was one of coming doom. To his dismay, the people of Nineveh take his message seriously, renounce their evil ways and throw themselves on the mercy of God. To his disgust:

"God repented of the evil which he had said he would do to them; and he did not do it" (3.10b).

Jonah would rather have died than see such heathen Ninevites experiencing the forgiveness of God (4.1-3). As he sat outside the city, moodily contemplating what the future might hold for Nineveh, God caused a plant to grow up to shield Jonah from the relentless heat of the sun. Jonah's delight at this unexpected shelter was short lived. Next day the plant withered and died, leaving him exposed to wind and sun. He was not amused. Into his fit of petulance, God spoke his decisive message. We may paraphrase it as follows. "Why are you upset about a mere plant, Jonah? Did you expend any labour on it? Why waste your pity on it? Have I not much greater cause to pity Nineveh, a great city of 120,000 ignorant people, not to mention their cattle?" (4.9-11).

Jonah in the story is Israel, the Servant of Yahweh, unwilling to face her high calling as the missionary of the one true God. What is at stake in God's relationship with his people is not Israel's self-respect or dignity, but something far greater, the compassionate outreach of God's concern for all people, even pagan oppressors like the Assyrians. In Jonah, the people of Israel are given a sharp reminder of the responsibility of the covenant people. As God had compassion, so must they. To fail to embody this divine compassion for the world was to miss their high calling as the people of God.

In the narrative of the giving of the covenant at Mount Sinai, there is a passage of uncertain date which underlines the same truth. God says to Moses:

"Thus you shall say to the house of Jacob, and tell the people of Israel: You have seen what I did to the Egyptians, and how I bore you on eagles' wings and brought you to myself. Now therefore, if you will obey my voice and keep my covenant, you shall be my own possession among all peoples; for all the earth is mine, and you shall be to me a kingdom of priests and a holy nation" (Exod. 19.3b-6a).

This is true covenant theology. The people are the people of

Yahweh's possession, a holy nation committed to obedience. But the relationship between Yahweh and Israel must be seen in a wider context. All the earth belongs to Yahweh. His people are to be a *kingdom of priests*. The priests in Israel formed a community within the community, their life controlled by strict regulations. But this priestly community existed solely for the well being of all Israel. They were the link between Yahweh and Israel, custodians of Yahweh's instructions to the people, interpreters of Yahweh's requirements. They were also the link between Israel and Yahweh, offering, on behalf of the people, sacrifice and prayer, thanksgiving and confession. So from Israel, Yahweh's priestly community, there is to flow Yahweh's instruction, a true faith for all the world, and through Israel the needs and desires of all mankind are to be brought to Yahweh.

Men of vision in Israel offered the life of their people to Yahweh in this faith. They may never have been wholly certain how this was to happen, but the vision remained. When the Jews found themselves increasingly a people dispersed to the far corners of the world, living their own life in Babylon, Alexandria or Rome, a Jewish Rabbi echoed this faith in the words, "God dispersed the Jews to facilitate proselytism".[1]

[1] Rabbi Eleazear, *Talmud Pesaḥim,* 87b.

Chapter Six

GOD AND WORSHIP

THE faith of the Old Testament which we have been examining, its interpretation of history, its understanding of the place of Israel in the purposes of God, springs ultimately from the witness of a minority, from Moses and the prophets. This faith, however, to be fruitful had to become part of the life of the nation, the shared privilege of the many. The point at which this happened was worship. Even when, with the canonisation of Torah, the Jews became the people of a book, the contents of this book were delivered and expounded to the people in the synagogue as the central act in corporate worship. If we would know the Old Testament aright we must seek to enter sympathetically into the experience of worship in ancient Israel.

1. Sacrifice

Every religion which makes any lasting impact upon the mind of man clothes itself in actions which express the inner reality of faith. Even the most violently anti-liturgical amongst us will go to a certain place at a certain time to worship, will adopt a certain attitude in prayer or will consciously engage in private meditation. What are these, but external actions expressing an inner reality? For the world of the Ancient Near East as for many other societies the most important of such external actions was sacrifice. Not only was sacrifice in some form or other common to the religions of the Ancient Near East, but certain of the technical names for different types of sacrifice were shared by Israel and her nearest neighbours, particularly the Canaanites. That does not mean that sacrifice had exactly the same significance for a Babylonian, a Canaanite and a Hebrew. Both in the Babylonian flood story in the eleventh

Tablet of the Epic of Gilgamesh and in the Biblical story in Genesis 7-8, deliverance from the flood is celebrated in the same way, the offering of a sacrifice to the gods.[1] Some form of sacrifice was the natural response to escape from seeming disaster. Both narratives speak of a sacrifice as a 'sweet savour' smelled by the gods. The type of sacrifice, however, differs; in Noah's case it is an animal offering, in the case of his Babylonian counterpart it is a vegetable offering more akin to incense. Nor must we assume that the description of sacrifice as a 'sweet savour' means the same thing in the two stories; that will depend on the overall Hebrew understanding of sacrifice on the one hand and the Babylonian on the other.

At least sacrifice was a shared religious experience for Babylonian and Hebrew. It is not a part of religious experience for most of us. From any form of animal sacrifice we tend to turn in disgust. To us it seems senseless butchery, a witness to the needless cruelty which has so often been perpetrated in the name of religion. Those parts of the Old Testament which deal with the different types of sacrifice and the details of sacrificial ritual, particularly the early chapters of Leviticus, we hastily skip over as being no longer of any interest or relevance. This is a pity. Such chapters, which to us are dead, were once alive with the warmth of a people's devotion. We must try to understand sacrifice as a natural form of worship, as natural as prayer is to the man of faith today. Sacrifice, it has been well said, ". . . is an essential act of external worship. It is prayer which is acted, a symbolic action which expresses both the interior feelings of the person offering it and God's response to this prayer . . ."[2]

Before looking at sacrifice in the Old Testament in the light of this statement, two general comments are worth making. Firstly, just as prayer is the expression of a rich variety of human needs and desires, acknowledgement of dependence upon God, joy, thanksgiving, confession, petition, so is it

[1] D.O.T.T., pp. 22-23; Gen. 8. 20-21.
[2] R. de Vaux, *Ancient Israel*, p. 451.

with sacrifice. In a sense there is no such thing as sacrifice, only many different kinds of sacrifice capable of expressing the many different tones in the dialogue between God and man. Secondly, the Old Testament documents which we possess span nearly a thousand years of a nation's religious history and describe a faith which, although possessing a basic unity, developed and adapted itself in the light of changing circumstances and new challenges. Much of the detailed information which we are given concerning sacrifice in Leviticus 1-7 probably represents sacrificial practice in the Jerusalem temple after the exile. Although religious practice is notoriously conservative, we have no right to assume that the particular emphasis we find there was always and everywhere the emphasis among the Hebrews. It is indeed very difficult to harmonise details in the sacrificial ritual in different parts of the Old Testament. This need hardly surprise us when we recall the controversy over the meaning and practice of the central Christian rite. The very fact that this may be differently interpreted, and be known by different names, Holy Communion, Eucharist, Mass, the Lord's Supper, should make us cautious in our handling of the various words for sacrifice in the Old Testament. But just as it is becoming increasingly clear that behind different forms and names there is a fundamental unity of faith in Christian celebration, so we may claim to find within the rich variety of sacrificial practice in the Old Testament three major emphases.

(a) Sacrifice as *a gift to God*

This seems to be the basic emphasis in two prominent types of sacrifice.

(i) *'Olah* (Lev. 1, burnt offering) literally means 'that which goes up', the sacrifice which is burnt upon the altar and rises in the smoke to God. The distinctive thing about this type of sacrifice, which always involves the offering of an animal or bird, varying in value according to the religious standing or wealth of the offerer, was the fact that the entire victim was given to God. Hence it was sometimes called the *kalil*, the whole offering. The blood of the animal, which in Old Testament sacrificial thinking is equivalent to its life (Lev. 17.14), was drained from the victim and poured out by the priest at the foot of the altar; the rest of the animal was cut up and burned upon the altar.

(ii) In certain of the latest codes in the Old Testament, the *'olah* was usually accompanied by a *minḥah* (Lev. 2, cereal offering). *Minḥah*, which means 'present' or 'gift' (cf. Gen. 32.13), was an offering normally of flour mixed with oil and various aromatics such as frankincense. This offering was brought by the worshipper to the priest, who took a handful of it and burned it upon the altar as an *'azkarah* 'memorial portion' (Hebrew *z-k-r* means 'remember'), a reminder to God of the complete offering brought into his temple.

Whether the offering was the priestly or the rich man's offering of a bull, the poor man's offering of young pigeons, or, in cases of extreme poverty, merely a cereal offering, it was always something which the worshipper brought and, through the agency of the priest, handed over entirely to God. It was his gift, something of his own possession, something costly, even if the cost could only approximate to the widow's mite. Such a gift might be an expression of joy (1 Sam. 6.14; 2 Sam. 6.17), of thanksgiving to God for favours received or promised (Ps. 96.8), or it might accompany a specific request to God (1 Sam. 7.9; 13.9; 1 Kings 18.38). In this latter case it is very doubtful whether Hebrew faith ever thought of such a gift sacrifice as a bribe to God. Rather this costly offering was an earnest of the worshipper's real desire for what he requested. Whatever the particular motive prompting such a sacrifice, it was a constant reminder to and acknowledgement by the people of something deep rooted in all true religious experience, the recognition of total dependence upon God. This is nowhere more finely expressed than in the prayer which the Chronicler puts into the mouth of David when he reveals to his people the plans for building the Jerusalem temple:

"Blessed art thou, O LORD, the God of Israel our father, for ever and ever. Thine, O LORD, is the greatness, and the power, and the glory, and the victory, and the majesty; for all that is in the heavens and in the earth is thine; thine is the kingdom, O LORD, and thou art exalted as head above all. Both riches and honour come from thee, and thou rulest over all. In thy hand are power and might; and in thy hand it is to make great and to give strength to all. And now we thank thee, our God, and praise thy glorious name. But who am I, and what is my people, that we should be able thus to offer willingly? For all things come from thee, and of thy own have we given thee" (1 Chron. 29.10b-14).

(b) Sacrifice as *communion with God*

The distinctive thing about this type of sacrifice, which involved the offering of an animal, was that it took the form of a meal shared by God, his priests and the worshippers; the fat, the kidneys and part of the liver being given to God, burned on the altar "as food offered by fire for a pleasing odour" (Lev. 3.16), the breast and right leg going to the priest, and the rest being shared by the worshipper and his family. Such a sacrificial meal was called a *zebhaḥ* (sacrifice) or *zebhaḥ shelamim,* that is, a sacrifice designed to promote *shalom* (peace), full harmonious fellowship between God and man. To share a meal with someone was, for the ancient world, in a very real sense, a sign and a pledge of brotherhood (cf. Gen. 31.54). Many different motives may have prompted participation in such a communion meal. The legislation in Leviticus distinguishes three different types, that which springs out of a sense of thanksgiving (Lev. 7.12), that which is the result of a vow (Lev. 7.16, cf. 1 Sam. 1.21) and that which is the expression of a spontaneous act of devotion (Lev. 7.16, the free will offering). Since the victim slaughtered for the sacrificial meal was provided by the worshipper, this sacrifice too was a gift to God, but it was a gift whose primary object was the sealing of that joyful sense of communion between God and man which lies very close to the heart of all faith. As far as our evidence goes, this seems to have been one of the most popular types of sacrifice in pre-exilic Israel. Nor is this surprising. It was the actualising in terms of personal experience of the covenant promise, "I shall be your God and you will be my people".

(c) Sacrifice as *a means of forgiveness and restoration*

It is a measure of the effectiveness of the prophetic witness to the judgement of Yahweh and the need for repentance that this type of sacrifice came to ever-increasing prominence in Israel, particularly after the exile. Not only must the people be thoroughly trained in obedience to Yahweh, but provision had to be made whereby the covenant with Yahweh could be renewed when it was broken by the sin of man. Two main types of sacrifice, not always clearly distinguished in the Old Testament, were the means to this end.

(i) *ḥatta'th*. This word means both 'sin' (literally, 'missing the mark') and the sacrifice which deals with sin, the sin-offering. As in the case of the *'olah*, the victim offered varied in value from a bull on behalf of the high priest or the entire community, to two turtle doves or pigeons in the case of the poor (Lev. 4-5.10). Though the form of the ritual varies, there is one constant factor, the significant part played by the blood of the victim. The blood, taken by the priest, was brought into the closest possible contact with God. Most of it was poured out at the foot of the altar, but some was smeared upon the four projecting corner pieces, the 'horns', of the altar. These horns of the altar, whatever their origin, had a special sanctity. A man on the run from his enemies sought asylum under the protection of God by grasping the horns of the altar (1 Kings 2.28). The nearest the Old Testament comes to giving us an explanation of the significance of this blood ritual in the sin offering is in Leviticus 17.11, where a prohibition on eating blood is backed up by the statement:

> "For the life of the flesh is in the blood; and I have given it for you upon the altar to make atonement for your souls; for it is the blood that makes atonement, by reason of the life."

If we ask what is meant by this 'by reason of the life', the answer is not wholly clear. It may be that the life of the victim was thought of as being accepted by God in place of the forfeited life of the sinner, on the analogy of the *lex talionis,* 'life for life . . .' It may be that the costly offering of the entire life of the victim to God was looked upon as a sign of the sinner's repentance, on the basis of which God took away his sin. As in the case of the *'olah,* the worshipper had no share in the victim. There was no sacrificial meal. There could be no new at-one-ment, no renewed communion with God until the sin which disrupted that communion was dealt with. Both the regulations in Lev. 4-5 and Num. 15.22 ff. make it clear that the *hatta'th* ritual availed only for certain types of sin, "unwitting" sins, inadvertent or accidental violations of the Torah of Yahweh. For anyone deliberately challenging the moral sovereignty of Yahweh, sinning "with a high hand" (Num. 15.30) there was no forgiveness through sacrifice; indeed according to Numbers 15.31, there was no possibility of renewal at all.

> "Because he has despised the word of the LORD, and has broken his commandment, that person shall be utterly cut off; his iniquity shall be upon him."

Many of the ideas surrounding the *hatta'th* ritual find their climax in the life of the community on one of the most significant occasions in the Jewish religious year, the 'Day of Atonement'.[1]

(ii) *'asham* (guilt offering, Lev. 5.14-6.7; Num. 5.5-8). The distinction between this and the *hatta'th* is not wholly clear. The *'asham,* however, seems usually to carry with it the idea of making reparation for a wrong done. This is well demonstrated in the story of what happened when the 'ark of the covenant' fell into the hands of the Philistines (1 Sam. 5). Strange things took place in the temple of the Philistine god Dagon; plague smote the Philistine cities. When priests and diviners were consulted as to the reason for such untoward

[1] cf. pp. 219 ff.

events, they indicated that it had something to do with the presence of Yahweh's ark in their midst. Yahweh was offended. It would not be sufficient, however, merely to return the ark to its rightful owners:

> "If you send away the ark of the God of Israel, do not send it empty, but by all means return him a guilt offering. Then you will be healed . . ." (1 Sam. 6.3).

Reparation had to be made for the affront offered to Yahweh. Within Israel the *'asham* sacrifice operated particularly in cases of theft, breach of faith or trust between members of the community; in just those cases where it was possible for tangible reparation to be made to the injured party. In such cases, as well as offering an *'asham* to God, repayment of what had been obtained by fraud plus one fifth had to be made to the person wronged. God was involved in the personal relationships of the members of his people. Not only must it be made abundantly clear that crime does not pay, but reconciliation must be sought with God.

In fulness of joy, when the need to say 'thank you' to God was compelling, when communion with God was seen to be the ultimate good, when the sense of dependence upon God was overwhelming, when the need for God's help or the word of forgiveness was urgent, men in Israel turned to sacrifice. Because sacrifice in Israel was regarded, not as some human invention, but as God's gracious provision for his people, it not only expressed the deepest needs and desires of the people, it carried with it the assurance that such desires and needs were met. "By sacrificial rite, the gift made to God *is* accepted, union with God *is* achieved, and the guilt of man *is* taken away."[1]

The more we stress the significance of sacrifice in the religious life of the Hebrews, the more we are left to face the question, "Why, then, is there so much in the Old Testament, particularly in the teaching of the prophets, which is bitterly

[1] R. de Vaux, *op. cit.*, p. 451.

critical of sacrifice?" One reason we have already seen. The prophets were the heralds of the moral kingship of Yahweh, challenging a corrupt society to decide for 'justice' and 'righteousness'. When Amos ironically invites his fellow countrymen to come to the temples and transgress (Amos 4.4-5), when he roundly declares that God detests their worship and will not accept the sacrifices which they bring, he is addressing people who cheat, bribe, oppress and live in the lap of luxury while the poor go to the wall. In such a society sacrifice must be a mockery since the lives of the worshippers are wholly out of tune with Yahweh and his demands. Sacrifice must never be allowed to degenerate into a form of religious magic, deluding the people into believing that all was well in their relationship with Yahweh, when all was not well. This does not mean that the prophets would have unconditionally advocated a society for the abolition of sacrifice. Isaiah of Jerusalem is equally scathing—and for the same reason—about prayer.

> "When you spread forth your hands,
>   I will hide my eyes from you;
>   even though you make many prayers,
>   I will not listen" (Isa. 1.15a).

Yet Isaiah knew full well the value and the reality of prayer. He condemns certain prayers for exactly the same reason as he condemns certain sacrifices.

> "Your hands are full of blood.
>   Wash yourselves; make yourselves clean;
>   remove the evil of your doings from before my eyes;
>   cease to do evil,
>   learn to do good;
>   seek justice,
>   correct oppression;
>   defend the fatherless,
>   plead for the widow" (Isa. 1.15b-17).

Failing that, any approach to Yahweh is a meaningless mockery. We need, moreover, to be careful in our interpretation of certain statements which seem to imply the unconditional rejection of sacrifice. It is characteristic of the Old Testament to say 'this and not that', where we would say 'this rather than that'. Thus Hosea declares in the name of Yahweh,

"I desire steadfast love *and not* sacrifice,
    the knowledge of God, *rather than* burnt offerings"
                (Hos. 6.6).

Both parts of this verse mean the same thing. It is a question of priorities. Without steadfast love, without true knowledge of God, there can be no acceptable sacrifice (1 Sam. 15.22).

There are, however, two passages in prophetic teaching, one in Amos, the other in Jeremiah, which seem to go further. Amos 5.25 is in the form of a rhetorical question which obviously expects the answer, 'No'.

"Did you bring me sacrifices and offerings the forty years in the wilderness, O house of Israel?"

The Jeremiah passage is even more explicit.

Thus says the LORD of hosts, the God of Israel: "Add your burnt offerings to your sacrifices, and eat the flesh. For in the day that I brought them out of the land of Egypt, I did not speak to your fathers or command them concerning burnt offerings and sacrifices" (Jer. 7.21-22).

Both passages appear to state categorically that in the formative period of Hebrew religion, the Exodus, Covenant, wilderness-wandering period, sacrifice played no part in the people's worship. This can hardly be correct. It is flatly contradicted in the earliest strands of Old Testament tradition. The clue to the correct interpretation is to be found in continuing the Jeremiah passage.

"I did not speak to your fathers or command them concerning burnt offerings and sacrifices. But this command I gave them, 'Obey my voice, and I will be your God, and you shall be my people; and walk in all the way that I command you, that it may be well with you' " (Jer. 7.22b-23).

Both Jeremiah and Amos are insisting that the vital, the

distinctive thing about Israel's religion from the beginning was not sacrifice, but obedience to the moral demands of Yahweh. Sacrifice as a religious rite the Hebrews shared with other people. Sacrifice was never the distinctive thing in Hebrew faith, *but* sacrifice was capable of expressing that distinctive faith. The sacrificial system in post-exilic Israel bears the marks of prophetic teaching in the seriousness with which it sought to make provision for the constant renewal of the covenant bond between Yahweh and his people, an emphasis which crept into all types of sacrifice. Religious institutions and rites may so easily degenerate till they blind men to the truth which they were intended to convey. They continually need to be exposed to the voice of prophetic criticism and challenge. Sacrifice was no exception. Under the impact of prophetic teaching, however, sacrifice was for many in Israel a true means of grace, sealing to them the central affirmations of their faith, enabling them to make a worthy response to God.

2. *The Religious Year*

Every community builds the rhythm of its corporate life round certain significant dates and festivals in the year. In many modern states such occasions may be basically secular, Independence Day or May Day, but for the communities of the ancient world and for religious communities to the present day, they are important religious festivals, highlighting the central religious convictions of the community. The importance of such recurring festivals can hardly be over-emphasised. They serve to remind the community of its destiny and provide occasions for renewed dedication to a common loyalty. Ancient Israel well knew the truth of this. In the great festivals of her religious year there was enshrined and passed on from generation to generation much that was distinctive in her faith.

It is often peculiarly difficult to trace the origin and meaning of some of the customs which gather round such festivals. The more popular a festival becomes the more it tends to attract to itself practices which originally had no connection with it. Christmas is a good example of this. We know that Christmas celebrates the birth of Jesus Christ, but how many of us, accustomed to a traditional Christmas, can say with certainty when and why there gathered round this Christian festival Santa Claus, holly and mistletoe, crackers and plum pudding? In dealing in the Old Testament with religious festivals which in many cases have gradually developed across the centuries, we may be far from certain about the original meaning of some practices, though the evidence of comparative religion, if judiciously handled, may be of assistance. Fortunately the evidence for the religious festivals of Ancient Israel comes from many different sources of different date. The main sources are Exodus 23.14-17, and 34.18-23, both dating from the early settlement in Canaan; Deuteronomy 16, seventh century B.C.; Leviticus 23 and certain passages in Numbers, e.g. 28-29, which in the main reflect post-exilic practice. This enables us to trace something of the development of these festivals, and in particular to see the distinctive meaning which many of these festivals took when they were ingrafted into the life of the covenant people.

(a) *Pesaḥ* (Passover). We begin with the only Hebrew festival which can with certainty be dated to the period prior to the settlement in Canaan. The ritual preserved in Exodus 12.1-20 bears all the marks of a festival originally celebrated by the semi-nomadic shepherd of the desert steppe. It seems to stem from a springtime sacrificial rite designed to ensure the fertility and well-being of the flock. Celebrated at full moon in the first month of the year, its central act is the sharing of a sacrificial meal, the victim being a young lamb. The blood of the lamb smeared on the tent posts was probably designed to ward off the demon of destruction who might attack the flock. The lamb, roasted in typical nomadic fashion over an open fire was eaten with unleavened bread, still characteristic desert food, seasoned with desert plants, the 'bitter herbs'.

Belt fastened, sandals on feet, staff in hand, the worshipper is ready to walk with the flock.

The curious thing is that, if Passover was originally a shepherd's sacrifice coming from Israel's nomadic past, it is no longer so in the Old Testament. The Hebrew word for Passover, *pesaḥ*, is of very uncertain meaning, but in the tradition in the book of Exodus it is explained in terms of the incident when the 'angel of death' sent by Yahweh 'passed over'[1] the blood-marked homes of the Hebrews on his death dealing mission.

"It is the sacrifice of the LORD's passover, for he passed over the houses of the people of Israel in Egypt, when he slew the Egyptians but spared our houses" (Exod. 12.27, cf. v. 23).

The fastened belt, the sandalled feet, the staff in hand are interpreted as signs of the haste with which the Hebrews celebrated the first Passover, ready to make a start to their march to freedom (Exod. 12.11; Deut. 16.3). According to Deuteronomy, the bitter herbs, the 'bread of affliction' recalls the harsh life of the Hebrews in bondage (Deut. 16.3) and the very date of the celebration of the festival is a memorial of the Exodus.

"Observe the month of Abib, and keep the passover to the LORD your God; for in the month of Abib the LORD your God brought you out of Egypt by night" (Deut. 16.1).

In early Israel, Passover was probably celebrated at home, as a family festival. From the time of the centralisation of worship in Jerusalem in 621 B.C. it became a national occasion celebrated at the temple in Jerusalem. It is this new Passover which is reflected in Deuteronomy 16 and in the account of Josiah's celebration of Passover in 2 Kings 23.22.

In Passover we see reflected something which is true of many of the great festivals of the Hebrew religious year. Whatever the origin of certain of the festivals, they became

[1] Elsewhere in the Old Testament *p-s-ḥ* means to 'limp' or 'jump' (2 Sam. 4.4; 1 Kings 18.21).

memorials of the historical events, notably the Exodus, upon which Hebrew faith was built. There is no more decisive witness to the essentially historical nature of the faith of the Old Testament.

(b) *The Agricultural Festivals*. All the liturgical calendars, including the two earliest (Exod. 23.14-17; Exod. 34.18-23), declare that there were three occasions in the year when all adult male Hebrews had to 'appear before Yahweh', that is to say, participate in a festival at the local shrine. These three festivals, all of them rooted in settled agricultural life, may well have been adopted by the Hebrews from the Canaanites. They are,

(i) *Maṣṣoth* (unleavened bread),

(ii) *Qaṣir* (harvest, Exod. 23.16) or *Shabhu'oth* (weeks, Exod. 34.22),

(iii) *'Asiph* (ingathering, Exod. 23.16; 34.23) or *Sukkoth* (huts, Deut. 16.13).

(i) *Maṣṣoth* marked the beginning of the harvest season when the first of the barley crop was reaped. According to Exod. 23.15 no one was to appear before Yahweh on this occasion empty handed. Part of the ritual was probably the offering of the first of the harvest to Yahweh (Lev. 23.9 ff.). The other feature of the festival, from which it takes its name, was the eating of unleavened or unfermented bread for seven days. Probably this custom is rooted in an ancient belief that the new harvest marked a time of new beginning. Nothing of the old must be allowed to come into contact with, and thus contaminate the new grain. Unleavened bread was also for a very different reason a feature of the celebration of Passover. This, and the fact that they were celebrated at roughly the same time of year, provided a link between the two festivals. So diverse in origin, the two became in Hebrew religion one sacrament of the people's deliverance from enslavement in Egypt (cf. Exod. 12.1-20; Deut. 16; Lev. 23.5-8). Even where, in early liturgical calendars, *Maṣṣoth* is mentioned without any reference to Passover, it has already become a witness to the Exodus:

"You shall keep the feast of unleavened bread; as I commanded you, you shall eat unleavened bread for seven days at the appointed time in the month of Abib, for in it you came out of Egypt" (Exod. 23.15).

(ii) *Qaṣir*, harvest festival, or *Shabhu'oth*, the festival of weeks, so called because it was celebrated "seven weeks from the time you first put the sickle to the standing grain" (Deut. 16.9), marked the end of the wheat harvest. It was a typical harvest festival, a time of joyous celebration when, according to Leviticus 23.15 ff. there were offered to Yahweh two loaves baked from the new grain. Harvest was safely gathered in; the first produce of the new grain was offered in thanksgiving to God. This festival was never very closely linked with the Exodus story, but among later Jewish groups, for example the Qumran community which has given us the Dead Sea scrolls, it came to be connected with the giving of the law at Mount Sinai. In the Deuteronomic version of the festival, however, the command to "rejoice before Yahweh your God" was placed in sharp relief against the background of former misery.

"You shall remember that you were a slave in Egypt; and you shall be careful to observe these statutes" (Deut. 16.12).

The wonder of the deliverance which had transformed their life could never be far from Hebrew thinking.

(iii) *'Asiph*, ingathering (Exod. 23.16; 34.23), was in many respects the most important of the three agricultural festivals. It marked the completion of the farmer's work for the season. Not only was the grain safely gathered in, but the olives and the grapes had been gathered and pressed. Not surprisingly, wine flowed freely and drunkenness was no uncommon sight on this joyous occasion. It was probably at *'Asiph* in the temple of Shiloh that the priest Eli mistook Hannah's lips moving in silent prayer as a sign of drunkenness (1 Sam. 1.12). Eli had obviously dealt with such situations before. As in the case of *Qaṣir* the ritual involved the offering of the produce of the good earth to Yahweh (Lev. 23.36). In Deuteronomy 16.13 the seven day celebration "when you make the ingathering from your threshing floor and your wine press" is called *Sukkoth,* 'huts', the word always denoting some rough temporary shelter, cf. Gen. 33.17; Jonah 4.5. The origin of this name for the festival and the significance of these huts are much disputed. Temporary shelters made of branches have for centuries been erected by Palestinian peasants in the fields during fruit harvest, and it is possible that the practice was in vogue even before the Hebrews settled in Canaan. Priestly tradition in the Old Testament, however, linked these huts with the story of the Exodus and the consequent period of wandering in the wilderness when the Hebrews had no permanent houses.

> "You shall dwell in booths for seven days; all that are native in Israel shall dwell in booths, that your generations may know that I made the people of Israel dwell in booths when I brought them out of the land of Egypt" (Lev. 23.42-43).

In these three agricultural festivals—*ḥaggim* as they are called because they originally involved pilgrimage to the local shrine —we may read something of the religious history of the Hebrews. The settlement in Canaan, with its change from the semi-nomadic to the agricultural life, meant that Yahweh had to be intimately related to the daily toil in field, orchard and vineyard. Harvest festivals already existing in Canaan were taken over. But the distinctive emphasis in Hebrew religion could not be changed. Yahweh was never merely the god who gave food to all in due season (cf. Ps. 145.15). He was the god who had brought his people out of slavery in Egypt. The liturgy of harvest time became in part a history lesson.[1] Tradi-

---

[1] cf. p. 17., Deut. 26.6 ff. a credal confession probably connected with *Maṣṣoth.*

tional features in the festivals took on new meaning in the light of this history-centred faith.

(c) *The Day of Atonement.* The festivals we have considered so far were all, whatever their origin, early baptised into the faith of Israel. The Day of Atonement (*Yom Kippur*), *the Day* as it came to be known, was somewhat different. Our only evidence for it in the Old Testament comes from priestly sources edited during or after the exile (Lev. 16; 23.27-33; Num. 29.7-11). We do not know when it was first celebrated in Israel. Inasmuch as it is designed to maintain the covenant relationship between Yahweh and Israel by making provision for dealing with the sins of the community, it may have sprung out of the experience of exile interpreted as Yahweh's inexorable judgement upon a sinful people. The ritual for *the Day*, as given in Leviticus 16, is a mixture of two rites probably originally quite distinct, which have been woven together to underline the truth that Yahweh has made provision for removing the sin which threatens to disrupt the covenant relationship. The ritual followed is the normal one for the offering of the *ḥatta'th* (sin offering) with one important exception. In the temple at Jerusalem the inmost chamber was called the 'holy of holies', the most holy place, the very abode of God himself. In it, according to tradition, stood the ark of the covenant surmounted by a gold covering. This covering (*kapporeth*, Hebrew *k-p-r*, probably originally means to 'cover', but in religious terminology in the Old Testament it carries the idea of 'to atone') has usually been described in English texts since the time of Coverdale as the 'mercy-seat' because of the part it plays in the ritual of *the Day*. Into the holy of holies, which was separated from the rest of the temple by a veil, only one man entered on one occasion of the religious year, the High Priest on the Day of Atonement. After carefully shrouding the 'mercy seat' with a cloud of incense, the High Priest took some of the blood of the *ḥatta'th* bull and sprinkled it upon the 'mercy seat' (Lev. 16.11-15).

Thus in the very presence of God, the sacred representative of the community presented the blood of the sin offering to make atonement "for himself and for his house and for all the assembly of Israel" (Lev. 16.17).

The second element in the ritual centres upon two goats, whose destiny is decided by lot, one being given to Yahweh as a sin offering for the people, the other allotted to Azazel (Lev. 16.7-8). Azazel is a mysterious figure known only from this narrative, probably some kind of desert demon or even a place of ill-omen in the desert. It was a common Hebrew belief that the wild, deserted spots were the haunts of demons (cf. Isa. 13.21; 34.11-16). One goat having been offered as a *hatta'th*, the other goat for Azazel was brought into the presence of Yahweh before the altar:

> "and Aaron shall lay both his hands upon the head of the live goat, and confess over him all the iniquities of the people of Israel, and all their transgressions, all their sins; and he shall put them upon the head of the goat, and send him away into the wilderness by the hand of a man who is in readiness. The goat shall bear all their iniquities upon him to a solitary land; and he shall let the goat go in the wilderness" (Lev. 16.21-22).

The idea of transferring the sins of the community to a public scapegoat is found widespread throughout the world in many primitive communities.[1] Whatever the origin or background of this rite we must look at its meaning in context in the ritual of the Day of Atonement. Both the offering of the blood of the *hatta'th* carried into the holy of holies and the scapegoat ritual stress in their different ways the same basic truth. The blood is accepted by Yahweh in the holy of holies; the fate of the goats is decided by lot—a well-known way of discovering God's will—and it is by Yahweh's command that the sins of the community are transferred to the goat for Azazel and driven out into the wilderness. Sin is a reality in the life of the people of Yahweh, and Yahweh provides the means of

[1] J. G. Frazer, *The Golden Bough* pp. 546-587 (abridged edition)

getting rid of it. To put it in more personal terms, forgiveness is needed and forgiveness comes from Yahweh.

If Passover and the agricultural festivals celebrated Yahweh's gracious initiative in delivering his people from enslavement in Egypt, the Day of Atonement symbolised and sealed in the life of the people his continuing gracious initiative ever bent on renewing and restoring his covenant bond with his people.

(d) *Purim* (lots). It is a curious fact that although the command to celebrate these festivals had the backing of Torah, the supreme authority for Jewish life and conduct, the festival which became, and in many ways still is, the most popular one in the Jewish religious year is not to be found in Torah. The festival of *Purim*, unknown apparently in Palestine before the second century B.C., is traced by the book of Esther to the Jews of the Eastern dispersion in Persia, who, thanks to Queen Esther and her uncle Mordecai, miraculously escaped a pogrom and turned the tables on their enemies. The name *Purim* is explained in Esther 3.7 and 9.24 as coming from an incident in the story where lots are cast to decide the fate of the Jews. *Purim* is, however, a loan word in Hebrew since it has to be explained by the usual Hebrew word for lot '*goral*'. Whatever the origin of the festival—features in it have been traced to many different sources, notably Persian and Babylonian—*Purim* was celebrated with uninhibited joy in something of a carnival atmosphere. Certain doubts were expressed by Jewish Rabbis about the possible effect upon Gentile neighbours of the virulent religious nationalism which pervades Esther, but *Purim* made good its place in the Jewish religious calendar. The history of the Jews ever since has strengthened that place. Haman, the Persian gauleiter in the story, is the prototype of the many persecutors of the Jewish people throughout the ages. *Purim* is a memorial to the eternal miracle of Jewish survival.

In modern Israel it is celebrated by balls and parties, by the giving of presents and by processions through the streets with effigies of the leading characters in the story of Esther, King Ahasuerus and his Jewish Queen Esther, wicked Haman filling the gallows which he had prepared for Mordecai. No wonder a Jewish children's song asks "Why is Purim not twice a week instead of only once a year?"[1]

3. Sabbath

The origin of this most famous of all Jewish institutions, Sabbath, is obscure. We must allow for a similar process operating here as in the case of the festivals of the religious year. Rest days are well authenticated in the Ancient Near East. The Egyptians seem to have had a fondness for the ninth and tenth days of the month, though there is no evidence that they had any religious significance. Attempts which have been made to link Sabbath with Babylonian days of ill-omen or the Akkadian full moon day *shapattu* are far from convincing. All that we can say with certainty is that Sabbath—the Old Testament links it with *sh-b-t* meaning 'to come to rest'—appears as a weekly day of religious significance in the earliest traditions of Israel, in the two early liturgical calendars (Exod. 23.12; Exod. 34.21) and in both versions of the charter of the covenant (Exod. 20.8-10; Deut. 5.12-14) as well as in priestly traditions (Exod. 31.12-17; Num. 15.32-36). It is with the religious significance of Sabbath for Israel that we are concerned. In this respect, as has been well said, "Its distinctive trait lies in the fact that it is a day made holy because of its relation to the God of the covenant; more it is an element in the covenant. Other religions had a day which was *tabu*; in Israel this day became a day consecrated to Yahweh, a tithe on time just as the first born of the flock and the first fruits of harvest were a tithe on the work of other days".[2]

How Sabbath came to reflect different aspects of the faith of the people of Yahweh may be seen by examining the

1 Quoted in *Overseas* (The Church of Scotland in other lands), Vol. 2, No. 4, December 1961.

2 R. de Vaux, *op. cit.,* p. 480.

different comments which have been attached to the law of the Sabbath in the charter of the covenant. The Deuteronomic version lays down an overall prohibition on work:

> "in it you shall not do any work, you, or your son, or your daughter, or your manservant, or your maidservant, or your ox, or your ass, or any of your cattle, or the sojourner who is within your gates, that your manservant and your maidservant may rest as well as you" (Deut. 5.14).

This humane concern that even the slave within the household may have rest is characteristic of the outlook of Deuteronomy. The passage goes on however, to make the Sabbath rest a reminder of the continuous burden of slave labour in Egypt from which Yahweh had delivered his people.

> "You shall remember that you were a servant in the land of Egypt, and the LORD your God brought you out thence with a mighty hand and an outstretched arm; therefore the LORD your God commanded you to keep the sabbath day" (Deut. 5.15).

So Sabbath becomes in this tradition the weekly reminder of the saving power of Yahweh.

The Exodus version (Exod. 20.8 ff.) shares with the priestly author of the hymn of creation in Genesis 1-2.4a a view which traces Sabbath right back to creation. There is to be no work on the Sabbath

> for in six days the LORD made heaven and earth, the sea, and all that is in them, and rested the seventh day; therefore the LORD blessed the sabbath day and hallowed it (Exod. 20.11, cf. Gen. 2.2-3).

Sabbath then belongs to the very nature of things, to the character and creativity of God, from whom all life comes. The observance of Sabbath thus is further illustration of one of the basic ethical principles governing the life of the covenant people, 'as God rested on the seventh day, so must you'.

As far as our evidence goes, Sabbath in pre-exilic Israel does not seem to have been a day hedged around with innumerable prohibitions. Normal work ceased, but the essential point of Sabbath was that it was Sabbath to Yahweh, a religious occasion recalling the goodness of Yahweh, his mighty acts both in history and in creation, and providing an opportunity to respond to such goodness in the sanctuary (2 Kings 4.23).

When in 586 B.C. Jerusalem and its temple were destroyed, the Jewish people exiled in Babylon were unable either to offer sacrifice or to celebrate at the temple the great occasions of the religious year. Much that had been of deep religious significance was lost. Sabbath therefore took on a new importance. It required no temple or elaborate ritual. Along with circumcision, it became one of the indispensable signs of the Jewish faith, distinguishing the Jew from his non-Jewish neighbour. With increasing importance, its character tended to change. The negative side of Sabbath was emphasised. Jeremiah 17.19-27, almost certainly a post-exilic addition to the oracles of Jeremiah, prohibits the carrying of any load in or out of Jerusalem, into or out of a private house on the Sabbath. Nehemiah 13.15-22 deals drastically with work or trade in any form on the Sabbath. The way is opening for later Jewish attempts to define precisely what constitutes work on the Sabbath. The Mishnah, a second century compilation of Rabbinic teaching, defines thirty-nine different kinds of work prohibited on Sabbath including loosening a knot, sewing two stitches and writing two letters (Mishnah Shabbath 7.2). Instead of being a weekly reminder of the mighty activity of the God of the covenant, Sabbath was in danger of becoming merely a monument to the negative piety of man. A similar fate has not infrequently befallen the Christian Sunday, a day quite distinct in origin from the Jewish Sabbath, but like it, intended to be a witness to a mighty act of God, the resurrection triumph of Jesus.

Sacrifice, the great festivals of the religious year, and Sabbath had this in common. All bore witness to the God of the covenant. They were intended to enable the people of Yahweh to make realistic and worthy response to the God whose gracious activity undergirded all life.

Chapter Seven

GOD IN THE PSALMS

WE have been examining what the Hebrews did in worship, and the significant occasions in their religious calendar. It is the Psalms, however, which bring us into contact with the living heart of worship in Ancient Israel. The present century has witnessed a revolution in our approach to the Psalms. For long, critical scholarship combed the Psalms in an endeavour to find references to specific historical events. There were two assumptions in this approach.

1. The Psalms were in the main to be treated as personal religious lyrics called forth by a specific situation in the life of the poet or of the community in which he lived. This is a very old approach to the Psalms, as may be seen from the headings given to many of the Psalms in Jewish tradition. Psalm 3, for example, is headed "A Psalm of David when he fled from Absalom his son"; Psalm 18 "A Psalm of David, the servant of the LORD who addressed the words of this song to the LORD on the day when the LORD delivered him from the hand of all his enemies and from the hand of Saul" (cf. Ps. 7, 30, 34, 51). Concerning the traditional titles to Psalms it has been judiciously stated, "It is perhaps no exaggeration to say that where their meaning is clear, we have reason to doubt their reliability, and that where they might provide us with valuable data about the history and use of the various psalms, their interpretation is debated or obscured".[1]

Into the former category fall most of the headings which give specific historical references; into the latter category, the

[1] G. W. Anderson in *Peake's Commentary on the Bible* (ed. M. Black and H. H. Rowley), 358a.

headings which refer to tunes and musical instruments (cf. Ps. 5 'for the flutes'? Ps. 7 'A Shiggaion'?).

2. Most of the Psalms were to be regarded as of late post-exilic origin, some as late as 100 B.C., most of them from 400 B.C. onwards. A recent supporter of this view claims that only Psalm 24.7-10 and Psalm 45 are definitely pre-exilic.[1]

Both these assumptions have been vigorously attacked in recent years. Increasing evidence from other cultures in the Ancient Near East enables us to say that the Psalms in the Old Testament stand within a tradition of liturgical poetry which flourished before the Hebrews settled in Canaan. There are many links in poetic structure, in language and in imagery between the Psalms and the Canaanite liturgical poems from Ugarit. In one of the poems it is said of Baal,[2]

> Behold thine enemies, O Baal,
> Behold thine enemies thou shalt smite,
> Behold thou shalt subdue thine adversaries.

We are reminded of Psalm 92.9,

> For, lo, thy enemies, O LORD,
> for, lo, thy enemies shall perish;
> all evil doers shall be scattered.

God is described in the Psalm as he "who rides upon the clouds" (Ps. 68.4, 33). 'Rider of the clouds' is a characteristic title of Baal in the Ugaritic poems. Psalm 29 is probably a very close Hebrew adaptation of a hymn to Baal, so marked are the resemblances in both structure and imagery to Ugaritic material. In Psalm 48.2 Jerusalem is described in the following terms:

> His holy mountain, beautiful in elevation,
> is the joy of all the earth,
> Mount Zion, in the far north,
> the city of the great King.

[1] R. H. Pfeiffer, *An Introduction to the Old Testament*, p. 633.
[2] D.O.T.T., p. 129.

It has always been difficult to understand the description of Mount Zion as being 'in the far north'. In the Ugaritic texts, however, the traditional abode of the gods lies in the 'crags of Zaphon', and Zaphon means north. It looks as if a phrase current in Canaanite mythology was taken over by the Hebrews, and used in the description of the abode of Yahweh.

> God has taken his place in the divine council;
>   in the midst of the gods he holds judgement (Ps. 82.1).

This picture of the assembly of the gods, where divine policy was discussed and decisions taken, is probably a reflection of the Ugaritic assembly of the gods presided over by El. It survives because it is traditional liturgical language, even though it fits rather uneasily into orthodox faith.

The closer the links with such Canaanite material the more unlikely it is that most of the Psalms are post-exilic. We must look for the origin of many of the Psalms in the worship of pre-exilic Israel. There is evidence within the Old Testament itself that Psalms found a place in worship at an early date. 1 Chronicles which, although it is a post-exilic priestly commentary on history, may preserve traditional liturgical material, links certain of the Psalms[1] with the coming of the ark to the temple at Jerusalem, the people responding to the singing of the Psalms by a guild of choristers (the sons of Asaph) with many a heartfelt 'Amen' and 'Hallelujah' (1 Chron. 16). Two Psalms are linked in their headings with the 'azkaruh, memorial offering, and reveal to us something of the urgent plea for God's help which must often have accompanied the sacrifice (Ps. 38; 70). Psalm 100 is entitled "A Psalm for the thank offering". This link has been doubted, but the dominant theme of the psalm, joy in worship and the certainty of God's goodness and faithfulness would appropriately accompany the sharing of a sacrificial meal as a response of thanksgiving for benefits received from God. Psalms 120-134 are designated 'Songs of Ascents', which may indicate that

[1] Ps. 105.1-15; Ps. 96.1-13; Ps. 106.1, 47-48.

they were traditionally sung by pilgrims making their way up to the temple at Jerusalem for one of the great religious festivals, Passover, according to later Hebrew tradition.

In recent years there has been a further attempt to give some of the Psalms a particular setting in the worship of pre-exilic Israel. A group of Psalms, including 47, 93, 95-100, have as their common theme the kingship of Yahweh, his sovereign rule over all the forces of nature and history. Their recurring theme phrase is 'Yahweh is king' (Ps. 47.8; 93.1; 96.10; 97.1; 99.1). Certain of the Ugaritic poems about Baal seem to preserve the liturgy of a Canaanite autumnal New Year festival in which there was dramatically enacted the triumph of Baal over all the forces of chaos and drought which threatened the well-being of the community. The kingship of Baal was the theme of such a Canaanite New Year festival; 'Marduk is king' was the theme of its Babylonian counterpart. In the light of analogies drawn widely from Ancient Near Eastern religion, Canaanite, Babylonian, and Egyptian, and on the basis of the language of these kingship Psalms and certain passages in the prophets, it has been argued that 'Asiph (Sukkoth) celebrated 'at the outgoing of the year' (Exod. 23.16; 34.22) was just such a New Year festival in Israel. Its celebration would include the re-enactment of Yahweh's victory over the forces of chaos, the declaration of his sovereignty in nature and history, and a joyous procession in which the ark of the covenant, symbol of Yahweh's presence, was carried into the temple at Jerusalem, where Yahweh was enthroned for the coming year. It is further claimed, in the light of parallels from other Ancient Near Eastern religions, that the ruling monarch in Israel had an important part to play in the ritual.

The case for such a New Year festival in Israel has powerful advocates, but it still lacks proof. If such a festival was as all important in pre-exilic Israel as some scholars suggest, it is surprising, to say the least, that no clear mention of it has survived in pre-exilic liturgical calendars. By no stretch of the imagination can the information concerning *Sukkoth* in such calendars be made to substantiate such a New Year festival. Nor is the language of the Psalms in itself sufficient evidence. We have no right to assume that when a Hebrew said "Yahweh is king", he meant basically the same thing as a Canaanite declaring "Baal is king" or a Babylonian acclaiming the kingship of Marduk; nor, lacking more explicit evidence, have we the right to place the acclamation of the kingship of Yahweh in the context of an autumnal New Year festival, celebrated with appropriate liturgy in the temple at Jerusalem. The thought of Yahweh's kingship over the forces both of nature and history was inherent in Hebrew religion from the time of the Exodus onwards. It is the underlying motif in most of the great occasions of the religious year. The Psalms which speak of the kingship of Yahweh must be interpreted in the light of the basic assertions of the covenant faith.[1]

Whatever view we take of such a New Year festival in pre-exilic Israel it remains true that the proper setting for most of the Psalms is worship, the worship of both pre-exilic and post-exilic Israel. ". . . the poetry of devotion is related to recurring situations in congregational life and in the life of the believer rather than to specific incidents in history."[2] If the analogy of a modern hymn book is of any relevance, this statement is true with this reservation. A hymn may begin life as the response of an individual to a specific incident or crisis. It becomes suitable for more general use because that specific incident contains elements which are part of common religious experience. Psalm 51 could have sprung, as its heading suggests, out of David's mood of contrition and confession consequent upon his adultery with Bathsheba, though there are good critical reasons for doubting this. It owes its position

[1] For the thesis of the autumnal New Year festival, cf. *Myth and Ritual* and *Myth, Ritual and Kingship*, ed. S. H. Hooke. A criticism is to be found in R. de Vaux, *Ancient Israel*, pp. 504 ff.

[2] G. W. Anderson, *A Critical Introduction to the Old Testament*, p. 174.

in the Psalter to the fact that confession and the need to be assured of God's forgiveness are a common religious experience. We are unlikely ever to be certain as to the origin of some of the Psalms; we do know that they enshrine the faith of the Hebrews as it found expression in worship.

1. We look first at a number of Psalms which were composed for state occasions, or particular events in the life of the royal household. Psalms 2 and 110 find their natural setting in the coronation service or some annual celebration of the king's accession to the throne. Both stress the universal power of Yahweh over the nations. Both speak of the peculiar bond that links Yahweh to the king of his people. The king is Yahweh's 'anointed', his adopted son, with a part to play in the worship of Yahweh (cf. Chapter Eleven, pp. 216 ff.). "You are a priest for ever after the order of Melchizedek" (Ps. 110.4). Although the king does not belong to the priestly families of Aaron and Levi, he has priestly functions which are traced back to the mysterious figure of Melchizedek, priest-king of pre-Israelite Jerusalem in Genesis 14.18 ff. Probably on certain important occasions the king led the people in worship and offered sacrifice on behalf of the community (cf. 1 Chron. 16). Psalm 72, equally at home in a coronation service, shows us something of what was expected from the ruling monarch. He is to be the embodiment of the twin prophetic ideals of 'justice' and 'righteousness'.

> "May he defend the cause of the poor of the people,
>   give deliverance to the needy,
>   and crush the oppressor" (Ps. 72.4).

After a characteristic prayer for long life and imperial greatness, there is voiced the hope that during the king's reign peace (*shalom*, completeness) will abound, that is to say, that the community will enjoy a complete, well-ordered, harmonious life uniting material prosperity, national greatness and social justice. This, the Hebrew ideal for the community, is firmly rooted in God since the Psalm opens with the plea,

"Give the king thy justice, O God,
and thy righteousness to the royal son"
(Ps. 72.1, cf. Ps. 21; and 45, the latter originally
composed for a royal wedding to a foreign princess).

Psalm 20 finds its original setting in a service of dedication
before the king rides forth to do battle against his enemies in
the name of Yahweh. It opens with a plea for Yahweh's powerful help (vv. 1-5), a plea which is capped by the assurance,
probably voiced by some temple prophet, that the prayers of
the people are answered:

"Now I know that the LORD will help his anointed;
he will answer him from his holy heaven
with mighty victories by his right hand.
Some boast of chariots, and some of horses;
but we boast of the name of the LORD our God.
They will collapse and fall;
but we shall rise and stand upright" (Ps. 20.6-8).

In all such Psalms composed for state occasions we see
intense faith in Yahweh, the God who will vindicate the cause
of his people, going hand in hand with the recognition that
the true well-being of the people depends upon a king who
will faithfully uphold Yahweh's demand for righteousness and
justice.

2. If we look beyond such royal Psalms, to Psalms which are
more generally concerned with the religious life of the community, we find that they reflect the faith of Israel in all its
rich variety.

(a) The Psalms witness to the living God who has confronted
his people in the decisive events of their history. In moments
of deep doubt and agony, assurance is sought by recalling where
faith is grounded, in the deeds of Yahweh, in his wonders of
old. Enslavement in Egypt, the miracle of deliverance across
the Reed Sea, the covenant at Sinai are the certainties of faith.

"Thy way, O God, is holy.
What god is great like our God?
Thou art the God who workest wonders,
    who hast manifested thy might among the peoples.
Thou didst with thy arm redeem thy people,
    the sons of Jacob and Joseph.
When the waters saw thee, O God,
    when the waters saw thee, they were afraid,
    yea, the deep trembled.
The clouds poured out water;
    the skies gave forth thunder;
    thy arrows flashed on every side.
The crash of thy thunder was in the whirlwind;
    thy lightnings lighted up the world;
    the earth trembled and shook.
Thy way was through the sea,
    thy path through the great waters;
    yet thy footprints were unseen.
Thou didst lead thy people like a flock
    by the hand of Moses and Aaron"

                            (Ps. 77.13-20; cf. Ps. 78).

If history witnesses to God, so does all creation seen through the eyes of faith. The whole world is claimed for Yahweh. His power is continuously and creatively at work therein. The language and imagery of Psalm 104 have often been compared with the Egyptian Hymn to Aten, the solar disk whose worship was fostered by the heretical Pharaoh Amenhotep IV (14th century B.C.), who changed his name in recognition of his new faith to Akhenaten. There are interesting parallels.

Hymn to Aten	Psalm 104
All beasts are satisfied with their pasture;	Thou makest springs gush forth in the valleys;
Trees and plants are verdant.	they flow between the hills,
The birds which fly from their nests, their wings are (spread) in adoration to thy soul;	they give drink to every beast of the field; the wild asses quench their thirst.
All flocks skip with (their) feet;	By them the birds of the air have their habitation;

All that fly up and alight	they sing among the branches
Live when thou hast risen (for) them. (31-36).	(vv. 10-12).

How manifold is that which thou hast made, hidden from view.	O LORD, how manifold are thy works!
Thou sole god, there is no other like thee.	in wisdom hast thou made them all;
Thou didst create the earth according to thy will, being alone:	the earth is full of thy creatures (v. 24).
Mankind, cattle, all flocks,	
Everything on earth which walks with (its) feet,	
And what are on high, flying with their wings	

$$(52-57)^1.$$

Yet the God of Psalm 104 is not the life-giving disk of the sun, nor anything else in all creation. He is the lord of all creation. Upon his creative spirit everything depends for life (Ps. 104. 30). Far from being but a reflection of an Egyptian original, Psalm 104 has been more truly described as "a symphony on the theme of Gen. 1.31—and God saw everything that he had made and behold it was very good." Not only so, but Psalm 104 sees God as the moral sovereign of the world, the Psalm ending with an impassioned plea that righteousness will be vindicated in all the world.

> "Let sinners be consumed from the earth,
> and let the wicked be no more!
> Bless the LORD, O my soul!
> Praise the LORD!" (Ps. 104.35).

In Psalm 136, one of the greatest Psalms of praise, creation and history join hands, both witnessing to the great reality undergirding all life, the steadfast love of Yahweh. The Psalm must have been sung responsively. Each call to worship (vv. 1-3), each remembrance of the mighty deeds of Yahweh

[1] D.O.T.T., pp. 146 and 147.

in creation (vv. 4-9) and in the history of Israel (vv. 10-22), each recollection of his continuing concern and providence (vv. 23-25) is answered by the response "for his steadfast love endures for ever". The Hebrew word *ḥesedh* translated 'mercy' in the A.V., 'steadfast love' in the R.S.V., is notoriously difficult to render adequately in English. At the heart of it there is the thought of loyalty and dependability, such loyalty as you have the right to expect from someone united to you by a covenant (cf. 2 Sam. 10.1-2 where David promises to 'do *ḥesedh*', to deal loyally with Hanun the new king of the Ammonites, as Nahash, Hanun's father, had dealt loyally with David). Yet there is perhaps more in *ḥesedh* than loyalty, especially when the word is applied to Yahweh. What brought the covenant between Yahweh and his people into being in the first place if not the unmerited, outgoing love of Yahweh? What could keep Yahweh loyal to that same covenant in face of his people's disloyalty if not that same love? 'Steadfast love' or 'loving dependability' is, therefore, perhaps as near as we can get to the meaning of *ḥesedh* when applied to God. This is the bed rock of faith for the Old Testament.

> "Our soul waits for the LORD;
> he is our help and shield.
> Yea, our heart is glad in him,
> because we trust in his holy name.
> Let thy steadfast love, O LORD, be upon us,
> even as we hope in thee"
> (Ps. 33.20-22; cf. Pss. 36, 57, 89, 117-118).

Many Psalms which do not use the word *ḥesedh* nonetheless have the steadfast love, the utter dependability of God as their theme (cf. Ps. 46). Such being God's nature, it is not surprising that there runs through the Psalms a deep undercurrent of joy which time and again bubbles to the surface to break forth into a torrent of unrestrained adoration and joy. 'Hallelujah'—Praise Yahweh. When worship is, as in Israel, man's response to the mighty deeds of God it cannot be dull or joyless.

"Praise the LORD!
Praise God in his sanctuary;
praise him in his mighty firmament!
Praise him for his mighty deeds;
praise him according to his exceeding greatness!
Praise him with trumpet sound;
praise him with lute and harp!
Praise him with timbrel and dance;
praise him with strings and pipe!
Praise him with sounding cymbals;
praise him with loud clashing cymbals!
Let everything that breathes praise the LORD!
Praise the LORD!"
(Ps. 150, cf. the other Hallelujah psalms,
111-113; 117; 135; 140-149).

(b) There are many Psalms which focus the needs of the community or of some individual within the community. It is not always possible to be certain whether a Psalm of this type refers primarily to the community or to an individual. The sharp distinction which modern man tends to draw between society and the life of the individual within society was not a natural distinction for the Hebrew. On the one hand, the Hebrew was conscious of being part of a community bound for weal or woe in the sharing of a very real corporate life; on the other hand the life of the community was embodied in the life of its members. This leads at times to a switch within a Psalm from the singular to the plural and vice versa. Psalm 102 begins

"Hear my prayer, o LORD;
let my cry come to thee!
Do not hide thy face from me
in the day of my distress!
Incline thy ear to me;
answer me speedily in the day when I call!"
(Ps. 102.1-2).

and continues in vividly personal terms to describe the plight of the worshipper in verses 3-11. Verses 12-22, however, are concerned with the community of Yahweh's servants. In verses 23-24 we return to the first person with its intensely personal description of tragedy and affliction.

> "He has broken my strength in mid-course;
> he has shortened my days" (Ps. 102.23).

It is possible that in many such cases the 'I' sections are spoken by a temple prophet or leading figure within the community, dramatically representing in his own person the plight and needs of the community.

In many cases, however, the content of the Psalm helps us to decide whether we are dealing with a community plea for help or with a cry wrung out of bitter personal experience. Psalm 44 is a good example of a community appeal to God, an appeal prompted by some national disaster in the history of the Hebrews—which we have no means of saying—and relevant thereafter to any national emergency. It begins (vv. 1-3) by recalling the past mighty acts of God,

> "We have heard with our ears, O God,
> our fathers have told us,
> what deeds thou didst perform in their days,
> in the days of old" (Ps. 44.1).

This ought to lead to present confidence and hope (vv. 4-8) yet circumstances make such confidence very difficult. God's people are 'cast off', 'scattered like sheep', 'sold for a trifle', 'the taunt of their enemies' (vv. 9-16),

> "a byword among the nations,
> a laughing stock among the peoples" (Ps. 44.14).

And all this has taken place without any reason for it (vv. 17-22).

> ". . . we have not forgotten thee,
> or been false to thy covenant.
> Our heart has not turned back,
> nor have our steps departed from thy way"
> (Ps. 44.17-18).

What can be the meaning of this suffering of God's faithful people? The Psalm ends with an impassioned plea to God to wake, to vindicate his afflicted oppressed people. It is a cry out of the depths of despair; but it is a cry possible only because the community believes that somewhere in the darkness there is the steadfast love of God which must triumph.

> "Rise up, come to our help!
> Deliver us for the sake of thy steadfast love!"
>   (Ps. 44.26, cf. Pss. 74, 79, 80, 83).

No type of Psalm is more common than that which springs out of some personal tragedy, loneliness, persecution, critical illness, the dark night of the soul. Faith is always a battlefield where the struggle is severe and victory hard won at the cost of many a wound. Doubt and assurance, faith and scepticism, bitterness and joy are closely woven together in the religious experience of Israel, notably in such personal Psalms. Many attempts have been made to reconstruct the background to such Psalms. Who, for example, are the 'enemies' or the 'workers of iniquity', who seem so often to be responsible for the Psalmist's plight? Many different people have been cast for this role, sorcerers whose evil spells need to be exorcised by God in the temple, the callous rich in society, people who bring false slanderous accusations in court, foreigners. All attempts to provide one answer to this question are doomed to failure. The threat to faith comes from many different directions, both from within and without the believer. The answer to such threats was to bring the doubt, the darkness and the bitterness to God, and there in his sanctuary seek reassurance.

Psalm 22, familiar in Christian tradition because its opening words were on the lips of Jesus during the dark night of his soul on the Cross, is a good example of this type of Psalm. The witness of past generations is clear. God has been mighty,

> "enthroned on the praises of Israel.
> In thee our fathers trusted;
> they trusted, and thou didst deliver them" (Ps. 22.3b-4).

But this is not the present experience of the Psalmist.

"My God, my God, why hast thou forsaken me?
Why art thou so far from helping me, from the
  words of my groaning?
O my God, I cry by day, but thou dost not answer;
and by night, but find no rest" (Ps. 22.1-2).

Scorned, despised, blasphemously taunted for his simple faith
(vv. 6-8), his vitality is now at a low ebb. Already as good as
dead in the eyes of those who gloat over his fall, the Psalmist
directs an urgent plea to God.

"But thou, O LORD, be not far off!
O thou my help, hasten to my aid!" (Ps. 22.19).

In verse 22 the mood of the Psalm changes from urgent plea
to rich assurance. Worship is no despairing attempt to storm
heaven, but the point where God meets the need of man.
Through the sacrifice which must have accompanied such a
plea—v. 26 "the afflicted shall eat and be satisfied" probably
described the healing experience which comes through sharing
in a sacrificial meal—through the word of temple priest or
prophet, the reality of God's presence and power is sealed in
the Psalmist's heart.

"You who fear the LORD, praise him!
all you sons of Jacob, glorify him,
and stand in awe of him, all you sons of Israel!
For he has not despised or abhorred
the affliction of the afflicted;
and he has not hid his face from him,
but has heard, when he cried to him" (Ps. 22.23-24).

From this assurance of the triumph of God's purposes in his
own life, the Psalmist reaches out in faith to the universal
triumph of God in the affairs of men and nations.

"All the ends of the earth shall remember
and turn to the LORD;
and all the families of the nations
shall worship before him.
For dominion belongs to the LORD,
and he rules over the nations" (Ps. 22.27-28).

This is the pattern of doubt and faith, perplexity issuing in new confidence which is characteristic of so many Psalms of this type (cf. Pss. 3-5; 7; 13; 15; 54, etc.).

(c) There are other Psalms in which the dominant mood is not the plea for help in time of trouble, but the glad acknowledgement of help received. The Psalmist's troubles and difficulties now lie in the past; it remains for him to acknowledge with thanksgiving the goodness of God. Many of these Psalms must have accompanied the bringing of a sacrifice of thanksgiving to the altar. Psalm 30 is such a Psalm, sung probably to mark recovery from a critical illness. The opening verses (1-3) set the tone for the rest of the Psalm. This man has cried to God for help and has been healed. He has been at the very gates of death—'Sheol' and the 'Pit' (v. 3, cf. v. 9) are both names for the shadowy underworld of no real life to which the dead went, in Hebrew thought—but his life has been restored. Summoning others to share in the praise of God, he confesses in an autobiographical fragment (vv. 6-10) how in time of prosperity he had been proudly self-confident. Affliction had humbled him and turned him to God. Nor had he been disappointed.

> "Thou hast turned for me my mourning into dancing;
> thou hast loosed my sackcloth
> and girded me with gladness,
> that my soul may praise thee and not be silent.
> O LORD my God, I will give thanks to thee for ever"
> (Ps. 30.11-12, cf. Pss. 34, 66, 92).

In all these Psalms, whether they express the mind of the community or the individual, we find enshrined the distinctively Old Testament insistence upon the initiative of God in all his dealings with men. His 'steadfast love' undergirds history and creation; his dependability meets life's perplexities. Doubt may be real, the threatening forces of evil powerful, yet it is the care and power of God which are life's greatest realities. Recall Psalm 23. Here is Yahweh the shepherd (vv. 1-4) leading his flock along safe paths, tending to their need for fresh life-giving water. So may a man be certain,

> "Even though I walk through the valley of the shadow of death,
> I fear no evil;
> for thou art with me;
> thy rod and thy staff,
> they comfort me" (Ps. 23.4).

Here is Yahweh, the gracious host making ample provision for his guests (v. 5). So may a man be certain,

> "Surely goodness and mercy shall follow me
> all the days of my life;
> and I shall dwell in the house of the LORD
> for ever" (Ps. 23.6; cf. Ps. 139).

This is one side of the covenant faith come to life in personal experience. The other side, the religious and moral responsibility of the people of Yahweh is equally stressed. Many Psalms underline the prophetic insistence that worship, unrelated to a life rightly ordered in response to God, is meaningless.

Psalm 24 was probably originally composed for some festive occasion when the ark, the symbol of Yahweh's presence, was carried into the sanctuary at Jerusalem. Yahweh, the King of glory, strong and mighty, mighty in battle (v. 8) is coming to his abode. Who may join him there truly to share in worship?

> "He who has clean hands and a pure heart,
> who does not lift up his soul to what is false,
> and does not swear deceitfully.
> He will receive blessing from the LORD,
> and vindication from the God of his salvation.
> Such is the generation of those who seek him,
> who seek the face of the God of Jacob" (Ps. 24.4-6).

Likewise in the moving confessional, Psalm 51, it is recognised that sacrifice in itself is not enough.

> "The sacrifice acceptable to God is a broken spirit;
> a broken and contrite heart, O God, thou wilt not despise"
> (Ps. 51.17).

This insistence in the Old Testament on the inescapably moral requirement for true worship is not a stern, self-defeating, moralistic attempt by man to make himself good enough to be acceptable to God. It is a man's glad response to what God has given. This is abundantly clear in the longest Psalm in the collection, Psalm 119, an acrostic poem (vv. 1-8 begin with the first letter of the Hebrew alphabet, vv. 9-16 with the second letter of the alphabet, and so on through the 176 verses of the poem) in the form of a meditation on the Torah of Yahweh. Torah enshrines Yahweh's precepts and statutes, his righteous ordinances and commandments. But this is not the cold forbidding voice of duty. This is Yahweh's gift to his people, his design for the good life. It calls forth delight, joy and love from his people.

> "I will delight in thy statutes;
>   I will not forget thy word"
>   (Ps. 119.16, cf. vv. 24, 35, 62, 70, 77).

> "for I find my delight in thy commandments,
>   which I love.
>   I revere thy commandments, which I love,
>   and I will meditate on thy statutes" (vv. 47-48).

> "Oh, how I love thy law!
>   It is my meditation all the day" (v. 97, cf. v. 113).

> "How sweet are thy words to my taste,
>   sweeter than honey to my mouth!" (v. 103).

> "Thy word is a lamp to my feet
>   and a light to my path"
>   (v. 105, cf. vv. 129-131; Ps. 19.7 ff.).

Limitations there undoubtedly are in the outlook of some of the Psalms[1] but in the Psalter we are in touch with the warm intense devotion of a people's response to God, with worship ever set in the light of the past, present and future activity of the living God.

[1] cf. p. 99 and p. 164.

Chapter Eight

GOD AND WISDOM

THERE has sometimes been a tendency to underestimate the place and the importance of the individual in Ancient Israel. The Old Testament, we are assured, presents us with a community faith. Man is important only as belonging to the community, or to the family within the wider community. As over against a false religious individualism, the Old Testment has something vital to say in its insistence on the people of Yahweh and the covenant relationship. But from an early date among the Hebrews a man was important, not merely as a member of the community, but in his own right. The demands contained in the charter of the covenant may be designed to create a true people of Yahweh, but they are directed towards the conscience of the individual members of the community, 'You (singular) shall not', 'You shall'. So with the teaching of the prophets. When Nathan appears before King David with the accusing words "You are the man" (2 Sam. 12.7), he is confronting David with personal guilt and responsibility. Nor does God's punishment for David's sin fall upon the community. It is directed personally at David through the child born of his illicit union. Thus personal guilt and personal responsibility were real factors among the Hebrews in the tenth century B.C. Likewise the sacrificial system and the Psalms express not only a community faith, but a wide range of intensely personal responses to God.

Nor was community life in the Old Testament static. It was often a community in transition—the semi-nomadic life giving way to the settlement in Canaan, small farming communities growing into commercial centres, the rise of a monied middle class not tied to the land, the growth of the monarchy and an increasingly centralised bureaucracy. While life for many a poor peasant farmer may have changed very little across the centuries in Old Testament times, others, especially in the towns, witnessed periods of rapid social change in which the problems of the individual were inevitably thrust to the fore. There is a good example of this in Genesis 18, part of the earliest 'J' strand in the Pentateuch. Behind the story lies the thought of communal responsibility widely accepted in the ancient world (cf. Joshua 7), the members of a particular social group bound together for weal or woe. Lot, Abraham's nephew, settles in Sodom, a Canaanite city. He is an alien in an alien community. It is hardly accidental that it is at this point that Abraham raises with God the question of distinguishing between the innocent (righteous) and the guilty (wicked) within the community. A new social factor has called in question the adequacy of the old doctrine of communal responsibility. The narrative does not reject communal responsibility entirely; indeed it restates it from a different angle. The righteous men would have been the salvation of the entire community. But it is Lot, the social intruder, who in his own person focuses a new problem.

Within the community faith of the Old Testament there was room for a very real interest in the individual, in the influences and motives which shaped human conduct, and in personal faith.

Alongside priest and prophet who each in his different way provided a link between God and the community—the priest as guardian of Torah, the prophet with his living word from God—there stood a third figure in the Old Testament, the sage, the wise man whose duty it was to give counsel, shrewd practical advice (cf. Jer. 18.18). Psalm 1, which has been added as a prologue to the Psalter, stands in the tradition of 'the wise' and reflects two of its important emphases.

1. It is intentionally didactic, being concerned to give practical advice which will lead to the good life. Such a life,

claims this Psalm, is only possible for the man whose

> ". . . delight is in the law of the LORD,
>   and on his law he meditates day and night" (Ps. 1.2).

2. It states a characteristic doctrine of the wise, the doctrine of the two contrasting ways, the way of the wicked and the way of the righteous (cf. Pss. 37; 49; 112).

There is no doubt that the wise men in Israel drew on a tradition of wisdom which we can document from Egyptian, Sumerian, Babylonian, Canaanite and Aramaic sources. Egyptian and Hebrew religion may have very little in common, but the wise men in both countries spoke in similar terms with the same practical purpose in view.

About the middle of the third millennium B.C., a certain Egyptian vizier Ptah-hotep, only too well aware that "old age has descended, feebleness has arrived, dotage is coming anew",[1] set down certain instructions for his son and designated successor to ensure that he would be a wise and efficient counsellor of state. The qualities needed for leadership, the social graces, true friendship, advice on how to behave both towards superiors and inferiors, are all deftly handled. As for domestic matters:

> "If thou art a man of standing, thou shouldst found thy household and love thy wife at home as is fitting. Fill her belly; clothe her back. Ointment is the prescription for her body. Make her heart glad as long as thou livest . . . keep her far from gaining control. Her eye is her storm wind. Let her heart be soothed through what may accrue to thee"[2]

In the same document we find the typical form of the brief wisdom saying in contrasting phrases,

> "He whom god loves is a hearkener,
>   He whom god hates cannot hear"

[1] A.N.E.T., p. 412.
[2] A.N.E.T., p. 413.

and the antithesis which echoes across the ages between the 'wise' and the fool.

> "The wise man rises early in the morning to establish himself,
> The fool rises early in the morning to agitate himself."[1]

Many centuries later, the scribe Ani, from a more humble social station, hands on to his son instructions which abound in salutary advice based on shrewd observation of life, e.g.

> "Do not talk a lot. Be silent and thou wilt be happy. Do not be garrulous. The dwelling of god, its abomination is clamour. Pray thee with a loving heart, all the words of which are hidden, and he will do what thou needest, he will hear what thou sayest and he will accept thy offering."[2]

Of more immediate interest for the Old Testament are the *Instructions of Amen-em-opet* which date back into the second millennium B.C. though our earliest extant copy is much later. There are numerous close parallels both in imagery and thought between the *Instructions* and one of the collections out of which the present book of Proverbs is built up, Proverbs 22.17-24.22. The *Instructions of Amen-em-opet* are divided into thirty chapters, the final one beginning with the words, "See then these thirty chapters, they instruct, they entertain." Proverbs 22.20 reads, "Have I not written for you thirty sayings of admonition and knowledge?"

The following parallels are typical:

Amen-em-opet	*Proverbs*
1. Give thine ears, hear what is said,	Incline your ear and hear the words of the wise,
Give thy mind to interpret them,	and apply your mind to my knowledge;
To put them in thy heart is beneficial.	for it will be pleasant if you keep them within you,
	if all of them are ready on your lips (22.17-18).

[1] A.N.E.T., p. 414.
[2] A.N.E.T., p. 420a.

VI. Remove not the landmark at the boundaries of the arable land,
Nor disturb the position of the measuring-cord;
Covet not a cubit of land,
Nor throw down the boundaries of a widow.

Do not remove an ancient landmark or enter the fields of the fatherless
(23.10, cf. 22.28).

IX. Associate not with the hot-head,
Nor become intimate with him in conversation.

Make no friendship with a man given to anger,
nor go with a wrathful man
(22.24).

XXIII. Eat not bread in the presence of a noble,
Nor apply thy mouth at the beginning.
If thou art satisfied—false chewings
Be a diversion for thy saliva!
Look at the cup which is in thy presence
And let it serve thy needs.[1]

When you sit down to eat with a ruler,
observe carefully what is before you;
and put a knife to your throat if you are a man given to appetite.
Do not desire his delicacies, for they are deceptive food
(23.1-3).

Sumerian, Babylonian and Aramaic sources provide wisdom sayings many of which bear a striking similarity to sayings in Proverbs. The Canaanite texts from Ugarit throw light on certain puzzling phrases in Proverbs and provide us with our only parallel in the Ancient Near East to a form of statement which we find occasionally in Proverbs, in which the first two lines contain different but parallel similes and the third line points their application.

> Like vinegar to the teeth,
> and smoke to the eyes,
> so is the sluggard to those who send him (Prov. 10.26).

So the goddess Anat's longing for Baal is described in the Canaanite text as follows:

[1] D.O.T.T., pp. 176 ff.

Like the heart of a wild cow for her calf,
Like the heart of a wild ewe for her lamb,
So (was) the heart of 'Anat for Baal.[1]

There is nothing that need surprise us in all this. Wisdom is not the monopoly of any one people. Sages of all nations have reached remarkably similar conclusions about every-day problems and the forces which make or mar human conduct.

Hebrew tradition makes King Solomon the royal patron saint of wisdom and attributes to him part, but by no means all, of the book of Proverbs (1 Kings 4.29-34; 10.1-10, 25 ff; Prov. 1.1; 10.1; 25.1). The truth in this tradition seems to be that the court and royal patronage provided the natural setting for the sages in Israel. Who more than the king stood in need of the shrewd practical advice they had to offer? The well-being of the community depended upon the king being well instructed in the ways of wisdom.

The Hebrew word translated proverb, *mashal*, has a much wider range of meanings than its English equivalent. It may mean a brief proverbial saying (1 Sam. 10.12; Ezek. 18.2-3), but equally it describes a prophetic vision or oracle, a ballad, riddle or allegory. Always it seems to carry with it the meaning 'authoritative instruction' whether couched in a brief proverbial saying or in longer form. Thus the book of Proverbs contains hundreds of brief epigrammatic sayings, but also longer units such as the warning against the harlot's wiles (5), meditations on wisdom (8-9), and the portrait of the efficient wife (31.10-31). Proverbs is not a book in the strict sense of the word, but an anthology of wisdom teaching culled from various quarters, a 'collection of collections'[2] as it has been described. It is very difficult to be certain about the date of any of these collections. Wisdom probably began to be fashionable in Israel under the early monarchy and it continued into post-exilic times. The very nature of the material in these

[1] A.N.E.T., p. 140.
[2] R. H. Pfeiffer, *Introduction to the Old Testament*, p. 645.

147

collections makes it impossible to summarise but we may indicate the main characteristics and emphases in each collection.

1. The first collection entitled "The proverbs of Solomon, son of David, king of Israel" runs from chapters 1-9. It is introduced by a prologue (1.2-6) which well indicates the interests and purposes of the teaching of the wise.

> "That men may know wisdom and instruction,
>   understand words of insight,
>   receive instruction in wise dealing,
>   righteousness, justice and equity;
>   that prudence may be given to the simple,
>   knowledge and discretion to the youth" (1.2-4).

The purpose of the wise is thus severely practical. It is not intended to encourage speculation or general philosophical reflection on the meaning of life. It is concerned with how a man is to act in daily life, how he can be disciplined in right conduct and sound habits and taught to distinguish between what is wholesome and what is harmful. Such was the purpose of the wise throughout the Ancient Near East. The distinctively Israelite emphasis on wisdom is sounded in 1.7.

> "The fear of the LORD is the beginning of knowledge" (1.7).

> "For the LORD gives wisdom;
>   from his mouth come knowledge and understanding"
>   (2.6; cf. 3.5-7, 11; 8.13).

Whatever the origin of the teaching of the wise in Israel, it was increasingly recognised that no life could be sound which neglected the instructions which Yahweh had given to his people. 'The fear of the LORD' implied submission to the sovereign claims of Yahweh upon the obedience of his people, claims which were outlined in Torah. To despise this discipline of Yahweh was to court disaster (3.11).

Within this first collection two themes are developed at length.

(a) There are frequent warnings of the dangers of being involved with the 'strange' or 'other' woman (cf. 2.16-19; 5; 6.20-25; 9.13-18). Attempts have been made to see in this a reference not to adultery or sexual licence, but to the allurement of foreign cults and heretical religious practices which are sometimes castigated in the teaching of the prophets as 'adultery', infidelity to Yahweh (cf. Hos. 1-3; Jer. 2). This is unlikely within the context of wisdom teaching which concerns itself primarily not with ultimate religious loyalties, but with everyday conduct. It is a revealing comment both on the standards of fidelity that were expected in Hebrew life and the extent to which these standards were flouted that there is so much in these opening chapters devoted to warning men against "the adventuress with her smooth words".

(b) Much of the first collection consists of a series of meditations on the meaning and value of wisdom. Stress is laid upon the treasures which wisdom has to offer.

> "She is more precious than jewels,
>   and nothing you desire can compare with her.
> Long life is in her right hand;
>   in her left hand are riches and honour.
> Her ways are ways of pleasantness,
>   and all her paths are peace.
> She is a tree of life to those who lay hold of her;
>   those who hold her fast are called happy" (3.15-18).

These meditations reach their climax in 8.22-31 where wisdom is personified as existing at God's side before the creation of the world, present and rejoicing with him in the work of his creation. There has been considerable discussion as to whether the figure of wisdom in such passages owes anything to non-Hebraic mythological and religious ideas, Oriental or Greek. It is difficult to be certain of influences. Once wisdom had become the supreme concern of sages in Israel, it was perhaps natural enough that in poetic imagery wisdom could be personalised as a figure standing side by side with God at the heart of all creation.

One feature of wisdom appearing in this collection and indeed throughout Proverbs must be noted since it was to be the source of considerable perplexity and mental anguish. Behind the injunction to follow wisdom there is often a strongly prudential motive.

> "My son, do not forget my teaching,
>   but let your heart keep my commandments;
>   for length of days and years of life
>   and abundant welfare will they give you" (3.1-2).

> "Honour the LORD with your substance
>   and with the first fruits of all your produce;
>   then your barns will be filled with plenty,
>   and your vats will be bursting with wine"
>   (3.9-10; cf. 1.22-33; 4.10; 19.17; 22.4).

On the contrary, the way of the wicked who despise wisdom is full of pitfalls. Premature death and disgrace await those who despise the instructions of Yahweh.

> ". . . The upright will inhabit the land,
>   and men of integrity will remain in it;
>   but the wicked will be cut off from the land,
>   and the treacherous will be rooted out of it"
>   (2.21-22; cf. 3.35; 5.22-23; 6.12-15).

In other words wisdom is commended as a good insurance policy, which can be guaranteed on maturity to bring riches, honour and long life. Sooner or later, someone out of bitter experience was bound to query the truth of this. Is it not often the wicked who seem to flourish and the righteous who go to the wall?

2. The second collection (10.1-22.16) is simply headed "The Proverbs of Solomon". It consists entirely of two-line proverbs, sometimes in *antithetic parallelism*, the thought of the second line standing in sharp contrast to the thought of the first; thus the collection begins:

> "A wise son makes a glad father,
>   but a foolish son is a sorrow to his mother" (10.1).

sometimes in *synonymous parallelism* in which the second line
both in form and thought repeats the first—

> "Pride goes before destruction,
>   and a haughty spirit before a fall" (16.18).

sometimes in *synthetic parallelism,* the second line carrying on
the thought of the first line and adding something to it:

> "Commit your work to the LORD,
>   and your plans will be established" (16.3).

There is little obvious sign of ordering of material in this
collection, though occasionally we find a small block of
material with a common theme. Proverbs dealing with 'the
king' are grouped together in 16.10-15. For the rest, we find
brief comments which range across the entire field of human
experience, shrewdly focusing attention on the follies and
greatness of men, giving advice which in many instances is
timeless, e.g.:

> "A soft answer turns away wrath,
>   but a harsh word stirs up anger" (15.1).

> "Better is a dinner of herbs where love is
>   than a fatted ox and hatred with it" (15.17).

> "A rebuke goes deeper into a man of understanding
>   than a hundred blows into a fool" (17.10).

> "A cheerful heart is a good medicine,
>   but a downcast spirit dries up the bones" (17.22).

> "The sluggard says, 'There is a lion outside!
>   I shall be slain in the streets!' " (22.13).

3. The third collection (22.17-24.22) we are already familiar
with as the Hebrew parallel to the *Instructions of Amen-em-
opet.* It remains to note that even in passages which are closely
paralleled we often find a distinctively Old Testament outlook
expressed.

> "Do not rob the poor, because he is poor,
>   or crush the afflicted at the gate" (22.22).

Why not?

> "for the LORD will plead their cause
> and despoil of life those who despoil them" (22.23).

Or take 23.10-11:

> "Do not remove an ancient landmark
> or enter the fields of the fatherless;
> for their Redeemer is strong;
> he will plead their cause against you."

In both cases we find in Proverbs the thought of a God who is actively concerned to protect and to vindicate the rights of those who might otherwise be defenceless in society, an attitude which is characteristic of Torah (e.g., Deut. 24.10 ff.) and the prophets of the eighth and seventh centuries B.C. The teaching of Proverbs, however, is not without its limitations. A notable example is 24.17-18, which starts to climb the ethical heights only to fall into a crevasse of self-regard.

> "Do not rejoice when your enemy falls,
> and let not your heart be glad when he stumbles;
> lest the LORD see it, and be displeased,
> and turn away his anger from him" (24.17-18).

In other words it is better not to take too sadistic a delight in the misfortune of your enemy lest God be displeased at your self-satisfied smirk, and withdraw his anger from that enemy.

4. The fourth collection (25-29) is entitled "These also are the proverbs of Solomon which the men of Hezekiah king of Judah copied", that is to say proverbs which have been handed down in court circles. Like the second collection, it consists in the main of brief proverbial sayings, though several blocks of material are evident, 25.2-7 dealing with royalty; 26.1-12 gathering together various proverbs concerning 'the fool', 26.13-16 dealing with 'the sluggard'. Otherwise memorable sayings drawn from a rich experience of life abound.

"As a door turns on its hinges,
so does a sluggard on his bed" (26.14).

"For lack of wood the fire goes out;
and where there is no whisperer, quarrelling ceases"
(26.20).

"Better is open rebuke
than hidden love" (27.5).

What more apt description of a nagging wife could be penned than this:

"A continual dripping on a rainy day
and a contentious woman are alike" (27.15).

5. The fifth collection (30) has the enigmatic title "The words of Agur, son of Jakeh of Massa". If this be the correct translation, we must confess to ignorance as to the identity of this Agur. Nor are we in any better position with Ithiel and Ucal mentioned in v. 1b. Chapter 30.2-6 are of interest since they contain a brief dialogue on faith and scepticism. In vv. 2-4 the sceptic, uncertain as to where or how a man can find any true knowledge of God, presents his challenge; vv. 5-6 are the reply of faith. This type of dialogue forms the basis of the book of Job. The temptations of too much wealth on the one hand and crippling poverty on the other are touched on in vv. 7-9. The rest of this collection consists of penetrating comments on life and character grouped around two key expressions, "There are those who" (literally 'the generation of') vv. 11-14; and a numerical scheme, e.g.:

"Three things are too wonderful for me;
four I do not understand:
the way of an eagle in the sky,
the way of a serpent on a rock,
the way of a ship on the high seas,
and the way of a man with a maiden" (30.18-19).

6. The sixth collection (31.1-9) is headed "The words of Lemuel, king of Massa, which his mother taught him". We may be groping in the dark as to the identity of Lemuel and

his wise mother, but the advice offered is clear and sound. It consists of a brief manual of kingship, warning the king against over-indulgence in women and wine (vv. 2-7), and concluding with a statement of that concern for the well-being of his subjects, particularly the weak within the community which ought to be the mark of a true king.

> "Open your mouth for the dumb,
> for the rights of all who are left desolate.
> Open your mouth, judge righteously,
> maintain the rights of the poor and needy"
> (31.8-9, cf. Jer. 22.13-17).

As if to redress the balance of the many severely critical things which have been said about women, Proverbs closes with a brilliant acrostic poem which has been described as "The Golden A.B.C. of the Perfect Wife", the perfect Hebrew wife naturally, industriously employed from morning to night seeing to the welfare of her husband and children (vv. 12-25, 27-28) a woman utterly devoid of that continually dripping contentiousness which is condemned in 27.15.

> "She opens her mouth with wisdom,
> and the teaching of kindness is on her tongue" (31.26),

a woman who adds to efficiency a deep piety,

> "Charm is deceitful, and beauty is vain,
> but a woman who fears the LORD is to be praised" (31.30).

This is woman in a patriarchal society. There is no thought of equality of status or rights. It is a pre-suffragette ideal, but none the less one which has an impressive nobility.

The wisdom literature, of which Proverbs is a good example, has been well described as "the documents of Israel's humanism",[1] not the humanism which denies or neglects the purposes of God, but that true humanism which regards with sympathetic interest human conduct in all its bewildering variety, the complex motives and purposes which shape the

[1] O. Rankin, *Israel's Wisdom Literature*, p. 3.

way people think and act. The wise in Israel observed, reported and thus held up to others a mirror in which they could see something of themselves. There is much that is eternally wise in their teaching. There are likewise certain assumptions in their teaching which were to be called in question.

The same humanism finds noble expression in the *Song of Songs,* that is to say 'the choicest song'. The uninhibited passion of its language, the frankly erotic nature of its imagery have raised many a question in people's minds as to why it was included in a Canon of Sacred Scripture. At the beginning of the Christian era there were certain Jews who regarded a banquet where the wine was flowing freely as the proper setting for Song of Songs. To Rabbi Akiba on the other hand "the whole world is not worthy of the day on which the Song of Songs was given to Israel. For all the writings are holy, but the Song of Songs is the holy of holies."[1]

Both Jews and Christians, particularly of the mystic tradition, have treated Song of Songs as an elaborate allegory describing, in the lover and his beloved, the relationship between God and Israel, Christ and the Church, or God and the human soul. Although the marriage symbol is used in the Old Testament to describe the relationship between Yahweh and Israel (e.g., Hos. 2; Jer. 31.32), the Song of Songs does not read like a conscious allegory, and its language is too boldly sensuous for a Hebrew to have used in describing God. Others have found the key to the book in reading it as a drama telling the story of the love of a beautiful country girl from Shulem (or Shunem 6.13) for her shepherd lad. Unfortunately the course of true love does not run smoothly. Attracting the attention of Solomon's servants, she is press-ganged into the royal harem at Jerusalem. None of the blandishments of life at court can make her forget her shepherd lover. In her dreams she sees him coming to rescue her and take her back home (5). The king, respecting her fidelity, eventually sends her home where she is

[1] *Talmud Yedaim,* 3.5.

joyfully reunited with her lover. The moral of the story is then to be found in the famous words in 8.6-7:

> for love is strong as death,
> jealousy is cruel as the grave.
> Its flashes are flashes of fire,
> a most vehement flame.
> Many waters cannot quench love,
> neither can floods drown it.

It is difficult however to find any real sense of dramatic development in Song of Songs. The reconstruction of this story demands too much reading between the lines to be convincing.

Whatever the origin of some of the imagery in Song of Songs, it seems best to treat the book as we certainly would treat it had it not been in a Canon of Sacred Scripture, that is to say, as a collection of love poems—perhaps even wedding songs—steeped in the depth and intensity of the strongest of all human emotions. Nor is there any reason—except a false religious asceticism or a modern cheapening of the concept of love—why such a collection of love poems should not have its place in the Old Testament Canon. Hebrew tradition traces the love which unites men and women back to the creative purposes of God (Gen. 1.27; 2.21 ff). Hebrew stories tell of how such love overcomes all obstacles—Jacob agreeing to serve his uncle Laban for seven years for the sake of Rachel, "and they seemed to him but a few days because of the love he had for her" (Gen. 29.20). Hebrew faith in the last analysis staked everything on the love of God, of which all human love is but a pale reflection. The wholesomeness and holiness of human love should never be in doubt in a religious tradition which sees such love as God's gift to man and celebrates it in the tender intensity of the poems which make up the Song of Songs.

Chapter Nine

GOD AND THE TROUBLED MIND

HISTORIANS and poets, prophets and priests, Psalmists and wisdom writers in the Old Testament all believed that in their different ways they were witnesses to a God who revealed himself personally to his people Israel. This central truth of Israel's faith had to be clothed in words and phrases, in a theology. All such theology is imperfect, a human witness to the truth, but never an adequate substitute for the living reality to which it points. Not only is it imperfect, but it is capable of being misunderstood or distorted. There were those in Israel who deepened and purified men's knowledge of God by challenging the theology of their day, by insisting that it did not make sense of their own experience. The French mystic Simone Weil declares in terms of Christian experience, "one can never wrestle enough with God if one does so out of pure regard for the truth. Christ likes us to prefer truth to him because before being Christ he is truth. If one turns aside from him to go towards the truth, one will not go far before falling into his arms."[1] It is with such wrestlers with God that we are now concerned, men who insisted that God was greater than current theology, men who challenged what others believed about God in their day out of a passion for truth. Through doubt they came to a deeper and more adequate faith. There was much that could be revealed only to the troubled mind.

I

It is surprising how little we really know about the prophets as men. We can place their teaching against the background of

---

[1] Quoted from *Waiting on God* by V. Gollancz, 'More for Timothy', p. 88.

the age in which they lived, but against their inner life a veil is drawn. Occasionally the veil lifts to allow us to glimpse some decisive moment in the prophet's life, particularly the moment when he felt called by God to be a prophet (cf. Amos. 7.15; Hos. 1-3; Isa. 6; Ezek. 3). Sometimes a certain amount of biographical information helps us to sketch in the broad outline of a portrait (cf. the stories about Elijah and material in the prophetic books such as Isa.36-38; Jer. 26 ff.). On the whole, however, the prophets are unpromising material for psychoanalysis except in so far as the character of a man may be deduced from the form and the content of his public utterances. This is no accident. Old Testament writers and editors were not primarily interested in prophetic psychology. The prophets were important because of the word they spoke. What God said through the man was of lasting significance, not the man himself.

In the case of Jeremiah, however, the situation is somewhat different. Not only is the decisive moment of his call to be a prophet recorded (1.4-10), not only are we singularly well provided with biographical information (26 ff.) thanks to the fact that during the latter years of his ministry he had a friend Baruch who became something of his biographer, but at intervals among his prophetic oracles there occur short autobiographical poems of an intensely personal nature. These disconnected and somewhat fragmentary passages have been described as his 'Confessions' or 'Intimate Papers'.[1] Not only do we know how the word of Yahweh came to Jeremiah, but we glimpse something of the stresses and strains that its coming brought. Not only do we have a record of Jeremiah's public utterances, but we hear him earnestly agonising in prayer. Not only may we admire the unflinching courage with which he defied kings, courtiers and other prophets in the last days of Judah, but we can see the inner battle which lay behind that courage, the nagging doubts, the black moods of depres-

[1] The main passages in question are 11.18-12.6; 15.10-21; 17.5-10, 14-18; 18.18-23; 20.7-18.

sion and bitterness which threatened to overwhelm him.

To understand the 'Confessions' we must retrace our steps to the moment when Jeremiah found himself confronted by God. Picked out for God's service, commissioned to be a prophet, Jeremiah can only reply,

> "Then I said, 'Ah, LORD GOD! Behold, I do not know how to speak, for I am only a youth' " (1.6).

Others before him had shrunk from answering the prophetic call. Moses pleaded among other things that he was not a persuasive orator (Exod. 4.10); Isaiah, faced with a vision of the burning splendour of Yahweh, was overwhelmed with a sense of personal and national guilt (Isa. 6.1-5). Neither the lack of oratorical gifts nor a sense of sin made Jeremiah resist God's call. Rather was it a deep feeling of personal inadequacy and inexperience which haunted him. "I do not know how to speak" does not mean "I am no orator". It is a plea that Jeremiah has had no experience whatever of standing before men as Yahweh's spokesman, nor did he feel that he had the necessary qualities for so doing. He was a mere 'youth' called to a man-sized task. He did not believe that he could measure up to the responsibility thrust upon him. Again and again in Jeremiah we meet with this clash between a diffident, sensitive personality and the demands of an inescapable burden placed upon him by God. This was reinforced by the sense of failure that Jeremiah carried with him in his ministry. For over forty years he pled with people to face the reality of God's judgement and live in the light of God's demands. He pled in vain. In certain quarters his teaching was so bitterly resented that he was persecuted. He had no sadistic delight in being the herald of his people's doom. On the contrary,

> "I have not pressed thee to send evil,
>   nor have I desired the day of disaster,
>   thou knowest;
>   that which came out of my lips
>   was before thy face" (17.16).

"I have not lent, nor have I borrowed, yet all of them curse
me. So let it be, o LORD, if I have not entreated thee for their
good, if I have not pleaded with thee on behalf of the enemy"
(15.10-11).

His experience of persecution was all the more disturbing
because at one stage in his career it came from his own relatives
and friends (cf. 11.19; 12.6). Such hostility, and worse, had a
profound effect on Jeremiah. It drove him in upon himself to
examine and re-examine the very foundations of his faith, to
scrutinise his own motives and above all to pray with an
honesty which is startling.

(a) Jeremiah experienced from time to time moods of deep
personal depression. Such was his immediate emotional response to failure and hostility. Bitterly he laments that he was
ever born.

> "Woe is me, my mother, that you bore me,
>   a man of strife and contention" (15.10).

> "Cursed be the day
>   on which I was born!
> The day when my mother bore me,
>   let it not be blessed!
> Cursed be the man
>   who brought the news to my father,
> 'A son is born to you',
>   making him very glad" (20.14-15, cf. 17-18).

This is a very un-Hebraic mood. Life to the Hebrews was
God's greatest gift, a sweet boon to be enjoyed to the full. All
else was uncertain. Even the author of Psalm 22 in the dark
night of his soul saw a gleam of hope in the remembrance that
Yahweh is:

> "he who took me from the womb;
>   thou didst keep me safe upon my mother's breasts"
>   (Ps. 22.9).

We have to turn to Job for any parallel to these crises of Jeremiah, and there again it is intense personal affliction which evoked it.

(b) More than Jeremiah's emotions were involved in the spiritual depression. There is evidence that Jeremiah's faith in God was severely tested, if not indeed shaken, and that in two ways.
(i) The apparent triumph of those who opposed him in defiance of God led him to query the moral ordering of the world. Like all the prophets before him, and like Deuteronomy which represented the orthodoxy of his day, Jeremiah believed that Yahweh was 'righteous'. The world was ordered by his right decision, in accordance with moral principles, evil receiving its due punishment. Yet how was it possible to make this square with Jeremiah's own experience? Jeremiah lodges his complaint,

> "Why does the way of the wicked prosper?
> Why do all that are treacherous thrive?
> Thou plantest them, and they take root;
> they grow and bring forth fruit" (12.1-2).

As far as we can judge, this is the earliest statement in the Old Testament of a problem which was increasingly to perplex the faithful (cf. Ps. 10.1-11, Ecclesiastes and in particular Job). Later it was to become an acute intellectual problem, but it is doubtfully so in the case of Jeremiah. He was not raising a speculative question; he was not seeking a philosophical discussion on the apparent triumph of evil in a divinely ordered world. It was the continued success of men who despised God's warnings and the only too obvious fruitlessness of his own witness which troubled him. Why do such wicked men flourish while God's servant is despised and persecuted?

> "If you have raced with men on foot, and they have wearied you,
> how will you compete with horses?
> And if in a safe land you fall down,
> how will you do in the jungle of Jordan?" (12.5).

Both the pictures in this, God's answer, say the same thing. There is worse to come. The jungle of Jordan was the belt of luxuriant growth along the banks of the Jordan, haunt of marauding lions which came to strike at the sheepfolds (Jer. 49.19; 50.44). It is a symbol of danger as opposed to the comparative safety of the open countryside. To be told that more strenuous effort and greater dangers lie ahead seems cold comfort. But it was only by being prepared to continue in his prophetic ministry whatever the cost that Jeremiah was to see his personal problem in its true perspective.

(ii) To go on with many a doubt unresolved implies that God can ultimately be trusted. But can he?

> "Why is my pain unceasing,
>   my wound incurable,
>   refusing to be healed?
>   Wilt thou be to me like a deceitful brook,
>   like waters that fail?" (15.18).

These words are all the more poignant since Jeremiah had already declared to his fellow countrymen that Yahweh, in striking contrast to the false gods of popular faith, was an unfailing fountain of living water (2.13). But if this fountain should prove in his time of need to be but a deceitful brook —one of the wadis which carry water in the rainy season, but are parched and dry when the traveller is most in need of refreshment—what then? In 20.7 Jeremiah bitterly complains that Yahweh has deliberately deceived him, turning him into the laughing stock of the day. How then can Yahweh be trusted? The answer given to this ultimate doubt is interesting.

> "Therefore thus says the LORD:
>   'If you return, I will restore you,
>   and you shall stand before me.
>   If you utter what is precious, and not what is worthless,
>   you shall be as my mouth.
>   They shall turn to you,
>   but you shall not turn to them.
>   And I will make you to this people
>   a fortified wall of bronze;

they will fight against you,
but they shall not prevail over you,
for I am with you
to save you and deliver you, says the LORD.
I will deliver you out of the hand of the wicked,
and redeem you from the grasp of the ruthless" (15.19-21).

Jeremiah is reassured at his point of greatest weakness. His prophetic ministry will succeed, but only on certain conditions. Jeremiah is summoned to 'repent', to turn back to Yahweh. With stabbing irony the message which Jeremiah has repeatedly proclaimed to others 'Repent, repent' (cf. 3.12, 22; 4.1; 7.15 ff.) is now directed to himself. As has been well said, Jeremiah had to learn that "the condition of victory over the world is victory over himself."[1] Repent, return, but to what? To renewed commitment to his calling as a prophet. He must steadfastly resist the temptation to ease present troubles by trimming his message to the mood of the day. This renewed demand is capped by a promise.

"I am with you to save you and deliver you, says the LORD" (15.20). This is no new promise. It echoes the promise made to Jeremiah at the very outset of his ministry (1.8, 18). Jeremiah needed to be reminded of the truth he already knew rather than to be taught new truth.

(c) Depression and doubt call forth a startling vindictiveness in Jeremiah. He did not react meekly to opposition; he literally screamed down curses upon his enemies, and called upon Yahweh to deal mercilessly with them.

> "Pull them out like sheep for the slaughter" (12.3).

> "Let those be put to shame who persecute me,
>   but let me not be put to shame;
>   let them be dismayed,
>   but let me not be dismayed;
>   bring upon them the day of evil;
>   destroy them with double destruction!"
>   (17.18, cf. 15.15; 20.11-12).

[1] J. Skinner, *Prophecy and Religion*, p. 21.

and most bitter of all,

> "Therefore deliver up their children to famine;
> give them over to the power of the sword,
> let their wives become childless and widowed.
> May their men meet death by pestilence,
> their youths be slain by the sword in battle.
> Forgive not their iniquity,
> nor blot out their sin from thy sight.
> Let them be overthrown before thee;
> deal with them in the time of thine anger"
>
> (18.21, 23b).

A parallel to this vindictiveness is to be found in certain of the Psalms, where the apparent triumph of the wicked calls forth a similar mood (cf. Pss. 55.12-25; 16.22-28; 137.8-9). Such bitterness has troubled many sensitive commentators. Jeremiah is indeed a very human prophet, not a stained glass window caricature of a saint. In his vindictiveness he does not scale the heights of the witness of the Old Testament, far less the New (cf. Luke 23.34). The portrait of the Servant of Yahweh in Isa. 40-55 is partly modelled on the experience of Jeremiah. The Servant

> was oppressed, and he was afflicted,
> yet he opened not his mouth;
> like a lamb that is led to the slaughter,
> and like a sheep that before its shearers is dumb,
> so he opened not his mouth (Isa. 53.7).

This picture comes from Jeremiah's description of himself as 'a gentle lamb led to the slaughter' (Jer. 11.19), but Jeremiah, unlike the Servant, was far from dumb. He opened his mouth and in the honesty of his sorely tried soul he cursed.

(d) There was one way out of this spiritual torment and Jeremiah was tempted to take it. Why not renounce his prophetic calling? Such was Jeremiah's natural inclination; but it foundered on the rock of an inescapable divine compulsion. This inner conflict surfaces in 20.7 ff. This passage begins with Jeremiah, in bitter disillusionment, accusing Yahweh of having deliberately deceived him. He is at the end of his tether. He wishes to quit Yahweh's service—only to find that he cannot.

> "If I say, 'I will not mention him,
>   or speak any more in his name,'
>   there is in my heart as it were a burning fire
>   shut up in my bones,
>   and I am weary with holding it in,
>   and I cannot" (20.9).

Jeremiah had reached the point where he thought it was impossible to go on; he discovered instead that it was impossible not to go on. The prophetic pathway might be pitted with doubts, depression and inner conflicts, but to turn aside from that pathway was to stumble into a jungle of torment from which there was no escape, except by returning to the pathway he had left. To go on mid lonely misunderstanding and with many problems unresolved, but to go on with Yahweh, this was the cost of being a prophet.

(e) To go on was possible because Jeremiah had an ultimate certainty. He himself was spiritually often a broken reed, and he knew it. But over against the baffling uncertainties of his own conflicting moods, he placed the certainty of a God who knew him and would ultimately vindicate his servant (17.9-10; 20.12). So he commits his cause to Yahweh (11.20); he prays for healing (17.14). Faced with the whispered threats of his enemies, he remembers,

> "But the LORD is with me as a dread warrior;
>   therefore my persecutors will stumble,
>   they will not overcome me" (20.11).

All the confidence in these words bursts forth into a paean of praise

> "Sing to the LORD;
>   praise the LORD!
>   For he has delivered the life of the needy
>   from the hand of evildoers" (20.13).

This upsurge of faith is rooted in prayer. Jeremiah in these

'Confessions' is not thinking his own thoughts aloud as in some Shakespearean soliloquy, he is in conversation with God. Doubt, despair and vindictiveness are all poured out to God in prayer to become in the end of the day more spiritually fruitful than the pious platitudes of lesser men. It was through a continuing dialogue with God that he won through to ultimate assurance.

Whatever the practical or intellectual difficulties in which it landed him, Jeremiah kept a firm hold on his belief in the ultimate righteousness of Yahweh (11.20; 12.1; 17.10). If Jeremiah had lost faith at this point the whole structure of his prophetic ministry would have crumbled. In many ways the easy thing for Jeremiah would have been to forget the righteousness of God, to deny that there was any divine purpose shaping events. It is characteristic of the Old Testament that, when facing the problem of evil, it refuses to take this path. For this it probably owes much to Jeremiah's wrestling with God.

Jeremiah might well have penned the prayer of a modern prophet martyr, words which are a profound commentary on the 'Confessions'.

> In me there is darkness,
> But with Thee there is light.
> I am lonely, but Thou leavest me not.
> I am restless, but with Thee there is peace.
> In me there is bitterness, but with Thee there is patience;
> Thy ways are past understanding,
>> but Thou knowest the way for me.[1]

II

Why do the wicked flourish, why do the righteous suffer in a world ruled by God? This was one of the problems faced by Jeremiah. In the book of Job, which belongs to the wisdom tradition, this problem comes to the centre of the stage to be debated vigorously in the light of Hebrew faith. It is an age-

[1] D. Bonhoeffer, *Letters and Papers from Prison*, p. 32.

old problem which has perplexed the human mind ever since man has thought at all seriously about the world in which he lives.

In the 'Babylonian Theodicy' from the late second millennium B.C. we find a dialogue between a sufferer and his friend. Why should it be, asks the sufferer that

> "Those who neglect the god go the way of prosperity,
>   while those who pray to the goddess are impoverished and
>   dispossessed."[1]

> "I have looked round society, but the evidence is contrary.
> The gods do not impede the way of a devil."[2]

From Egypt nearly a thousand years earlier there comes a text called 'A Dispute over Suicide', a dialogue in which a man who is weary of life and the injustice with which society is riddled seeks to convince his soul that death is much to be preferred to life.

> Hearts are rapacious,
> No man has a heart upon which one can rely.
> To whom shall I speak today?
> There are no righteous men.
> The land is left over to workers of iniquity . . .[3]

The problem became acute in the Old Testament because of the unwavering Hebrew insistence upon the moral sovereignty of Yahweh over all life and because of certain ways in which that moral sovereignty was safeguarded in what came to be orthodox Hebrew theology. The link between obedience to Yahweh and national prosperity, disobedience and national disaster was deeply embedded in the teaching of Torah and the prophets. Whatever the nation sowed, that would it reap. Furthermore in the wisdom tradition as reflected in Proverbs, righteousness was commended as a good insurance policy for personal prosperity, while wickedness was said to bring inevitable disaster. From this it is but a short, if not wholly

[1] *Babylonian Theodicy*, 70-71, D.O.T.T., p. 100.
[2] ibid. 243-244, D.O.T.T., p. 101.
[3] D.O.T.T., p. 165.

logical step, to the belief that the man who prospers is the man whose life is in tune with God, while the man who suffers grievous affliction is a notorious sinner. Sooner or later the assumptions behind this viewpoint were bound to be called into question at the bar of human experience. It happens in *Job*.

Wonder and bewilderment are natural responses to this literary masterpiece. No one can fail to be moved by the infinitely varied mastery of words and imagery which the book displays. Equally, certainly, a student of the book is often accompanied by an uneasy feeling that in his attempt to understand Job he may have been wandering in a maze of unanswered and indeed half-formed questions. The Hebrew text is notoriously difficult. The date of the composition of the book is uncertain. There has been vigorous debate as to whether the book which we now possess is the work of one creative mind or a mosaic of contributions from different sources.

A brief outline of the structure of the book will indicate some of the problems. Chapters 1-2 are a prose prologue introducing us to Job, the man of outstanding integrity, his misfortunes and his immediate response to misfortune. Chapters 3-27 present us with three cycles of poetic speeches in which Job and three friends, Eliphaz the Temanite, Bildad the Shuhite and Zophar the Naamathite debate the meaning of the affliction which has befallen Job. After an opening statement (3) in which Job pours out some of the pent up bitterness in his soul, the first two cycles consist of a speech from each of Job's friends, each speech being answered by Job. The third cycle, however, is fragmentary. It lacks any speech from Zophar, and some of the material in it, particularly 27.7-23, seems to have been attributed wrongly to Job.

Chapter 28 is a fascinating hymn to wisdom which would in many respects be more at home in the first wisdom collection in the book of Proverbs. Its relevance to the theme of Job is not immediately obvious, though it has been defended on the grounds that it "has something of the character of a chorus in a Greek tragedy, commenting on the theme of the debate just ended."[1] Chapters 29-31 contain speeches by Job in which he compares former felicity and prosperity with present misery and gives a moving *apologia pro vita sua*. These chapters conclude with the cryptic sentence "The words of Job are ended". Many have seen in this the original ending to Job, or the ending of the first draft of the book to which the author, dissatisfied with the inconclusiveness of what he had written, returned at a later date. In fact 29-31 do give us the last set speeches from Job. Only two brief awe-struck responses to the challenge of God are later found on his lips.

Chapters 32-37 introduce a newcomer to the debate, young Elihu son of Barachel who, scornful of the wisdom of the men who have hitherto tried to convince Job of the error of his ways, proceeds to defend the wisdom and providence of God and to challenge Job anew, Job meanwhile remaining uncharacteristically silent. Elihu's arguments are followed by two speeches from Yahweh to Job (38.2-40.2 and 40.6-41), each capped by a few hesitant words from Job (40.3-5 and 42.1-6). The basic similarity in theme of the two speeches has raised the question as to whether they are not simply variant versions of one original divine speech. The book is completed by a prose epilogue 42.1-17 which describes how Job is restored to God's favour and to worldly prosperity.

The kernel of the book is to be found in the speeches between Job and his three friends (3-27). The author of these speeches seems to have made use of a traditional folk tale about a blameless and upright man called Job as a text round which to weave his discussion. Job in the prologue exemplifies the Hebrew ideal of the good life, piety and prosperity, righteousness and well-being, walking hand in hand. In the heavenly court, one of the angels 'the adversary' (Satan) suggests to Yahweh that Job's much vaunted piety can hardly be described as disinterested (1.6-10). Permission is given for Job to be stripped of all the worldly props to his piety. One by one the

[1] G. W. Anderson, *A Critical Introduction to the Old Testament*, p. 184.

blows fall. The loss of wealth and family call forth from Job submissive resignation:

> "Naked I came from my mother's womb, and naked shall I return; the LORD gave, and the LORD has taken away; blessed be the name of the LORD" (1.20-21).

Loathsome sores and a wife at the end of her tether call forth an equally pious response.

> "Shall we receive good at the hand of God, and shall we not receive evil?" (2.10).

In chapters 29-31, basically the same situation is sketched. In 29, Job looks back on what is now for him an idyllic past. Then he was sheikh in some small community, prosperous and highly respected by young and old alike. Confidently he looked forward to a vigorous and lengthy life. Chapter 30 describes in painful and moving contrast Job's present plight. The community whose welfare he once guaranteed has gone to ruin. Those who once revered him, taunt him. They spit contemptuously at the sight of him. Despised and lonely, Job says

> ". . . my soul is poured out within me;
> days of affliction have taken hold of me.
> The night racks my bones,
> and the pain that gnaws me takes no rest"
>
> (30.16-17).

Stark reversal of fortune is not Job's only problem. His present plight can only mean that God who was once his friend has become his enemy.

> "Oh, that I were as in the months of old,
> as in the days when God watched over me;
> when his lamp shone upon my head,
> and by his light I walked through darkness;
> as I was in my autumn days,
> when the friendship of God was upon my tent;
> when the Almighty was yet with me,
> when my children were about me" (29.2-5).

> "God has cast me into the mire,
> and I have become like dust and ashes.
> I cry to thee and thou dost not answer me;
> I stand, and thou dost not heed me.
> Thou hast turned cruel to me;
> with the might of thy hand thou dost persecute me"
>   (30.19-21).

But why? This is Job's problem. What has he done which could possibly merit this tragic reversal of his life? What can have turned his divine friend into an enemy, a cruel capricious enemy utterly heedless of Job's plight? Nothing, so far as Job is aware; his life hitherto had followed the highest Hebrew ideals, humble before God, honest, unflagging in his concern for the unfortunate within the community (31). If Job of the prologue was quietly submissive, the Job of the rest of the poem is defiantly rebellious. It is in this setting that we must look at the dialogue between Job and his friends.

Job provokes the dialogue by bitterly cursing the day of his birth (cf. Jer. 20.14 ff.). It is a measure of the extremity of his pain and suffering that the twilight existence in Sheol, the shadowy underworld of the departed, seems to him preferable to life. There at least

> ". . . the wicked cease from troubling,
> and there the weary are at rest" (3.17).

Eliphaz, the senior and in some ways the most sympathetic of Job's friends, tries (4-5) to inject into Job's disturbed condition a shot of religious and theological sanity. He begins by suggesting that Job's outburst is really unworthy of himself. Job had often given good advice to others in affliction. Can he not swallow his own medicine (4.1-5)? His faith and a clear conscience ought to be his support. Recall, says Eliphaz, what we believe—the innocent never perish, the wicked never flourish (4.6-11). Of course no one is wholly perfect, not even the angels of God, therefore a certain element of suffering is part of our human lot,

man is born to trouble
as the sparks fly upward (5.7).

Faced with affliction there is only one thing man can do; commit his cause to God, nor will he be disappointed (5.8, 18).

It is important to do justice to Eliphaz' argument. It represents the orthodox standpoint at its best and obviously contains a large element of truth. Sin is universal. Suffering is therefore part and parcel of our human lot. None the less, God being righteous, the good will prosper, the wicked will fall. If by chance a good man meets with unexpected misfortune, it can only be temporary. God will restore.

However rational and plausible, this argument suffers, as far as Job is concerned, from one fatal defect. It is, if we may so put it, land-based theology while Job is storm-tossed at sea. It has no word to say to a man who is at the end of his tether and alienated from God:

"the arrows of the Almighty are in me;
my spirit drinks their poison;
the terrors of God are arrayed against me" (6.4), cries Job.

Surely God can get no pleasure out of hounding one of his frail creatures. When God does change his attitude, says Job, it will be too late; he will have passed from this mortal scene (7.17-21).

Bildad appeals to the past. The experience of the ages, he claims, proves that "the hope of the godless man shall perish" (8.13), but "God will not reject a blameless man" (8.20). Job admits that he accepts this traditional doctrine. But how can a man possibly prove his innocence to God? God is omnipotent, but omnipotence is not enough:

"Lo, he passes by me, and I see him not;
he moves on, but I do not perceive him" (9.11).

It is difficult to argue with God but, apparently, he destroys both the blameless and the wicked (9.22). God must know that I am innocent, says Job, but for some inexplicable reason he has got his knife into me.

The mounting exasperation of the friends is well voiced by Zophar. No one likes to have cherished theological convictions called into question. He accuses Job of self-righteousness and of having committed some heinous sin.

> "Know then that God exacts of you
> less than your guilt deserves" (11.6).

Facts must be made to fit the theory. Job is suffering greatly, therefore he must have sinned greatly. This is the first indication of an attitude which Job's friends are increasingly to adopt. Rather than revise their theology, they are prepared to rewrite Job's life. Job counters by calling into question the arrogant certainty of his friends. He deplores their total lack of sympathy (12.5). The whole universe may underline the wisdom and power of God (12.13 ff.), but his friends are indulging in specious arguments in their attempt to defend the ways of God.

> "Your maxims are proverbs of ashes,
> your defences are defences of clay" (13.12).

Over the heads of his friends Job makes a twofold appeal to God. In the first place he asks God to stop hounding him:

> "withdraw thy hand far from me,
> and let not dread of thee terrify me" (13.21).

In the second place he wishes to know exactly what he has done to merit his present misfortune and alienation from God.

> "How many are my iniquities and my sins?
> Make me know my transgression and my sin.
> Why dost thou hide thy face,
> and count me as thy enemy?" (13.23-24).

This first cycle of speeches clearly states the point at issue. Job's friends strongly defend the orthodox viewpoint on the relationship between sin and suffering. Job heretically denies that this makes sense of his own experience. Future speeches add little new, but they do serve to sharpen the issue and to increase the personal tension between Job and his friends.

Increasingly the friends are tempted to slant the truth, indeed to invent facts to fit their reliefs. Job *must* have sinned. In his final speech (22), Eliphaz goes so far as to catalogue the sins of which Job is guilty, abuse of power, callous indifference to the needs of others (22.5-11). In the light of Job's apology in 31 this can only be a complete fabrication. Truth has not infrequently been sacrificed on the altar of a theological theory. As the arguments of his friends become more dogmatic and their personal attitude to him more hostile, Job's logic becomes sharper and his insight clearer. He flatly rejects the orthodox viewpoint, not only in terms of his own experience, but in terms of the world at large. You say, says Job to the friends, that the wicked "are swiftly carried away" (24.18), I say that God "prolongs their life" and "gives them security" (24.22, 23).

> "If it is not so, who will prove me a liar,
>   and show me that there is nothing in what I say?" (24.25).

More and more he turns from his "miserable comforters" (16.2) to God. Here Job is filled with a strange mixture of fear, despair and hope. Unshaken in his belief in his own integrity, Job can only continue to assert that God must have some personal spite against him (16.6-17; 19.6-12); yet he cannot but believe that this must rest on some tragic misunderstanding. If only he could break through to God and state his case surely all would be well.

> "Oh, that I knew where I might find him,
>   that I might come even to his seat!
> I would lay my case before him
>   and fill my mouth with arguments.
> I would learn what he would answer me,
>   and understand what he would say to me.
> Would he contend with me in the greatness of his power?
>   No; he would give heed to me.
> There an upright man could reason with him,
>   and I should be acquitted for ever by my judge" (23.3-7).

But how can a man possibly find God? (23.8-9). At one moment Job seems to be reaching out to God in the hope that God would vindicate him; at the next he is groping his way blindly through the darkness of despair. Does he ever get beyond this to a certainty which not even continuing suffering nor recurring doubts can touch? There are two well-known passages in the A.V. which seem to suggest that he does. Both need careful handling.

(a) In 13.15 Job according to the A.V. says, "Though he slay me yet will I trust in him". Unfortunately the Hebrew text will not bear this translation. R.S.V. more correctly renders, "Behold, he will slay me; I have no hope", a cry not of unshakeable faith, but of abject despair.

(b) Much more debatable is the famous passage in 19.25-26, translated with some hesitation by the R.S.V. as

v. 25.   "For I know that my Redeemer (or Vindicator) lives,
              and at last he will stand upon the earth;

v. 26.   and after my skin has thus been destroyed,
              then without my flesh I shall see God."

The footnote to v. 26 reads 'the meaning of this verse is uncertain', a masterpiece of understatement. We must first take note of the context in which this passage occurs. Job (v. 21 ff.) makes a despairing appeal to his friends for sympathy and understanding, but even as he makes it he knows that his appeal will be in vain. Hence in vv. 23-24 he considers an appeal to the generations to come. If only his story can be indelibly recorded for the future, then one day the truth for which he stands will be vindicated. This thought is continued in vv. 25-26. He will be vindicated; but by whom, when, and how? Is the vindicator God or some heavenly figure whom Job at another point imagines as pleading his case before the heavenly council (16.19)? Is it perhaps no more than some kinsman—this is the basic meaning of the word translated Redeemer—who will survive Job and witness the rehabilitation of his good name and honour? The first half of v. 26 is hopelessly corrupt; in the second half the words translated "without my flesh" could equally well be rendered "from my flesh", that is to say, while I am still alive. Job may therefore be looking for vindication either after death or in this life at the eleventh hour, when all seems lost. Whatever interpretation we adopt—and none is without difficulty—the passage is one of the most vehement declarations by Job that somehow the rightness of his cause will prevail.

The Elihu speeches (33-37) may well be the second thoughts of the author of the earlier speeches or the contribution to the debate of another author. They are an attempt to restate the arguments of the friends in a more congenial form and with a different emphasis. To Job's protestations that he is innocent and that God is deaf to his appeals, Elihu replies that God has his ways of speaking to men, through dreams and visions, and always his word is a warning against human presumption, a call to repent (33.12-18). Further, there stands between man and God an angelic mediator who instructs man in his duty and intercedes to God on his behalf (33.23-25). Against this background a man may humbly pray and confess in the certainty of restoration. Just because we may not understand the ways of God, that does not mean that God has no purpose (34). Elihu makes a significant contribution to the discussion when in chapter 35 he puts forward a view which is at one and the same time a criticism of Job and of his friends. When Job complains, and his friends cling to their orthodoxy, are they not falling into the same error of regarding religion as something that ought to pay dividends? But God is so great that man's goodness or otherwise has very little effect on him. He *is* to be found, but only by those who seek him for his own sake with disinterested desire. When the good are caught in the cords of affliction it is so that they may learn and repent. Suffering is part of God's educative purposes in the world. In all circumstances man should approach God with a song of praise, because his greatness is writ large in the world of his creating:

"God is clothed with terrible majesty.
The Almighty—we cannot find him;
he is great in power and in justice,
and abundant righteousness he will not violate.
Therefore men fear him;
he does not regard any who are wise in their own conceit"
(37.22b-24).

Job had appealed to God to be allowed to state his case. His appeal is answered in one sense when God speaks to Job out of the whirlwind (38.1). The two speeches which follow (38-40.2 and 40.6-41) have this in common; both seem monumentally irrelevant to Job's particular problem. There is not a word in them about sin or suffering—which may be a strong argument for their genuineness. The poetry of these chapters is of superb literary quality. Job wishes to put God in the dock; he finds himself there instead.

"Who is this that darkens counsel by words without knowledge?
Gird up your loins like a man,
I will question you, and you shall declare to me" (38.2-3).

In question after rhetorical question, God confronts Job with his divine majesty, power and wisdom, evidenced in the entire creation. How can Job dare pick fault with the way God orders this universe? In response, Job admits his presumptions, confesses that God is all powerful and concludes:

"I had heard of thee by hearing of the ear,
but now my eye sees thee;
therefore I despise myself,
and repent in dust and ashes" (42.5-6).

What contribution does the book of Job make to the problem it raises?

(a) The speeches of God (38 ff.) are irrelevant to the intellectual dimensions of Job's problem. They offer no explanation as to why an upright and pious man like Job should experience such horrible affliction. But they do speak to Job's condition from another angle. In some respects the hardest cross Job had

177

to bear was his sense of alienation from God, the fact that God cruelly and silently mocked his prayer. Job appealed to God and in these speeches the lines of communication between God and Job were reopened. Within this renewed fellowship with God, much of the bitterness and much of the meaninglessness of life lifts from Job's shoulders. Nothing is said in the speeches which had not already been said by the friends, but what Job cannot accept from his unsympathetic friends he does accept in renewed fellowship with God. It is in the light of this fellowship restored that we must look at the Epilogue. There is from the Hebrew point of view, nothing incongruous in this picture of Job having all his former possessions and more given back to him. It is not merely a slick ending to something that might otherwise be intolerable. The good life rooted in the friendship of God must normally, in Hebrew thought, have its full share of the good things of this world. They are God's gift.

(b) Within this experience of fellowship with God, there is nothing irrational in a man admitting that there are limits to his understanding of God's purposes. To know God is to acknowledge a greatness beyond our fullest understanding, a mystery which is veiled. This must never become an easy escape from wrestling seriously with the problems of life, but it is a valid religious insight.

(c) In the dialogue between God and the angelic adversary (Satan), another view of suffering is put forward. It is not God's will for his servants; but God permits it as a test of faith. The same point is made by Elihu in chapter 35 when he stresses that faith in God is an end in itself, and that within such faith suffering may have an educative value. As H. W. Robinson says,[1] "Whenever a man can say in his own heart, this calamity is not anything I have directly deserved, and when he can further say, I have learned from the suffering all that I am able to learn and yet it continues, then he is warranted in claiming for

[1] H. W. Robinson, *The Cross in the Old Testament*, p. 67.

himself the great theme of the book of Job, the thought that this suffering serves some larger purpose such as the vindication of disinterested piety.''

(d) The book is an attempt to kill stone dead a far too simple orthodox view of the relationship between sin and suffering. It is a view which dies hard (cf. John 9.2). Nowhere in the entire book is the orthodox thesis of the friends upheld. Indeed in the epilogue God says to Elihu:

> "My wrath is kindled against you and against your two friends; for you have not spoken of me what is right, as my servant Job has" (42.7).

Only the intercession of Job saves them. The intellectual honesty which brings orthodoxy to the touchstone of facts and finds it wanting is an act of faith which in the end is justified. "The basic fact for an understanding of the Dialogue is that Job is represented, not in a theological position, but in a spiritual pilgrimage away from the uncritical current orthodoxy towards a faith and hope deep grounded in experience."[1] There may be more of faith in a deep and questing scepticism than in a shallow orthodoxy.

The book of Job can hardly claim to have provided a satisfactory intellectual answer to the problem it tackles. Unmerited suffering remains a mystery. The greatness of the book lies in the fact that it raises the problem in an acute form, rejects too easy an answer offered by the faith of the day, and pushes its protest to the limit of human understanding without denying that in life we face the living God. It is the witness of a troubled mind to God.

III

A troubled mind of a rather different type confronts us in Ecclesiastes. Ecclesiastes had to knock very firmly on the door

---

[1] W. A. Irwin in *Peake's Commentary on the Bible* (ed. M. Black and H. H. Rowley), p. 356b.

of the Old Testament Canon before it gained admittance, and some of the guardians of Old Testament tradition admitted it only with the greatest reluctance.

Traditionally the book was ascribed to Solomon on the basis of 1.1, "The words of the Preacher, the son of David, king in Jerusalem" (cf. 1.12, 16; 2.7, 9). The language, however, is that of a man who thought and spoke naturally in Aramaic — though he writes in Hebrew — and this brings us down to late post-exilic times, perhaps the third century B.C. The picture that we get of Koheleth (the preacher) is that of a man of some standing in Jerusalem, perhaps a professional teacher in the tradition of the wisdom school (cf. 12.9-10). The book contains the typical wisdom admixture of sayings, shrewd and memorable in their brevity. This is particularly so in chapters 4, 5, 7, 10 and 11.

A good name is better than precious ointment;
and the day of death, than the day of birth (7.1).

Better is the end of a thing than its beginning;
and the patient in spirit is better than the proud in spirit (7.8).

If the serpent bites before it is charmed,
there is no advantage in a charmer (10.11).

Even in your thought, do not curse the king,
nor in your bedchamber curse the rich;
for a bird of the air will carry your voice,
or some winged creature tell the matter (10.20).

Cast your bread upon the waters,
for you will find it after many days (11.1).

He who observes the wind will not sow;
and he who regards the clouds will not reap (11.4).

We meet with the repeated wisdom contrast between the wise and the fool (7.4-6; 10.1-3, 12). What distinguishes Ecclesiastes, however, from the wisdom collection in Proverbs is that here the sayings are set within the framework of personal confessions of a marked individuality, the product of a restless sceptical mind which has looked keenly at the world and human life and has decided that life has no discernible meaning. His motto text is:

"Vanity of vanities, says the Preacher,
vanity of vanities! All is vanity" (1.2).

It is all to no purpose (2.11, 17, 26; 4.8, etc.). What led him to this conclusion? Koheleth is keenly aware of the many anomalies in life. Whatever orthodoxy may say, he agrees with Job that it is just not true that the righteous flourish and the wicked perish.

> There is a vanity which takes place on earth, that there are righteous men to whom it happens according to the deeds of the wicked, and there are wicked men to whom it happens according to the deeds of the righteous (8.14, cf. 9.1-6, 11-12).

Endowed with all the material resources to make the good life possible, Koheleth has discovered through bitter experience that life yields no ultimate satisfaction. Life for him is the same ceaseless round of experience that it has always been and always will be. It has nothing new, nothing compelling to offer. Where a Psalmist will look at nature and break into a hymn of praise to its creator (Ps. 104, 136), Koheleth can only read in the regularity of nature a parable of the monotonous, meaningless round of life.

"The eye is not satisfied with seeing,
nor the ear filled with hearing.
What has been is what will be,
and what has been done is what will be done;
and there is nothing new under the sun
(1.8b-9, cf. 3.15).

Here is a man who has denied himself nothing. Great possessions, pleasure, wine, women and song, all have been his, but his verdict is still 'vanity'. Nothing either shocks or surprises him. He is well aware that corruption and oppression are rife (3.16; 4.1). Long before Parkinson applied his mind to the devious ways of bureaucracy, Koheleth had noted some of the dangers inherent in its growth.

> If you see in a province the poor oppressed and justice and right violently taken away, do not be amazed at the matter; for the high official is watched by a higher, and there are yet higher ones over them (5.8).

But he views it all with a cool detachment. There is a time and a place for everything (3.2-9). Life must simply be accepted for what it is, a patchwork of varied and contradictory experiences.

Wisdom has its value. The wise man is always to be preferred to the fool (2.13-14; 7.19; 9.16). Yet wisdom has its limitations and brings with it its own perplexities and problems. It does not guarantee fame, nor is it likely to be properly honoured. Koheleth quotes the example of a poor man who through his wisdom saved his community in an hour of crisis. His reward was this, "no one remembered that poor man" (9.13-15). Furthermore wisdom cannot discover the ultimate secrets of God's ordering of the universe; it cannot tell you what divine purpose, if any, runs through life. Although he has searched night and day, and taken a good look at all the works of God, he can only conclude

> that man cannot find out the work that is done under the sun. However much man may toil in seeking, he will not find it out; even though a wise man claims to know, he cannot find it out (8.17, cf. 3.10-12).

If, baffled by the mystery of the universe, you turn the spotlight of wisdom on human nature, you end up a cynic.

> "One man among a thousand I found, but a woman among all these have I not found. Behold, this alone I found, that God made man upright, but they have sought out many devices" (7.28-29).

Both Koheleth's agnosticism and cynicism feed upon the one thing in life concerning which a man may be utterly certain, the fact of death. Brooding over his entire philosophy is this sense of the brevity and transitoriness of our human life which wends its way inexorably to a dark mystery about which a man may say nothing.

> For the fate of the sons of men and the fate of beasts is the same; as one dies, so dies the other. They all have the same breath, and man has no advantage over the beasts; for all is vanity. All go to one place; all are from the dust, and all turn to dust again. Who knows whether the spirit of man goes upward and the spirit of the beast goes down to the earth (3.19-21).

Death is no respecter of persons. The wise and the fool, the good and the sinner are alike struck down (2.14-16; 3.19-21; 9.10). His last word on the fleetingness of life is to remind the young that a time will come when pleasure, strength and desire will fail,

> the dust returns to the earth as it was, and the spirit (life) returns to God who gave it (12.7).

To Koheleth all human aspirations are mocked by this last enemy.

Yet a man cannot live by scepticism alone. What does Koheleth enjoin as the positive good in life?

> There is nothing better for a man than that he should eat and drink, and find enjoyment in his toil. This also, I saw, is from the hand of God (2.24, cf. 3.13; 5.18; 8.15; 9.7-10).

Accept life as it is; ask no unnecessary questions; take what enjoyment you can get out of it—all else is uncertain. This is no new philosophy. We can trace it back into the history of thought in the Ancient Near East, well into the second millennium B.C. where it appears in the Epic of Gilgamesh which had wide currency in Mesopotamia. In the Epic, Gilgamesh is warned off his search for immortality by an ale-wife in the following terms:

> "The life thou pursuest thou shalt not find.
> When the gods created mankind,
> Death for mankind they set aside,
> Life in their own hands retaining.

Thou, Gilgamesh, let full be thy belly,
Make thou merry by day and by night.
Of each day make thou a feast of rejoicing,
Day and night dance thou and play!
Let thy garments be sparkling fresh,
Thy head be washed; bathe thou in water.
Pay heed to the little one that holds on to thy hand,
Let thy spouse delight in thy bosom!
For this is the task of mankind."[1]

It is, however, an astonishing philosophy of life for a Jew nurtured in the faith of Moses and the prophets. How does faith in God fit into it? The answer to this is peculiarly difficult because it is widely believed that the book of Ecclesiastes has been extensively annotated by later more orthodox writers who have toned down his radical scepticism. This may well be so, but it is worth remembering that not everyone who speaks of God has a living faith. Perhaps the crux of Koheleth's religious outlook is to be found in certain advice he gives concerning worship. The less you say in the temple, he claims, the better, "for God is in heaven, and you upon earth" (5.2). For Koheleth this means that an infinite gulf separates God and man. There is no possibility of vital contact. Substitute 'Fate' or 'Chance' for God in many of the sayings in Ecclesiastes and it would make little difference to the substance of the book.

Attempts have been made to see in Ecclesiastes the acids of Greek scepticism corroding Hebrew faith. It is doubtful if we need this explanation. If Ecclesiastes comes from the third century B.C. the influence of Greek thought is certainly beginning to be felt, but there were other factors within Judaism itself which would go some way to explaining Ecclesiastes' mood. The voice of prophecy was silent. The Jewish people seemed to be stagnating under foreign occupation. There were few burning issues in the day to call forth ultimate loyalties.

Koheleth and Job have much in common. Both stand within the wisdom tradition. Both are intensely personal protests against certain over-simplifications in orthodox theology.

[1] A.N.E.T., p. 90.

There is one vital difference. Job tried to save faith in a God-ordered world; Koheleth gave up the attempt. Job still believed in a living personal relationship between God and man; Koheleth did not. If only Koheleth had believed like Job that God had his knife in him he would not, however troubled, have become so cynical.

By a strange religious insight, Judaism made Ecclesiastes prescribed reading on the third day of *Sukkoth*, the great harvest thanksgiving festival whose dominant mood is joy. If joyous faith in the mighty acts of Yahweh is the major emphasis in Old Testament thinking, it is well to be reminded that faith is often hard won, for some impossible, and that joy needs to be tempered and deepened by the witness of the troubled mind.

Chapter Ten

GOD AND MAN

IT is commonly asserted that the Hebrews, unlike the Greeks, had no genius for philosophy. They were essentially practical in outlook, not given to speculation. This is a truth which can be overstated. There is evidence within the Old Testament that there were those who pondered daily upon the ultimate meaning of life and sought to interpret Israel's history within the framework of God's purposes for all mankind. Their commentary on the ultimate meaning of all life is to be found in Genesis 1-11, the prologue to the story of Israel's encounter with God. Like all good prologues it was written, after the plot of the drama was known, to direct our attention to some of the most important elements in the drama.

From the literary standpoint, Genesis 1-11 is not originally a unity. It has been built up from two different sources, the priestly source ('P') and the earliest non-priestly source ('J'). These sources, however, have been so skilfully unified that together they provide us with an introduction to the Old Testament doctrine of God and man. It is a great mistake to regard these early chapters of Genesis as primitive pre-scientific speculation about the origin of things. They contain the insights of some of the greatest theologians in Israel. We cannot always be certain what lies behind some of the stories in Genesis 1-11, but we know enough to be able to assert that in these chapters Israelite thinkers are handling themes and ideas which had a wide currency in the Ancient Near East, particularly in Mesopotamia, the home, according to tradition, of the forefathers of the Hebrew people. But if they handle traditional currency, it comes from their hands reminted, changed in many instances almost beyond recognition by the distinctive faith of Israel.

The term 'myth' has been, and is, so frequently applied to material in Genesis 1-11 that we may well begin by seeking to understand its meaning. Myth is one of these words of respectable ancestry which have come down in the world. We speak of something as a myth, or mere myth, when we mean that it is not true. There are still those who, whenever they see the word myth used of a Biblical passage, assume that the truth of the Bible is under attack and rush to its defence.[1] But the problem of myth is deeper than that of popular misunderstanding. The word is used in different senses in scholarly discussion.

1. "Myth is to be defined as a complex of stories—some no doubt fact and some fantasy—which for various reasons human beings have regarded as demonstrations of the inner meaning of the universe and human life. Myth is quite different from philosophy in the sense of abstract concept, for the form of myth is always concrete—consisting of vivid sensually intelligible narratives, images, rites, ceremonies and symbols."[2] Two points are worth stressing in this definition. Firstly, the form which myth takes is that of the story or narrative whether that story be told in words or in actions. Secondly, the purpose of such stories is not merely entertainment. They are attempts to tell us something about the meaning of life and the world which surrounds us. Such stories may be traditional, popular stories handed down from generation to generation, or they may be the creation of a literary artist or teacher.

It is usually in this sense that the word 'myth' has been applied to some of the material in Genesis 1-11. In terms of this approach it would be quite wrong to try to locate the Garden of Eden, or to hunt for relics of Noah's ark. Adam is

[1] Hence A. Richardson, *Genesis 1-11* (Torch Commentaries) suggests that we use 'parable'.

[2] A. W. Watts, *Myth, Ritual and Christianity*, p. 3.

not the first man, living at a particular time in human history; he is Everyman, the Everyman in us. Such stories may draw on pure fantasy (the Garden of Eden?) or they may draw on fact. If the story of Noah and the flood (6.5-8.22) is a myth, none the less behind it may be the memory of disastrous flooding in the Mesopotamian valley. Similarly, if the Tower of Babel story (11.1-9) be myth, the myth-maker may have used the *ziggurats* or towered temples of Mesopotamia as the starting point for his myth. Myth in this sense is a purely literary term, like prophetic oracle, hymn or parable. In itself it says nothing about the truth or otherwise of what is conveyed by the myth.

2. The world of the Ancient Near East, however, which is Israel's cultural home, was dominated by myth of a different kind such as we find in the Babylonian Creation story, Enuma Elish, or the Ugaritic poems concerning Baal. Myth in this sense has been defined as "a form by which the existing structure of reality is understood and maintained . . . Existing world order is maintained through the actualisation of the myth in the cult."[1] The definition may become clearer if we look at two characteristic features of such myths. In the first place they serve a severely practical purpose, the everyday needs of man and the society in which he lives. One of the basic needs of the farmer is for assurance that when he sows his seed the fertilising rain will fructify the earth. Thus the theme of many such myths is the recurring conflict between life and death, drought and fertility; their central figure a dying and rising god. A creation myth is not evidence of man's curiosity about the origin of things. Its annual recital served a present need. Ordered life now existed because so it was ordained at the beginning of things when the gods of order triumphed over the forces of chaos. But life was ever precarious. Chaos was ever threatening to break in. Therefore periodically the triumph of order over chaos must be re-

[1] B. S. Childs, *Myth and Reality in the Old Testament*, p. 29.

enacted. In such myths, man sees himself as part of the world in which he lives, he is aware of an unbreakable link between himself and what we would call 'Nature', but what he personalised as gods and goddesses. Man's basic problem is how to control and harness for his own good the unpredictable forces in the world around him. Myth and its inseparable twin ritual are the means to this end.

This brings us to the second important feature of such myths. Myth and ritual are originally part of an indivisible whole. Myth is what is spoken or recited as the ritual is performed, the libretto of a religious drama. Myth declares in words what the ritual ensures through action. Ritual is not simply performed in pious hope. If the correct fertility ritual is faithfully performed, fertility is ensured for the coming year. When creation is re-dramatised at the New Year festival, the well-being of the community is guaranteed for the year ahead. We are here on the borderline between magic and religion.

Myth and the accompanying ritual are generally concerned with what we would call natural forces. In the myths, however, such forces are never 'it', but always personal. Thus in Canaanite myth, the interplay of fertility and drought is depicted in the struggle between Baal and his adversary Mot. It is debatable whether the worshippers drew any distinction between Baal and the fertilising rain. It is certain that, in terms of the myth-ritual pattern, there is no thought of god as 'transcendent', standing over and apart from the world. The claim has been made that myth in this sense is to be found in Genesis 1-11, more particularly in Genesis 1 which has been regarded as the myth accompanying a creation ritual at the Israelite version of the New Year Festival, the feast of Tabernacles. We have already seen reason to doubt whether such an annual New Year Festival played any part in Hebrew faith;[1] it remains now to see how the God of Genesis 1 is significantly different from the gods of the myths.

[1] cf. pp. 128 ff.

The Creation Hymn (Genesis 1-2.4a).

Both in style, vocabulary, background and theological emphasis, this opening section of Genesis is to be distinguished from the narrative which follows it.[1] In its present literary form it may be post-exilic—it comes from the priestly source ('P')—but it contains the Hebrew answer to many of the presuppositions of Ancient Near Eastern myth and ritual as they confronted the Hebrews in Canaanite religion.

The Mesopotamian creation story, which we know at its fullest in the Babylonian version called Enuma Elish from its opening words 'When above';[2] was part of the ritual of the New Year Festival. Between it and Genesis 1-2.4a there are certain marked similarities. Both describe the creation of heaven and earth, the various planets and man; both imply a certain kinship between man and god. Genesis 1.2 implies that before the creative activity of God began, there existed a dark formless chaos of water, which is precisely the picture drawn in the opening stanzas of Enuma Elish. The picture of primordial watery chaos is thought to be a reflection of geographical conditions in lower Mesopotamia where large tracts of country were extensively flooded in winter, dry land beginning to reappear in spring when the New Year Festival was being celebrated. Yet the more we discover points of contact between Genesis 1-2.4a and a Mesopotamian background, the more remarkable the Genesis story becomes. Instead of an "exuberant and grotesque polytheism" we find "a severe and dignified monotheism".[3] In a sense, however, the polytheism of the Mesopotamian creation myth is not grotesque; it is the inevitable consequence of thinking of religion in terms of man's natural environment, with its conflicting forces of life and death, chaos and order. The gods and goddesses are but personifications of such forces. Genesis 1 strips the creation story of its mythological flavour. It must do so because the

[1] For details, cf. S. R. Driver, *Genesis* (Westminster Commentary).
[2] cf. D.O.T.T., pp. 5 ff.
[3] S. R. Driver, *op. cit.*, p. 30.

God of Genesis 1 is the sovereign lord of all life, not one aspect of nature, not even Nature with a capital N. He cannot be equated with the world or anything in it. Source of all life, he stands over and above the world of his creating. The waters of chaos may lurk behind the language of Genesis 1.2, but they are the passive backcloth against which the Hebrew drama of creation is enacted. There is no longer any conflict between the forces of chaos and good order.

"In the beginning God created" (Gen. 1.1). Over the dark primeval chaos there 'hovered' or 'soared' (R.S.V., moved) the 'Spirit of God'. The word used in Hebrew for 'created', *bara'*, is a word which in this form is used only of God and his mighty creative activity. The same point is underlined in the phrase the 'Spirit of God'. The basic meaning of *ruaḥ* (spirit) seems to be wind, the wind which may sweep with terrifying force across the desert, symbol of irresistible power and energy. The *ruaḥ* of *God* is God creatively and powerfully at work in the world, source for the Old Testament of all exceptional skill or strength in man (Gen. 41.28; Exod. 31.3; Judges 15.14) and in many passages the giver of all life (Isa. 44.3 ff.; Ps. 104.30). All is here traced back to the mighty energy of one transcendent God.

This creative activity of God is seen within the framework of six days (Gen. 1.3-31).

Day one—light (vv. 3-5)
Day two—the firmament of heaven (vv. 6-8)
Day three—(a) earth, (b) vegetation (vv. 9-13)
Day four—the planets, sun and moon (vv. 14-19)
Day five—fish and birds (vv. 20-23)
Day six—(a) mammals, (b) man (vv. 24-31).

There is a basic literary pattern to which the whole chapter, with minor variations, conforms. Each section begins "And God said . . ." The fulfilment of this divine word is described in the laconic "And it was so" or in a slightly fuller form

(vv. 3, 21, 27). Concerning six of the acts of creation—there are eight altogether, two on the third day, two on the sixth—there is pronounced the verdict "And God saw that it was good", and over the whole there is set the seal of divine approval in v. 31, "And God saw everything that he had made, and behold, it was very good." Each section ends "And there was evening and there was morning, a xth day," the form of this statement being dictated by the fact that for the Hebrews the new day began at sunset.

This pattern stresses the lordly supremacy and power of the God of Hebrew faith. No conflict between rival gods precedes creation. This God but speaks and his word is power-charged, effective. Likewise it stresses the very positive attitude which the Hebrews had to the world. Throughout the Old Testament there runs a rich vein of rejoicing in the world God has created (e.g., Ps. 104; 148). It is a good, a very good world. There is never any suggestion that the world we see and handle is evil or illusory, a stumbling-block to the life of the soul. The Old Testament has a much more radical diagnosis to make of man.

God's creative activity in Genesis 1 reaches its climax in the creation of man (Gen. 1.26 ff.). The place of man in the universe and his relationship to the gods is a recurring theme in Ancient Near Eastern myth. Enuma Elish describes how after the defeat of *Tiamat* (primeval watery chaos) by the Babylonian champion of the gods, Marduk, Marduk informs his father Ea of his intention to create man to ease the lot of the vanquished gods who have been assigned menial tasks in the service of their victors.

> "Blood will I compose, bring a skeleton into being,
> Produce a lowly primitive creature, 'Man' shall be his name;
> I will create *lullu-amelu*—an earthly 'puppet'-man.
> To him be charged the service that the gods may then have rest."

After discussion it is agreed that men shall be made out of the blood of one of the rebel gods, Kingu.

They (formally) bound him, held him fast before Ea,
Laid the (total) crime upon him, cutting into his blood:
Thereupon from his blood (he cre)ated mankind,
Imposed the service upon him, released the gods who must else
    have served.[1]

Man has thus divine blood flowing in his veins. His primary task is to see that provision is made for suitable dwellings for the gods, and to ensure that the cult of the gods is faithfully maintained.

In Genesis 1 man, created after the rest of creation, stands in a peculiar relationship to God.

Then God said, "Let us make man in our image, after our likeness" (Gen. 1.26a).

So God created man in his own image, in the image of God he created him; male and female he created them (Gen. 1.27).

". . . in our image, after our likeness"—these words have been described as the Magna Charta of Humanity,[2] but what do they mean? 'Image' and 'likeness' are here synonymous terms used cumulatively for emphasis. Only once in the Old Testament outside this passage do we find the phrase man 'created in the image of God', in Genesis 9.6, where it seems to stress the sanctity of human life (cf. Gen. 5.3 which coming from the same priestly source as Genesis 1 probably implies that Adam handed on to his descendants the image of God with which he had been endowed).

The temptation has always been to interpret the 'image of God' in the light of what each age has regarded as being most distinctive in man. Thus a Jewish-Greek writer of the first century B.C. interprets it to mean that man is made to be immortal;[3] while for the late nineteenth and early twentieth centuries it stands for man's 'self-conscious reason'[4] which

<hr>

[1] D.O.T.T., p. 12.
[2] J. H. Hertz in the Soncino Bible, ad loc.
[3] Widom of Solomon, 2.21.
[4] S. R. Driver, Genesis, ad loc.

includes all his artistic and intellectual faculties. But what does the expression mean in context in Genesis 1? Some have argued that it refers to man's bodily form. God is consistently spoken of in human terms in the Old Testament. It would thus be natural for the Hebrews to think of God as having a body, the human body being a replica of the divine prototype. It is doubtful whether the thought of Genesis 1 is quite as naïve as this. There are two further possibilities.

1. The meaning of "in our image" may be defined by what follows in v. 26:

> and let them have dominion over the fish of the sea, and over the birds of the air, and over the cattle, and over all the earth, and over every creeping thing that creeps upon the earth.

Just as God is lord over all creation, so man reflects this lordship in his relationship to the rest of creation. The thought is developed in Psalm 8:

> "When I look at thy heavens, the work of thy fingers,
> the moon and the stars which thou hast established;
> what is man that thou art mindful of him,
> and the son of man that thou dost care for him?
> Yet thou hast made him little less than God,
> and dost crown him with glory and honour.
> Thou hast given him dominion over the works of thy hands;
> thou hast put all things under his feet,
> all sheep and oxen,
> and also the beasts of the field,
> the birds of the air, and the fish of the sea,
> whatever passes along the paths of the sea" (Ps. 8.3-8).

This is man's destiny, to exercise authority under God over the rest of creation. The further we advance in science and technology, the more exciting and the more dangerous the possibilities in such a lordship become.

2. There is, however, another clue to the meaning of "the image of God" in Genesis 1. The distinctive thing about man in this chapter is not merely that he is given dominion over the rest of creation, but that after God has created male and female

"God blessed them, and *God said unto them*" (v. 28). To man and to man alone of all that he creates, God speaks. Between God and man there can be a conversation. This is the distinctive mark of man in the Old Testament. He has been so made that there exists between him and his creator a personal relationship which is seen in God addressing man, and in man's ability to respond (cf. Gen. 3.9-10; Exod. 3.4, etc.). One of the most famous of Jewish Rabbis, Rabbi Akiba, once declared, "Man is of God, and what is far more, he knows he is of God".[1] This 'knowing' comes to him as he hears God's word and responds to it in faith or rebellion.

Genesis 1 is no scientific textbook. There is no more reason for attempting to fit the six days of creation into a modern evolutionary scheme than there is for trying to square vv. 26-27 with a physiologist's account of man. The chapter is best treated as a *hymn* written out of faith to convey certain abiding theological truths about the world and man in relationship to God.[2]

The Enigma of Man (Gen. 2.4b-3.24)

To pass from Genesis 1 to Genesis 2.4b ff. (from the words "in the day that") is to enter a very different world. In place of the studied, rhythmic, hymn structure, we find a vivid, simple narrative style, the work of one who is both a literary artist of high merit and a penetrating theologian. It belongs to the 'J' source.

Whatever this narrative may be, it is impossible to describe it as history. The characters in the story do not have proper names, Adam means Man, Eve means Life. The trees in the garden are not ordinary trees but magical trees. Strange creatures appear, a talking serpent, cherubim with a flaming sword. The location of this Garden of Delight (Eden) is given in the vaguest fashion in a passage (Gen. 2.10-14) which has the appearance of being a quaint learned addition to the

---

[1] *Soncino Bible, loc. cit.*
[2] For a discussion of Sabbath (Gen. 2.2-3), cf. pp. 122 ff.

original story. The purpose of the narrative is not to explain what once happened but to focus attention on certain features of life as the author knew it. It may, therefore, well be described as 'myth' in our first sense of that word. Let us look at such a myth from a culture which has no connection whatever with Israel. The Namaquas or Hottentots of South Africa say that:

> Once upon a time the Moon wished to send mankind a message of immortality, and the hare undertook to act as messenger. So the Moon charged him to go to men and say, "As I die and rise to life again, so shall you die and rise to life again." Accordingly the hare went to men, but either out of forgetfulness or malice he reversed the message and said, "As I die and do not rise to life again, so you shall also die and not rise to life again." Then he went back to the Moon, and she asked him what he had said. He told her, and when she heard how he had given the wrong message, she was so angry that she threw a stick at him which split his lip. That is why the hare's lip is still cloven. So the hare ran away and is still running till this day. Some people, however, say that before he fled he clawed the Moon's face, which still bears the marks of the scratching, as anybody may see for himself on a clear moonlight night. But the Namaquas are still angry with the hare for robbing them of immortality. The old men of the tribe used to say, "We are still enraged with the hare, because he brought such a bad message, and we will not eat him." Hence from the day when a youth comes of age and takes his place among the men, he is forbidden to eat hare's flesh, or even to come into contact with a fire on which a hare has been cooked. If a man breaks the rule, he is not infrequently banished from the village. However, on the payment of a fine he may be readmitted to the community.[1]

This well illustrates the popular narrative style of myth, and the fact that such a story may seek to answer not one question, but many questions. The important central question which the Namaqua's story seeks to answer is "Why do men die, and unlike the Moon, never come to life again?" But equally it gives popular answers to several other questions. Why does the hare have a cleft lip? Why does the hare always seem to be on

[1] J. G. Frazer, *Folklore in the Old Testament* (abridged edition), p. 20.

196

the run? Why does the Moon have marks on its face? Why do adult male Namaquas never eat hare's flesh? If Genesis 2.4b ff. is a myth of this kind, we may well expect it to wrestle with certain central questions, and at the same time to give us popular Hebrew answers to other questions.

It is wrong to speak, as is sometimes done, of two creation stories in Genesis 1-3. Genesis 2.4b ff. is not a creation story. The arid waste transformed by subterranean water (Gen. 2.5-6) —a different background picture from Genesis 1.2 and one more natural to the Palestinian landscape—merely provides the setting for man. The interest of the narrative is focused firmly on man. Certain duplications (e.g., the tree of the knowledge of good and evil, *and* the tree of life) suggest that various traditions may lie behind Genesis 2-3, but the narrative comes to us as a unity with two well-defined themes.

1. *The nature of man.* "Then the LORD God formed man of dust from the ground" (Gen. 2.7a). Yahweh is here depicted as a divine potter shaping man out of the dust from the ground. An etymological link is claimed between man (*'adham*) and the ground (*'adhamah*). Man's essential 'earthiness' is here stressed. He is just as much part of the world as every beast of the field and bird of the air who are likewise formed 'out of the ground' (Gen. 2.19).

Having fashioned man, Yahweh

"breathed into his nostrils the breath of life; and man became a living being" (Gen. 2.7b).

It is as if an inanimate statue now has breathed into it the gift of life. Man thus becomes a 'living being'. The A.V. translation of this phrase 'living soul' is quite misleading if it brings to our mind the thought of man being equipped with a 'soul' as well as a body. The narrative is but stressing man's total dependence upon God for the gift of life. If anything, Genesis 2.7b underlines the earthiness of man, the transitoriness of life, since the Old Testament is well aware that this 'breath of life' which Yahweh gives to man may be withdrawn at any time (Pss. 103.14-16; 104.29; Eccl. 3.19-20). Yet this frail creature man is still, as in Genesis 1, lord over the rest of creation. This is the point of Genesis 2.19-20 where all the birds and beasts are brought to man so that he may name them. To know someone's name, in ancient thinking, is to possess power over that person.

2. *The disobedience of man.* The essential difference between man and the rest of creation is to be found in the story of the Garden of Delight (Eden) which turned to disenchantment through man's disobedience. The story touches upon a theme which had been long familiar to the Ancient Near East, man's quest for immortality (Gen. 3.22). Two well-known Mesopotamian texts, the *Adapa* myth and the *Gilgamesh Epic,* deal with this quest. Adapa, summoned to appear before the supreme judge Anu, is warned by the god Ea not to eat 'the bread of death' or drink 'the water of death' which will be offered him. He faithfully obeys, only to discover too late that what he has been offered was in reality 'the bread of life' and 'the water of life'.[1] In the Gilgamesh Epic, Utnapishti, the one man who has achieved immortality by surviving the disastrous flood, offers to Gilgamesh 'a hidden thing', a marvellous plant which guarantees life.

"Its name shall be 'Man becomes young in old age'."

On the way home, however:

"Gilgamesh saw a well whose water was cool.
He went down into it to bathe in the water.
A serpent snuffed the fragrance of the plant.
It came back (from the well) and carried off the plant,
Going back to shed its slough."[2]

We find here a widespread belief that the serpent is immortal —it always renews its youth by casting its old skin—and that the serpent achieved immortality by cheating man out of what

[1] A.N.E.T., p. 101.
[2] A.N.E.T., p. 96.

ought to have been his by right. The serpent is cast for an equally fatal but rather different role in Genesis 2-3.

The author of Genesis 2.15-3.24 is handling familiar themes, but he has reshaped them. The plot centres not on a life-giving plant, the tree of life, but on "the tree of the knowledge of good and evil" (Gen. 2.17). "The knowledge of good and evil" is a phrase capable of many different interpretations. It is hard to believe that an Old Testament writer, in making God place an embargo on the eating of the fruit of the tree of knowledge of good and evil, meant to suggest that man should never possess one of his highest faculties, the power of moral choice and discernment. For the Old Testament it is part of man's glory that in response to God's challenge he can choose good rather than evil. In Hebrew, however, good and evil are not necessarily moral terms (cf. Gen. 2.9; 3.6 "good for food", i.e., pleasant to taste). Furthermore, a typical Hebrew idiom employs opposites to express everything that comes in between the opposites. We sometimes speak of hot and cold when we mean in fact any temperature. 'Good and evil' in many an Old Testament phrase means 'anything' or 'everything' (Gen. 24.50; Num. 24.13). "The knowledge of good and evil" could mean 'all knowledge'. Man is forbidden to grasp at the totality of knowledge which belongs to God. He must be prepared to accept that he is a finite creature and that certain things lie beyond his ken. Having deliberately disobeyed and trespassed this limit, man now, according to the story, naturally knows the location of the mysterious 'tree of life' and is therefore in danger of usurping another prerogative of God, immortality. He has therefore to be thrown out of the Garden of Delight, the way back to the tree of life being barred by a vigilant divine security guard (Gen. 3.23-24). This is an attractive interpretation, but it is doubtful whether the Hebrews were as concerned with the problem of 'knowing all things' as this suggests.

Two Old Testament passages which use the phrase 'knowing good and evil' suggest a different approach. In Deuteronomy

1.39 and Isaiah 7.14-15, 'knowing good and evil' is used to describe a certain stage of maturity in life in contrast to infancy or childhood. May it not be that the author of Genesis 2.15 ff. thinks of the true status of man in the light of God as one of childlike dependence? Instead of gladly accepting his childlike dependence, man wishes to be independent, seeking a maturity of his own, defiantly thrusting his own will before that of his creator. This attempt to win a false independence from God proves his ruin. All now goes wrong. The Garden of Delight becomes the garden of disenchantment. Childlike trust becomes the guilty conscience (3.9-11); harmony turns to friction (3.12 ff.); the life of rewarding toil becomes an irksome struggle for survival (3.17 ff.); death enters.[1]

To the question "What is wrong with Man?" Genesis 2.15 ff. returns the answer. Man is a creature in revolt against his Creator, seeking an independence which he may grasp but only at tragic cost. If this concern with the tragic flaw in man is central to the story, none the less, like the Namaquas' myth, the story suggests answers to many other questions.

Why was woman created? Why was marriage instituted? Answers to these questions are traced back to God's intention in creation. Woman is designed to be a suitable 'helper' to man (2.18). Man ('ish) and Woman ('ishah)—both Hebrew and English have the linguistic link between the words, the Hebrew narrative naïvely explaining this by claiming that woman was made from a rib taken from man—together by God's design form one 'flesh' (basar), rather one personality (2.21 ff.).

> Therefore a man leaves his father and his mother and cleaves to his wife, and they become one flesh (2.24).

Other puzzling features of life are directly related in the story to man's revolt against God. Why death (2.17; 3.3, 22-24)? Death, claims the story, is an intruder into God's world, the

[1] For a different interpretation cf. S. H. Hooke in *Peake's Commentary on the Bible, ad loc.*

tragic fruit of man's disobedience to God. It is worth noting how Hebrew tradition at this point is cast in an utterly different mould from the Greek Platonic tradition where the body is the prison-house of the soul, and death often a consummation devoutly to be wished. The Hebrews never regarded death as a friend, nor did they see the quest for immortality as the supreme goal of religion. For long enough, Hebrew thinking about what lay beyond death was vague and rudimentary. Death was an enemy, the destroyer of God's life-giving purposes.

In Genesis 3.14-19, a series of questions of very different character are likewise answered in terms of man's revolt against God. Why is the snake such an odd creature, crawling about in the dust (v. 14)? Why is there an instinctive antipathy between man and the snake family (v. 15)? Why is child-bearing painful (v. 16)? Why is man the dominant partner in the marriage relationship (v. 16)? Why is the lot of the farmer so hard (vv. 17-19)? Some of these questions, e.g., those concerning the snake, are on much the same level as the Namaquas' explanation as to why the hare has a cleft lip, but this must not blind us to the central truth of Genesis 2-3. The witness of the Old Testament does not stand or fall by what it has to say about snakes; it does stand or fall by what it has to say about man and God. The claim that man is a creature in revolt against his Creator is a very radical analysis of the human situation: that is to say, it is something which penetrates to the very roots of man's nature. If it be true, it is something that neither education nor advancing technology nor human idealism can answer. It is the conclusion to which Hebrew thinkers were driven as they pondered the mystery of Israel's strangely stubborn resistance to the will of a gracious God. There must be something radically wrong with man. We have little reason to think otherwise. The central ethical challenge of the Old Testament is therefore 'repent', reorientate life so that it looks towards God instead of being in revolt against him.

A similar emphasis is to be found in the *Tower of Babel* story (Gen. 11.1-9). Unlike the Creation story or the Garden of Eden story, nothing remotely similar to this story is to be found in Mesopotamian mythology. Yet the Mesopotamian location of the story is unmistakable. Burnt brick and bitumen (Gen. 11.3-4) were used for building projects in Mesopotamia from an early age. These were never natural building materials in Canaan. Behind the tower with 'its top in the heavens' there lies a characteristic feature of the Mesopotamian landscape, the *ziggurats* or towered temples, the most famous of them being the three-storied ziggurat at Ur dedicated to Nannar Sin, the moon god, and Etemenanki 'house of the foundations of heaven and earth', the seven-storied shrine at Babylon. Such temple towers were the cathedrals of Mesopotamia. On their top was a shrine where the god and the chosen representative of man, often a priestess, consorted. They were built as an expression of faith to ensure contact between heaven and earth, god and man.

The Tower of Babel takes on a quite different character in the light of Hebrew faith. Genesis 11.1-9 on one level provides us with the popular Hebrew explanation of a phenomenon which has always puzzled men. Why do people speak different languages? Why can't we understand what the people on the other side of the mountains say? Quite erroneously the story links the name Babel, which means 'the gate of the god' with the Hebrew verb *b-l-l*, meaning to confuse. The diversity of languages is said to come from the confusion which followed man's attempt to build this tower up to heaven. But this is not the central point of the story. Like Genesis 2-3, it is the story of man's attempt to overstep the limits of his creaturely dependence upon God, "the effort of the restless, scheming, soaring human mind to transcend its divinely appointed limitations."[1]

"Come, let us build ourselves a city, and a tower with its top in the heavens, and let us make a name (reputation) for our-

[1] J. Skinner, *Genesis* (International Critical Commentary), p. 229.

selves, lest we be scattered abroad upon the face of the whole earth" (Gen. 11.4).

This is the Genesis version of Swinburne's "Glory to Man in the Highest, for Man is the master of all things", and the result is not peace and goodwill, but chaos and confusion. In the fear which prompted the act "lest we be scattered abroad upon the face of the earth" we see symbolised man's feverish search for security, a search which, when undertaken apart from God, inevitably fails.

Cain and Abel (Gen. 4.1-14)

This story provides us with fresh insight into the intention of the theological authors of Genesis 1-11. Originally it may have had nothing to do with Genesis 2-3; the genealogical link in 4.1 is probably an editorial addition. It invites the hoary question 'Where did Cain get his wife?' Certain Jewish traditions assume that incest was originally permissible (cf. Jubilees 4.4). The story of the murder of Abel by Cain has many curious features. The origin of the mark set by God upon Cain has been sought in tribal identification marks which make blood revenge possible, or in a ritual sign. The story has been interpreted as the clash between two ways of life, the agricultural represented by Abel, the semi-nomadic and pastoral represented by Cain. Whatever the original form of the story it has been deliberately placed side by side with the story of man's revolt against God in Genesis 2-3. In this setting it finds new meaning. The hand raised in anger and jealousy against a brother is the consequence of man's challenge to the sovereignty of God. 'Self' having asserted itself against God now turns against a brother. The wrong in human relationships is a by-product of the wrong in man's relationship to God. That is why, when the Bible seeks to redress the human situation, it confronts man, as in the Decalogue, with a twofold demand, the sovereignty of God and the needs and rights of one's neighbours. The lawyer's summary of the Old Testament message in this respect is wholly sound,

"You shall love the LORD your God with all your heart, and with all your soul, and with all your strength, and with all your mind; and your neighbour as yourself" (Luke 10.27).

The Old Testament takes the fact of evil in the world with a deadly seriousness. It insists that God can never be indifferent to such evil. Cain, fresh from the murder of Abel, is challenged by God, "Where is Abel your brother?" (Gen. 4.9); as Adam, hiding from the consequences of his disobedience, heard God say, "Where are you?" (Gen. 3.9) God's judgement is a stern reality as prophets had insisted throughout Israel's history. But there is another element in the story. When Cain, compelled to be a friendless fugitive, protests "my punishment is greater than I can bear" (or "my guilt is too great to be forgiven") (Gen. 4.13), God places upon him a protective mark. Cain's reply to God's question concerning his brother has become a classic expression of irresponsibility. "I do not know; am I my brother's keeper?" (4.9). Yet in spite of everything God remains Cain's keeper. The mark placed upon him was the sign of God's concern even for his evil children. Cain may wash his hands of Abel, but God, however real his judgement, would never wash his hands of Cain.

The Flood (Gen. 6.5-8.22)

Stories of a catastrophic flood inundating the world occur in the folk lore of many nations.[1] There are marked similarities between the Genesis story and other flood stories from the Ancient Near East. The earliest version of a Near Eastern flood story we possess is the fragmentary Sumerian account which tells how king Ziusudra, being forewarned by the gods, builds a boat and thus escapes a divinely ordained flood which sweeps across the earth seven days and seven nights.[2] There seems little doubt that this provides the outline for the later

[1] J. G. Frazer, op. cit., pp. 46-143.
[2] A.N.E.T., pp. 42 ff.

Babylonian version which survives remarkably complete in Tablet XI of the Epic of Gilgamesh. Like Noah, Utnapishti is warned of an impending flood and told to take aboard ship "the seed of all creatures" (Tablet xi, line 28, cf. Gen. 6.19). The boat is built and caulked with pitch (lines 64-65, Gen. 6.14). Both narratives describe how the same technique was used to discover whether the flood was subsiding.

Epic of Gilgamesh	Genesis
On the seventh day's arriving, I freed a dove and did release him. Forth went the dove but came back to me; there was not yet a resting-place and he came returning. Then I set free a swallow and did release him. Forth went the swallow but came back to me: there was not yet a resting-place and he came returning. So I set free a raven and did release him. Forth went the raven— and he saw again the natural flowing of the waters, and he ate and he flew about and he croaked, and came not returning (Tablet XI, lines 145-154).	At the end of forty days Noah opened the window of the ark which he had made, and sent forth a raven; and it went to and fro until the waters were dried up from the earth. Then he sent forth a dove from him, to see if the waters had subsided from the face of the ground; but the dove found no place to set her foot, and she returned to him to the ark, for the waters were still on the face of the whole earth. So he put forth his hand and took her and brought her into the ark with him. He waited another seven days, and again he sent forth the dove out of the ark; and the dove came back to him in the evening, and lo, in her mouth a freshly plucked olive leaf; so Noah knew that the waters had subsided from the earth. Then he waited another seven days, and sent forth the dove; and she did not return to him any more (Gen. 8.6-12).

Noah and Utnapishti celebrate their deliverance in the same way.

So all set I free to the four winds of heaven, and I poured a libation, and scattered a food offering, on the height of the mountain. Seven and seven did I lay the vessels, heaped into their incense basins sweet-cane, cedarwood and myrtle. And the gods smelled the savour, the gods smelled the sweet savour, the gods gathered like flies about the priest of the offering
(Tablet XI, lines 155-160).

Then Noah built an altar to the LORD, and took of every clean animal and of every clean bird, and offered burnt offerings on the altar . . . the LORD smelled the pleasing odour
(Gen. 8.20-21).

The Babylonian narrative ends with the god Enlil blessing Utnapishti and his wife:

Hitherto Utnapishti has been but a man; but now Utnapishti and his wife shall be as gods like ourselves. In the Far Distance, at the mouth of the Rivers, Utnapishti shall dwell (Table XI, lines 193 ff.).[1]

It is not surprising that in Mesopotamian mythology a man should achieve immortality by surviving a disastrous flood. On the evidence of flood deposits in various Mesopotamian city states such as Ur, Kish, Shuruppak, severe flooding was common enough. Such floods, however, occurred at different times at different places, archaeology providing us with no evidence to substantiate the Genesis story of a universal flood which

prevailed so mightily upon the earth that all the high mountains under the whole heaven were covered; the waters prevailed above the mountains, covering them fifteen cubits deep (Gen. 7.19-20).

Just as in Mesopotamian mythology the experience of disastrous floods is used to describe man's quest for immortality, so the Bible, drawing on the same tradition, uses it for its own purposes. The present story in Genesis comes from two closely

[1] D.O.T.T., pp. 22 ff.

interwoven sources ('P' and 'J'), but a uniform spirit pervades the narrative, a spirit in sharp contrast to that of the Babylonian version. The Genesis narrative is monotheistic, while its Babylonian counterpart swarms with gods and goddesses, frightened out of their wits by the deluge storm and gathering like flies round Utnapishti's sacrifice. The reason for the sending of the flood is far from clear in the Babylonian version; in Genesis it is directly attributed to the wickedness of men (Gen. 6.5). But neither the monotheism of the Genesis narrative, nor its deeply ethical spirit take us to the heart of the difference between the two narratives. The entire orientation of the narrative is different. The Gilgamesh Epic's theme of man's quest for immortality has in Genesis been replaced by three of the central themes of Old Testament theology, judgement, deliverance and covenant.

Judgement

We have traced the Rake's Progress of Man from his revolt against God through Cain's murder of his brother Abel. The flood story is immediately preceded by a brief incident which takes the evil in man a stage further. The strange story of the involvement of the sons of God and the daughters of men (Gen. 6.1-4)—which can only mean liaisons between angelic or divine beings and mortal women, a common enough theme in pagan mythology—seems to be used in Genesis 1-11 to stress that there is a cosmic dimension to evil. It infects even the heavenly places. The point is reached where the narrator comments

> The LORD saw that the wickedness of man was great in the earth and that every imagination of the thoughts of his heart was only evil continually (Gen. 6.5).

But evil never goes unchecked. Adam is expelled from the garden; Cain is banished to lead a fugitive existence; a limit is placed on the life expectancy of man (Gen. 6.3), and now the decision is taken to "blot out man whom I have created from the face of the ground" (Gen. 6.7). The Rake can only progress to destruction. God's judgement on human wickedness is a stern reality. To summon the people of Yahweh to face the reality of God's judgement upon evil was one of the marks of the prophetic witness in the Old Testament. The Hebrew theologians who gave final shape to Genesis 1-11 are steeped in prophetic teaching and thinking.

Deliverance

Judgement is not the sole reality. In the flood narrative, the folly and wickedness of men call forth grief and disappointment in the heart of God. God cannot look with stony indifference upon the destruction of all that he has made. His purposes are not ultimately destructive but constructive. The mystery of God's love finds expression in the statement, "Noah found favour in the eyes of the LORD" (Gen. 6.8). Noah is spared so that through him and his descendants God's gracious purposes for the world may be fulfilled.

Covenant

This is expressed more fully in the *Covenant* theme which runs through the flood story.[1] When universal destruction is threatened, Noah is assured by God

> "But I will establish my covenant with you; and you shall come into the ark, you, your sons, your wife, and your sons' wives with you" (Gen. 6.18).

Once the flood has subsided, God says to Noah:

> "Behold, I establish my covenant with you and your descendants after you, and with every living creature" (Gen. 9.9-10).

> "I establish my covenant with you, that never again shall all flesh be cut off by the waters of a flood, and never again shall there be a flood to destroy the earth" (Gen. 9.11).

The covenant carries with it a 'sign', the bow in the clouds, not in the first instance a sign to man, but regarded, quite

[1] cf. Chapter Two.

naïvely, as a sign to God guaranteeing that God will never forget.

"When I bring clouds over the earth, and the bow is seen in the clouds, *I will remember my covenant*" (Gen. 9.14-15, cf. 16).

As in Israel's historical experience this covenant is rooted in God's gracious initiative and built everlastingly upon the rock of the utter dependability of God.

A few firm strokes of the theologian's brush and there is painted for us in Genesis 1-11 the broad outline of the faith of the Old Testament. Here is God, transcendent, creator of all that is. Here is man, lord over the rest of creation, yet sharing in the frailty of all living things: man made in the image of God to find life's fulfilment in dependence upon and in fellowship with God. This serene background is overlaid with the sombre hues of tragedy, as man restlessly seeks to overstep the limits God has placed upon him. He deifies his own will; he seeks to find his own security. Instead he finds chaos and insecurity, and the ever pressing reality of God's judgement. But the darkness is pierced by the light of hope. Rebellious man is not utterly cast off. The protecting mark is placed on Cain; Noah is spared. This light of hope flashes from Israel's experience as a nation from the moment when with the call of Abraham God's saving initiative was made known to his people.

Chapter Eleven

GOD AND THE FUTURE

A MARKEDLY optimistic strain runs through the Old Testament. It is not a facile optimism which turns a blind eye to the evil in the world and man. It hardly encourages us to believe that increased further education or more intelligent economic planning will inaugurate an age of lasting peace and prosperity. It is not man-centred at all, but God-centred. Because the man of faith in Israel looked back to the mighty acts of God in the history of his people, because he experienced the ever present reality of God's grace in worship or had first-hand knowledge of the severity of God's judgement, he looked forward in hope. In and through Israel God had begun a good work which would inevitably find its fulfilment. The past, the present and the future belonged to God. This confidence about the future is expressed in the Old Testament in many different pictures, all with one thing in common. These pictures are never mere dreams or fantasies. They take their starting point from the certainties of Israel's faith, and push these certainties to their logical conclusion.

I

1. *The Spirit of God*

As the past for Israel centred upon the mighty acts of God, so shall the future. The dynamic, creative activity of God in the world and in the lives of man is described in the Old Testament as the Spirit (*ruah*) of God.[1] To this spirit of God is attributed all outstanding human wisdom, skill or strength. The spirit of God enables Joseph to interpret dreams (Gen.

[1] cf. p. 191.

41.38), or a judge such as Othniel to deliver his people from the hand of the oppressor (Judges 3.10). It is the source of Samson's strength (Judges 14.6), of Bezalel's skilled craftsmanship (Exod. 31.3), of Saul's religious enthusiasm (1 Sam. 10.10; 11.6). Prophets and kings are equipped by the spirit for their vocation in Israel (Ezek. 3.12; 10.5). Israel can only fulfil her mission as the Servant of Yahweh when she is endowed with the spirit (Isa. 42.1). The spirit of God is indeed the source of all life (Gen. 1.2; Ps. 104.30) and of all that is creative within life.

The prophet Ezekiel brought by the spirit of God (Ezek. 37.1) finds himself in the weird valley of dry bones, a battlefield strewn with the bones of men long dead. "Can these bones live?" is the incredible question hurled at Ezekiel by God (Ezek. 37.3). Yes, life, the spirit can be breathed anew into them by God. The vision is a parable; the dry bones are Israel, her national life destroyed, her people scattered in exile. No wonder they say

"Our bones are dried up, and our hope is lost; we are clean cut off" (Ezek. 37.11).

But hope can never be lost. From the graveyard of exile Yahweh can bring his people home.

"And I will put my Spirit within you, and you shall live, and I will place you in your own land; then you shall know that I, the LORD, have spoken, and I have done it, says the LORD" (Ezek. 37.14).

In a world where God's creative and recreative spirit is at work, the despair and hopelessness of men can never have the last word.

There is a strange story in Numbers 11.24 ff. which tells of the coming of God's spirit upon seventy elders of the people, enabling them to prophesy. Apparently the proper place for such prophetic activity was considered to be at the 'tent', the portable tabernacle outside the camp. Two of the elders, however, were for some reason detained within the camp. To the surprise of many, the spirit came upon them in the midst of the camp, and they began prophesying. Joshua who, like many a later ecclesiastic, seems to have been very concerned that everything should be done decently and in order and in the correct place, asks Moses to forbid the two to prophesy in the camp. Moses replies:

"Would that all the LORD's people were prophets, that the LORD would put his spirit upon them!" (Num. 11.29).

The prophet Joel, in one of his pictures of the days which will herald the fulfilment of God's purpose in the world, echoes these words of Moses.

"And it shall come to pass afterward,
that I will pour out my spirit on all flesh;
your sons and your daughters shall prophesy,
your old men shall dream dreams,
and your young men shall see visions.
Even upon the menservants and maidservants
in those days, I will pour out my spirit" (Joel 2.28-29).

The prophetic gift, once the prerogative of the few, is to become the possession of the many, young and old alike. All are to share in the true vision and knowledge of God. Nothing short of this could do justice to the wonder of Israel's experience of God. It must, it will, be universalised. And this will be God's doing, the fruit of his outpoured spirit.

2. The New Covenant

The covenant was God's gift to Israel, a relationship established by his gracious initiative, its beginning and continuance rooted in his loving dependability (hesedh). Yet the covenant relationship was constantly being threatened from the people's side by their disobedience and failure to respond to the covenant demands. No one was more aware of this than Hosea; its truth found an echo in his own bitter experience. What exactly happened in Hosea's tragic marriage to Gomer the daughter of Diblaim has been much discussed. There is no doubt that Gomer broke her marriage bond with Hosea, but how and in what circumstances we know not. Hosea describes the birth to Gomer of three children. Whether Hosea was their father or whether they were the fruit of their mother's participation in the debasing fertility rites is uncertain. The three children are given by Hosea symbolic names which underline the tragic reality of Yahweh's judgement upon a faithless people; *Jezr'el* (Hos. 1.4) recalls a particularly bloody massacre through which Yahweh's judgement once fell upon the royal house (2 Kings 9-10), *Loruḥamah* (Hos. 1.6) 'not pitied' heralds the end of Yahweh's compassion on the present community, *Lo'ammi* (Hos. 1.8) 'not my people' signifies Yahweh's repudiation of the covenant relationship. Like Amos, Hosea is the herald of Yahweh's stern judgement. He has no illusion about his nation. Its conduct deserves nothing less than that Yahweh should finally and utterly wash his hands of it.

"Hear the word of the LORD, O people of Israel;
for the LORD has a controversy with the inhabitants of the land.
There is no faithfulness or kindness,
and no knowledge of God in the land;
there is swearing, lying, killing, stealing, and committing adultery;
they break all bounds and murder follows murder.
Therefore the land mourns,
and all who dwell in it languish" (Hos. 4.1-3a).

"I know Ephraim,
and Israel is not hid from me;
for now, O Ephraim, you have played the harlot,
Israel is defiled.
Their deeds do not permit them to return to their God,
For the spirit of harlotry is within them,
and they know not the LORD" (Hos. 5.3-4).

Gomer had turned out to be a wife of harlotry (Hos. 1.2); so had Israel, the wife of Yahweh. The shallowness and the fickleness of Irael's *ḥesedh* are well described in Hosea 6.4:

"Your love (*ḥesed*) is like a morning cloud,
like the dew that goes early away."

"Your love (*ḥesedh*) is like a morning cloud,

But what of God? Here the word of God came to Hosea through his own attitude to Gomer.

> "And the LORD said to me, 'Go again, love a woman who is beloved of a paramour and is an adulteress; even as the LORD loves the people of Israel, though they turn to other gods and love cakes of raisins'. So I bought her for fifteen shekels of silver and a homer and a lethech of barley. And I said to her, 'You must dwell as mine for many days; you shall not play the harlot, or belong to another man; so will I also be to you'."
> (Hos. 3.1-3).

If this, as seems likely, refers to a later stage in Hosea's marriage than chapter 1, it points us to the fact that although Gomer had proved unfaithful, Hosea remained faithful. At cost to himself, Hosea was prepared to reclaim Gomer, and discipline her again to be his wife. Was God's loving faithfulness less than Hosea's? Israel may have played fast and loose with her loyalty to Yahweh but there could be no divine tit for tat. Judgement must be severe, but:

> "How can I give you up, O Ephraim!
> How can I hand you over, O Israel!
> How can I make you like Admah!
> How can I treat you like Zeboiim!
> My heart recoils within me,
> my compassion grows warm and tender.
> I will not execute my fierce anger,
> I will not again destroy Ephraim;
> for I am God and not man,
> the Holy One in your midst,
> and I will not come to destroy" (Hos. 11.8-9).

There will be a new beginning to Israel's history (Hos. 2.14-15), a renewal of the covenant marriage bond between Yahweh and Israel at Yahweh's initiation (Hos. 2.19-20).

Hosea spoke as the Northern Kingdom of Israel was tottering to destruction. Jeremiah and Ezekiel in the hour of crisis for the Southern Kingdom of Judah had likewise a message of hope centred on the covenant theme. Jeremiah had the heart-searching experience of living through a national religious reformation which promised much and achieved little.[1] The reformation of 621 B.C. eliminated certain abuses, but new ones crept in to take their place. Jeremiah appealed in vain for a radical reordering of the life of society which would show that the people were facing their covenant responsibilities. There seemed to be a strange perversion in the hearts of men, what Jeremiah called 'a stubborn evil will' (Jer. 16.12; 23.17) which made a mockery of the best intentions of men. It was one thing to recall the nation to its loyalty to Yahweh, quite another to ensure that such a loyalty would be forthcoming. Such a loyalty could spring only from a new experience of God, and this God alone could make possible.

> "Behold, the days are coming, says the LORD, when I will make a new covenant with the house of Israel and the house of Judah, not like the covenant which I made with their fathers when I took them by the hand to bring them out of the land of Egypt, my covenant which they broke, though I was their husband, says the LORD. But this is the covenant which I will make with the house of Israel after those days, says the LORD: I will put my law within them, and I will write it upon their hearts; and I will be their God, and they shall be my people. And no longer shall each man teach his neighbour and each his brother, saying, 'Know the LORD', for they shall all know me, from the least of them to the greatest, says the LORD; for I will forgive their iniquity, and I will remember their sin no more" (Jer. 31.31-34).

The covenant of Mount Sinai had failed, shattered on the rock of the people's disloyalty. The charter of the new covenant will have to be written not on tablets of stone, but upon the hearts of the people, Yahweh's Torah, engraved upon their very will so that no longer is there an unbridgeable gulf between what Yahweh demands and what his people can give. This can only be rooted in a deep personal knowledge of God, a living communion with God within which forgiveness and

[1] cf. pp. 90 ff.

renewal are a reality. This God could do as Jeremiah knew full well from his own troubled religious pilgrimage.[1]

Ezekiel held out to his stricken people the same covenant hope. Yahweh will make with his people "a covenant of peace" (Ezek. 34.25; 37.26), a covenant which will guarantee anew his people's welfare, security from fear and oppression in a land abundantly fertile and prospering.

> "And they shall know that I, the LORD their God, am with them, and that they, the house of Israel, are my people, says the LORD God" (Ezek. 34.30).

But Ezekiel, like Jeremiah, was far too great a moral realist to believe that this covenant could simply take over where the old covenant had broken down. That would be to invite the same recurring pattern of disloyalty leading to inevitable judgement. There was one condition for a future true covenant relationship between Yahweh and the people.

> "A new heart I will give you, and a new spirit I will put within you; and I will take out of your flesh the heart of stone and give you a heart of flesh" (Ezek. 36.26).

There was needed a deep inner transformation, replacing the stony hardness of disloyalty by wills which were sensitive and responsive to Yahweh. This is to be the work of God's spirit (Ezek. 36.27, cf. Ps. 51.11-13).

The prophets may despair of man, but they never despair of God. He remains faithful amid all his people's infidelities. The love which reached out to call into being the covenant at Mount Sinai would find its fulfilment in a new covenant in which the covenant promise would be truly realised. "You shall be my people, and I will be your God" (Ezek. 36.28).

3. The Messiah

In the world of the Ancient Near East, kingship was no mere political convenience, it was an essential element in the divinely ordered structure of the universe. "In Egypt from

[1] cf. pp. 158 ff.

earliest times, the ruling Pharaoh was the incarnation of the god, not merely god-like, but god. In terms of Osiris worship the ruling Pharaoh was Horus, the divine son and avenger of Osiris, and on death he became Osiris. By the coronation rites, the new Pharaoh became not only legitimate king, but a god, directly linked to all his royal predecessors, the company of ancestors that stretched in unbroken line to the first god king, and his position and authority were unassailable."[1] The king-god had an important part to play in the religious ritual of the community. Through it he maintained and confirmed the existing world order established by the gods at the beginning of time. The picture from Mesopotamia is not so clear. The king seems to have been regarded in the main as the 'tenant farmer' of the gods, responsible to the gods for the care and use of the land under his control. He had, however, an important part to play in ritual, particularly the sacred marriage ritual when, on certain occasions, the king played the role of the god and his daughter the role of the goddess. The king was an indispensable link in the chain which bound the community and the gods. Likewise among the Hittites, the king became on his accession, not merely the supreme military commander and the guardian of law and order, but the priest of the gods.

An immediate military threat to the continued existence of the Hebrews led them to adopt kingship (1 Sam. 11, cf. p. 72), but the king was soon more than a military leader. This is clear both from historical narratives and from the 'Royal Psalms'. Psalm 2 begins by depicting the insurrection of vassals, a frequent happening at the accession of a new king. Such insurrection will be in vain. They are in revolt "against the LORD and his anointed" (Ps. 2.2). The Hebrew word rendered 'anointed' is *mashiah,* hence our English Messiah. The title implies a rite such as we find in 1 Samuel 16.13 where

Samuel took the horn of oil, and anointed him (i.e. David) in the midst of his brothers.

[1] H. W. Fairman in *Myth, Ritual and Kingship* (ed. S. H. Hooke, p. 81).

This anointing was the sign that this person had been specially marked out by Yahweh to be the ruler of his people. It was usually accompanied by an outpouring of the Spirit of Yahweh upon his chosen agent,

> and the Spirit of the LORD came mightily upon David from that day forward (1 Sam. 16.13b; 24.6, 10; 26.9, 11, 16, 23; 2 Sam. 23.1-7).

How else could he fulfil his high calling? The person of the king was regarded as sacrosanct because he was the *mashiah* of Yahweh (1 Sam. 26.9). Put in another way, the king at his accession became the adopted son of Yahweh,

> "I will tell of the decree of the LORD:
> He said to me, 'You are my son,
> today I have begotten you' " (Ps. 2.7).

There is no evidence, however, that the king of the Hebrews was ever thought of as divine, like his royal counterpart in Egypt. Hebrew thought was too conscious of the gulf between God and man, even the greatest of men, ever to blur this distinction. The king, as the *mashiah* of Yahweh and his adopted son, did however, on occasion, lead his people in worship. He had certain priestly functions and privileges, cf. Samuel 6 where David brings the ark to Jerusalem, wearing the priestly ephod, sacrificing and pronouncing the priestly blessing upon the people (cf. 1 Kings 3.4; 8.14 ff.; Ps. 110.4 and the discussion on p. 130). Psalm 2 ends on the note of the dominion that Yahweh's Messiah is expected to exercise over all his enemies. But more than military prowess and priestly functions were expected of the king in the eyes of a community committed to fulfil the charter of the covenant. The king must be the guarantee and embodiment of Yahweh's righteousness and justice, caring for the needy, crushing the oppressor, defending the poor and the weak (Ps. 72). When Absalom, David's son, conspires to overthrow his father, he appeals for support on the grounds that David is neglecting to dispense justice to his people.

"See, your claims are good and right; but there is no man deputed by the king to hear you. Absalom said moreover, 'O that I were judge in the land! Then every man with a suit or cause might come to me, and I would give him justice' " (2. Sam. 15.3-5).

From the ruling monarch in Israel, therefore, great things were expected. As the Messiah of Yahweh, endowed with Yahweh's spirit, he was responsible for the right ordering of society in the light of the covenant; he represented his people on occasion before God; he was expected to lead the people to triumph over their enemies. Such hopes were strengthened by the belief that there existed between Yahweh and the legitimate royal house, the house of David, "an everlasting covenant, ordered in all things and secure" (2 Sam. 23.5, cf. 2 Sam. 7.16). The reality was often far different. It is in the tension between the reality and the expectation of faith that there is born the hope of a future Messiah, a king anointed by Yahweh who would truly bring to his people a rich fulness of life. We may trace this tension in the teaching of two of the prophets.

In the year 735 B.C., attempts were made by neighbouring states to force King Ahaz of Judah into joining an anti-Assyrian coalition. Ahaz, his throne in jeopardy, saw no other remedy than to appeal for help to the Assyrians. The prophet Isaiah challenged him to have faith instead in Yahweh's promises, and offered him the choice of any sign to confirm the truth of such promises. Ahaz, however, had made up his mind. He side-steps the offer of a sign, clothing his refusal in words which can only be described as pious cant, "I will not ask, and I will not put the LORD to the test" (Isa. 7.12). With his heart and the heart of his people shaking "as the trees of the forest shake before the wind" (Isa. 7.2), Ahaz is convinced that the situation demands not faith in Yahweh, but the maximum military power he can muster. Isaiah is adamant. A sign shall be given, whatever Ahaz' attitude.

Therefore the LORD himself will give you a sign. Behold, a young woman shall conceive and bear a son, and shall call his name Immanuel   (Isa. 7.14).

The identity of the young woman, not necessarily a virgin as in the A.V., has been endlessly discussed. Most likely she was one of the favourite members of Ahaz' harem, present on the fateful occasion of Isaiah's interview with Ahaz. But the heart of the sign is not the identity of the young woman. It is the birth of a son to the royal house, a son whose name, Immanuel, 'God with us', enshrines all the promises which Ahaz as Yahweh's anointed theoretically believed but will not put to the test in the hour of crisis. Within a few short years, the danger from the anti-Assyrian coalition will have passed, and Ahaz and his people will know the truth of the promise in the child's name, 'God with us'. But Ahaz, having invoked Assyrian help, will find that the price to be paid for refusing to trust Yahweh is heavy.

Ahaz, to Isaiah, is the example of a king who might as well not have been the *mashiah* of Yahweh. In two passages, oracles suitable for the accession to the throne of a new king, the prophet paints for us his picture of the true Messiah. Light breaks upon the people's darkness. There is joy as at a harvest festival or some notable victory. Oppression has disappeared.

> For to us a child is born,
> to us a son is given;
> and the government will be upon his shoulder,
> and his name will be called
> "Wonderful Counsellor, Mighty God,
> Everlasting Father, Prince of Peace."
> Of the increase of his government and of peace
> there will be no end,
> upon the throne of David, and over his kingdom,
> to establish it, and to uphold it
> with justice and with righteousness
> from this time forth and for evermore.
> The zeal of the LORD of hosts will do this (Isa. 9.6-7).

> There shall come forth a shoot
> from the stump of Jesse,
> and a branch shall grow out of his roots.
> And the Spirit of the LORD shall rest upon him,
> the spirit of wisdom and understanding,
> the spirit of counsel and might,
> the spirit of knowledge and the fear of the LORD.
> And his delight shall be in the fear of the LORD.
> He shall not judge by what his eyes see,
> or decide by what his ears hear;
> but with righteousness he shall judge the poor,
> and decide with equity for the meek of the earth;
> and he shall smite the earth with the rod of his mouth,
> and with the breath of his lips he shall slay the wicked.
> Righteousness shall be the girdle of his waist,
> and faithfulness the girdle of his loins (Isa. 11.1-5).

Nearly one hundred and fifty years after Isaiah confronted Ahaz, Jeremiah had to deal with an equally irresolute Judaean monarch who dithered into disaster, desperately looking for help everywhere except in Yahweh. On his accession, this king had been given the name 'Zedekiah', a name full of promise and hope, "Yahweh is righteous"; and acted as if the name were meaningless. In sharp contrast to this vacillating monarch, Jeremiah draws his portrait of the true Messiah.

> "Behold, the days are coming, says the LORD, when I will raise up for David a righteous Branch, and he shall reign as king and deal wisely, and shall execute justice and righteousness in the land. In his days Judah will be saved, and Israel will dwell securely. And this is the name by which he will be called: 'The LORD is our righteousness' " (Jer. 23.5-6).

The name which Zedekiah is unworthy to bear will one day be rightly bestowed.

In these portraits of the true Messiah, there keep appearing characteristic features of the ruling monarch. He will belong to the legitimate royal family, whose future is guaranteed by the covenant with Yahweh, a scion of David, a shoot from the stem of Jesse, David's father (cf. Mic. 5.2; Zech. 3.8; 6.12). He will be mightily endowed with the spirit of Yahweh

(2 Sam. 23.2). He will bring his people a fulfilment of life rooted in 'justice' and 'righteousness'.

Even after Judah ceased to exist as an independent national state, and no national king sat upon the throne, the Messianic hope remained. It is hardly surprising that, in periods of national humiliation, the nationalistic emphasis came ever more strongly to the fore, till the Messiah became the symbol of all the suppressed patriotism of the Jewish people, the rallying cry of many an ill-starred politico-religious insurrection.

4. A Renewed World

So far, we have traced the hope of the Old Testament along fairly well defined national lines—the outpouring of God's spirit upon his people, a new relationship between God and his people based on a new covenant, the rule of a coming, perfect king. But just as the life of Israel was seen, in faith, as the means by which all mankind would be brought to the knowledge of God (cf. p. 91 ff), so the Old Testament hope for the future embraces not only Israel but the whole created universe.

To understand this, we must look at the Old Testament attitude to what we call 'Nature'. We tend to think of 'Nature' as an impersonal 'it', a closed system of laws operating inflexibly, irrespective of how we feel or act. This at least is the layman's picture, however far removed it may be from the latest complexities of the scientific understanding of our universe. We know, of course, that if we neglect certain fundamental laws of nature, nature takes its revenge, for example in the creation of dust-bowls or deserts. This is nevertheless but another sign of nature following inexorably its own laws. The Old Testament outlook is very different. Nature and man in the Old Testament form one indivisible whole, both utterly dependent upon and pliable in the hands of God and linked in destiny to each other.[1] For good and for

[1] cf. H. W. Robinson, *Inspiration and Revelation in the Old Testament*, pp. 1-33.

ill, nature reflects the condition of man. Thus in the myth in Genesis 2-3, Adam's disobedience reacts upon the whole world in which he lives.

> "Because you have listened to the voice of your wife,
> and have eaten of the tree
> of which I commanded you,
> 'You shall not eat of it,'
> cursed is the ground because of you;
> in toil you shall eat of it all the days of your life;
> thorns and thistles it shall bring forth to you"
>
> (Gen. 3.17-18a, cf. Deut. 28).

To a prophet like Amos, famine, drought, ruined crops, plague and earthquake (Amos 4.6-11) are not merely natural phenomena, but God's warning signals, signs in creation of the disharmony within Israelite society. Jeremiah graphically describes the flight from justice into anarchy and moral chaos in terms of the return of primeval darkness and desolation.

> "I looked on the earth, and lo, it was waste and void;
> and to the heavens, and they had no light.
> I looked on the mountains, and lo, they were quaking,
> and all the hills moved to and fro.
> I looked, and lo, there was no man,
> and all the birds of the air had fled.
> I looked, and lo, the fruitful land was a desert,
> and all its cities were laid in ruins
> before the LORD, before his fierce anger" (Jer. 4.23-26).

It would be a mistake to regard this as merely poetic imagery. It is more harshly realistic. Man has made a desolation not only of the society in which he lives, but of the very creation to which he is linked by unbreakable ties.

The converse also holds good. When the Old Testament looks for a renewed people of God enjoying a rich fulness of life, then it cannot but speak of this fulness of life in terms of a recreated universe from which all pain, disharmony and ruthlessness have been banished. The age of the true Messiah will be an age when

The wolf shall dwell with the lamb,
and the leopard shall lie down with the kid,
and the calf and the lion and the fatling together,
and a little child shall lead them.
The cow and the bear shall feed;
their young shall lie down together;
and the lion shall eat straw like the ox.
The sucking child shall play over the hole of the asp,
and the weaned child shall put his hand on the adder's den.
They shall not hurt or destroy
in all my holy mountain;
for the earth shall be full of the knowledge of the LORD
as the waters cover the sea (Isa. 11.6-9).

A world flooded with the knowledge of God is, for the Old Testament, a world of renewed trust and innocence even in nature. Nature red in tooth and claw gives way to the marauding wolf happily settling down with the lamb, formerly the object of its prey. A child fearlessly fondles poisonous snakes. The perpetual enmity between woman and the snake family which the Garden of Eden story traces to man's defiance of God is now a thing of the past. Instead of a world in which the farmer's lot is a wearisome struggle against 'thorns and thistles' (Gen. 3.18) there is to be a time of superabundant crops and fertility:

"Behold, the days are coming," says the LORD, "when the ploughman shall overtake the reaper and the treader of grapes him who sows the seed; the mountains shall drip sweet wine, and the hills shall flow with it" (Amos 9.13, cf. Joel 3.18).

Not the least interesting or curious is the picture which Ezekiel draws, following an ancient mythological theme, of a river of water issuing from the temple in Jerusalem to transform the sterile waters of the Dead Sea. The now lifeless waters will teem with fish of 'many kinds, like the fish of the Great Sea' (i.e., the Mediterranean). Along its shores fishermen will spread their nets (Ezek. 47.10).

However strange this may at first appear to us, it springs from the Old Testament doctrine of creation by a good God who saw everything that he created and passed upon it the verdict 'good, very good' (Gen. 1.31). But the world as the Hebrews well knew was not unqualifiedly good. There were earthquakes and deserts, plague and the Dead Sea. They saw the world as reflecting and being infected by the evil in man. They looked for a renewed and recreated universe, as they looked for a renewed and recreated people of God.

II

We have been looking at the future through the eyes of prophetic faith. There is within the Old Testament another type of literature which claims to have a God-centred word to speak about the future—*Apocalyptic,* which became of ever-increasing importance in the years leading up to New Testament times. Short apocalyptic additions have been added to several prophetic books in the Old Testament but there is only one complete example of Apocalyptic, the book of Daniel. Apocalyptic, so called because it claims to 'unveil' (Greek *apokaluptein*) the future, has been the fertile breeding ground for rash, if pious, speculation. The use which it makes of apparently cryptic symbolism and mysterious numbers is an open invitation to that misplaced ingenuity which delights to find the events of our own day hidden in Scripture. A true appreciation of the book of Daniel must take account of certain facts. It was produced in an hour of crisis. It is deliberately pseudonymous, claiming to be the work of Daniel in the exilic age, sixth century B.C., but in fact written by an unknown author at a much later date. In the interests of faith it makes use of imagery and symbolism drawn partly from other Old Testament books and partly from non-Jewish, particularly Persian, sources.

The hour of crisis was the Maccabean revolt, provoked by the attempt of the Seleucid emperor Antiochus IV (175-163 B.C.) to crush the Jewish faith in the interests of religious and political uniformity throughout his empire. The worship of

Yahweh in the Jerusalem temple was proscribed, an altar to the Greek god Zeus replacing the altar to Yahweh.[1] Jews faced martyrdom for professing their faith or even possessing a copy of Torah. Some Jews were genuinely attracted by the ideals of Hellenism which Antiochus represented; some were prepared to compromise; others resisted to the death, some of them from the outset with the sword, some passively. It is from the ranks of these loyalist Jews that the book of Daniel comes.

From the point of view of content, the book falls into two distinct sections, each designed to steel the nerve of the faithful. Chapters 1-6 recount certain stories, probably long current among the Jews, about Daniel and his exiled friends who were forced to live amid the pagan splendours of imperial Babylon. There are two major themes in these stories. Chapters 1, 3 and 6 describe how Daniel and his friends found themselves in situations where they had to choose between denying the faith of their fathers or death. In every story, uncompromising loyalty to Yahweh is vindicated by a miraculous deliverance. Chapters 2, 4 and 5 face the problem presented to faith by the seeming triumph of pagan imperialism. All declare that the pomp and glory of such imperialisms are doomed to pass away. The final reality in human history is not the kingdom of Nebuchadnezzar, nor Belshazzar, nor Darius but the kingdom of God:

> his dominion is an everlasting dominion,
> and his kingdom endures from generation to generation
>
> (Dan. 4.34; cf. 4.3; 6.26).

This theme of the kingdoms of this world and the kingdom of God is further dealt with in the visions of chapters 7-12, through symbolism, the detail of which sometimes eludes us,

---

[1] There is a punning reference to this in the 'abomination which desolates' (Dan. 9.27; 11.31). The Semitic equivalent of Zeus is 'Baal Shamaim', Lord of heaven. Baal, the name of the Canaanite god, is frequently changed and satirised by pious scribes of the Old Testament. Here it becomes 'Shiqquz', shame, and 'Shamaim' is turned into a similar sounding word 'meshomem' meaning 'making desolate'.

but which would be meaningful to the contemporaries of the author of Daniel. The visions have this in common, they all reveal a very rudimentary and imperfect knowledge of the history of the exilic and immediately post-exilic age, but a very detailed and much more accurate knowledge of the career of Antiochus IV down to 164 B.C.

The first vision (chapter 7) may be taken as typical in its outlook on history. Four great beasts, a lion figure with eagle's wings, a bear crunching three ribs in its teeth, a leopard with four wings on its back, a fourth monster with iron teeth and ten horns, appear in turn before a heavenly tribunal presided over by 'one that was ancient of days', there to be judged and destroyed. Universal dominion and glory is then handed over to "one like a son of man" (Dan. 7.13). As for the interpretation of the vision we are not left to wander in the dark. "These four great beasts are four kings who shall lord it over the earth" (Dan. 7.17) evidently intended by the author to represent four imperialisms under which the Jews had lived since the exile, Babylon, Media, Persia and the Greek empire founded by Alexander the Great.

The vision concentrates, however, on the fourth beast, and in particular on the one little horn which destroys three others. It has

> eyes and a mouth that spoke great things, and (it) seemed greater than its fellows. As I looked, this horn made war with the saints, and prevailed over them, until the Ancient of Days came, and judgement was given for the saints of the Most High (Dan. 7.20-22).

The reference is to Antiochus IV, his success over rival claimants to the Seleucid empire, and his persecution of the Jews.

The 'one like a son of man' (Dan. 7.13), a human figure as opposed to its bestial adversaries, is not the Jewish Messiah, or any individual, but, as the context makes quite clear, 'the saints of the most high', either Jewish loyalists facing martyrdom at the hands of Antiochus, or perhaps the holy angels who watch over the Jewish people. Dominion is to be taken from the persecutor and given to them.

> And the kingdom and the dominion
> and the greatness of the kingdoms under the whole heaven
> shall be given to the people of the saints of the Most High;
> their kingdom shall be an everlasting kingdom,
> and all dominions shall serve and obey them (Dan. 7.27).

Apocalyptic is not other-worldly escapism. It is an attempt to apply the great affirmations of prophetic faith to a dark age of persecution. The persecuting regime is only too real. It seems to triumph, but it can never have the last word. Ultimately, God's purposes and God's faithful people will be vindicated. Apocalyptic can never allow human history to run out meaninglessly into the sands of time. Nor can it envisage the final triumph of evil. All human history stands under the sovereignty of God. His will shall be done on earth, however dark present appearances. This conviction is the strength of Apocalyptic. Its weakness lies in a tendency not to be content with such a declaration of faith, but to try to establish a precise time-table for the fulfilment of God's purposes. Having enthroned God over evil, it makes him the slave of the calendar (cf. Dan. 8.13-14; 9.24 ff.; 12.11 ff.).

But what of the faithful who die before 'the time of the end'? Are they who have defended the faith even unto death to be excluded from God's kingdom when it comes in triumph? If we insist on the triumph of God's righteousness in human history, must we not equally insist on its triumph in the life of the individual? At this point Apocalyptic makes its distinctive contribution to the faith of the Old Testament.

To those who think that the primary task of religion is to provide men with a faith for dying, it must seem curious that we have passed in review the thought of the Old Testament without saying anything positive about its attitude to death. Yet this is true to the witness of the Old Testament. For long enough, the Hebrews were very inarticulate in their attitude towards death, partly perhaps because they were surrounded by fertility cults which dealt with life and death and had highly immoral associations. Provided the family 'name' was handed down from father to son across the generations, the fate of the individual beyond this present life seems to have roused little interest among the Hebrews. Traditionally the Hebrews thought of the dead as going via the grave to a vague shadowy abode under the earth called *She'ol*, the Pit, or *'Abhaddon,* the place of ruin. It was the antithesis of real life, "regions dark and deep" (Ps. 88.6) where men were forgotten by God.

> "Dost thou work wonders for the dead?
>   Do the shades rise up to praise thee?
>   Is thy steadfast love declared in the grave,
>   or thy faithfulness in Abaddon?
>   Are thy wonders known in the darkness,
>   or thy saving help in the land of forgetfulness?"
> (Ps. 88.10-12).

—such is the cry of a man who has suffered much and is in the grip of black despair (cf. Ps. 62; Isa. 38.16-19).

The faith of the Old Testament, however, could not remain content to leave the realm of the departed outside the jurisdiction of Yahweh. Amos insists that there can be no escape from the judgement of God even in Sheol (Amos. 9.2). One of the most intensely personal of all the Psalms insists that even in Sheol there is no avoiding the active presence of God.

> "Whither shall I go from thy Spirit?
>   Or whither shall I flee from thy presence?
>   If I ascend to heaven, thou art there!
>   If I make my bed in Sheol, thou art there!" (Ps. 139.7-8).

In certain other Psalms there is described an experience of God beside which all the treasures that earth affords pale into insignificance, and all the sorrows of life lose their sting (cf. Ps. 73.21-28). We are on the verge of something that was bound to shatter the narrow confines of this present life. It is only in Apocalyptic, however, that the prison of death is burst open, significantly not in terms of anything that man himself is, e.g., the possessor of an immortal soul, but in vindication of the righteousness of God.

> At that time (i.e., the time of God's final triumph) shall arise Michael, the great prince who has charge of your people. And there shall be a time of trouble, such as never has been since there was a nation till that time; but at that time your people shall be delivered, everyone whose name shall be found written in the book. And many of those who sleep in the dust of the earth shall awake, some to everlasting life, and some to shame and everlasting contempt (Dan. 12.1-2).

There is no unqualified statement here of life for all those who are dead. The concern of the author of Daniel is to ensure that those who deserve reward, the faithful martyrs, and those who deserve punishment, the persecutors of God's people, will receive their due. Hence there must be a resurrection for some at least of those who sleep in the dust (cf. Isa. 26,19, part of an apocalyptic fragment which has been added to the book of Isaiah). The particular form in which this hope is expressed in Daniel is not of vital importance. What is important is the conviction that even death itself cannot be allowed to gainsay the righteous purposes of God.

It was on God, on his known character, and on the necessary fulfilment of his purposes that Israel's hope both in life and in death was built.

EPILOGUE

THE Old Testament points beyond itself. The main stream of Judaism has always known this. Once Torah became the supreme authority for faith and conduct in the Jewish community after the exile, it was recognised that "The book of the Torah of Moses might be a final law, but it was not a finished law."[1] In Jewish theory, side by side with written Torah, there had existed from the time of Moses onwards a living oral tradition supplementing and explaining the written word, ensuring its continued relevance. It was the task of the later Rabbis to steep themselves in this tradition and to examine the meaning of Torah for the life of the Jewish community in each succeeding age. Judaism has survived into the present as the religion of a book, the religion of a people seeking to be truly obedient to the Torah of a God, a people waiting still in patient hope for the coming of the Messiah and the final fulfilment of God's purposes.

Within Judaism, however, there have always been groups which have adopted a more radical attitude to the Old Testament. The sectarian community of Qumran[2] claimed to be the people of the new covenant, a reform movement within Judaism separating itself physically and spiritually from the corruption of the world and contemporary Judaism, a community claiming a new obedience to the Torah of Moses. It took the prophetic literature of the Old Testament, for example the book of Habakkuk, and read therein references to contemporary events and to the life of the community. The day of fulfilment was at hand.

[1] G. F. Moore, *Judaism*, Vol. I, p. 30.
[2] F. M. Cross, *The Ancient Library of Qumran*. For the relation of this community to the New Testament, cf. M. Black, *The Scrolls and Christian Origins*.

Another Jewish sect made even more startling claims. Unlike the Qumran community, it sought not withdrawal from the world, but the evangelisation of the world. Its missionary message was steeped in the faith of the Old Testament. The true Messiah had come in Jesus of Nazareth. He had inaugurated the New Covenant. His followers were the new Israel upon whom God had poured out his spirit. In the life, death and resurrection triumph of Jesus, the Old Testament had come to its full fruition. For the Christian, therefore, the Old Testament should never be an alien or unimportant book. Abraham, Isaac and Jacob, Moses and the prophets are his own ancestors in the faith. He will see the story of the church, the people of God, beginning when Abraham journeyed forth in faith from Ur of the Chaldees. He will see in the story of God's deliverance of his people out of enslavement in Egypt the pattern of all God's gracious dealings with men which reach their climax in that greater deliverance offered in Jesus Christ. But, if he is wise, he will not regard the Old Testament merely as a preparation for the New. He will turn humbly to the Old Testament knowing that Hebrew historians and prophets, priests, poets and story-tellers have much to teach him. Their hard-won faith is, in its own right, one of the most significant contributions to the spiritual pilgrimage of mankind. Though dead, their words are still alive, able to challenge and stimulate, calling into question many of the accepted values by which we live, offering us a faith which stakes all on God, on his mighty acts and gracious purposes. No one can fail to be immeasurably enriched by walking in the company of this goodly fellowship.

BIBLIOGRAPHY

Background to the Old Testament
  J. B. Pritchard (ed.), *The Ancient Near East* (Oxford University Press, 1958)
  R. de Vaux, *Ancient Israel* (McGraw-Hill Book Co., 1961)
  H. H. Rowley, *The Modern Reader's Bible Atlas* (Association Press, 1961)

Archaeology and the Old Testament
  G. E. Wright, *Biblical Archaeology* (Westminster Press, 1957)
  J. Gray, *Archaeology and the Old Testament World* (Thomas Nelson & Sons, 1962)

History of Old Testament times
  M. Noth, *The History of Israel* (Harper & Bros., 1958)
  J. Bright, *A History of Israel* (Westminster Press, 1960)
  H. M. Orlinsky, *Ancient Israel* (Cornell University Press, 1960)

Introduction to the Literature of the Old Testament
  G. W. Anderson, *A Critical Introduction to the Old Testament* (Duckworth & Co., 1959)
  C. Kuhl, *The Old Testament, Its Origin and Composition* (John Knox Press, 1961)

The Faith of the Old Testament
  G. E. Wright, *God Who Acts* (Henry Regnery Co., 1952)
  W. Eichrodt, *Theology of the Old Testament* (Westminster Press, 1961)
  E. Jacob, *Theology of the Old Testament* (Harper & Bros., 1958)
  J. Muilenburg, *The Way of Israel* (Harper & Bros., 1962)

Useful commentaries for the non-specialist student are to be found in the *Layman's Bible* (John Knox Press) series and the *Torch* (The Macmillan Co.) series.

Wm. Neil's *Harper's Bible Commentary* (Harper & Bros., 1963) gives an excellent commentary survey of the thought of the Bible.

The new *Peake's Commentary* (ed. M. Black and H. H. Rowley, Thomas Nelson & Sons, 1962) gives an up-to-date survey of Old Testament scholarship both in its general articles and in the commentaries on individual books.

INDEX

Abraham, Blessing of, 94 f.
  Call of, 23 f., 37
  Covenant with, 41 f.
Adam, 197
Adapa myth, 198
Agag, 73
Ahab, 29, 53, 74 f., 85
Ahaz, 54, 219 ff.
Akhenaten, 132
Alexander the Great, 22
Amen-em-opet, 145 f.
Amenhotep IV, 132
Amos, 70, 76 f., 86 ff., 111 f., 223
Anat, 49
Ani, 145
Antiochus IV, 225
Apocalyptic, 225 ff.
Archaeology, 36 ff.
'asham, 109 f.
Asherah, 49, 53
'asiph, 116, 117 f.
Athirat, 49
Atonement, Day of, 119 f.
Azazel, 120
'azkarah, 106, 127

Baal, 49 ff.
  prophets of, 53, 84
  Melqart, 53
Baalism, 75 ff.
Babel, Tower of, 202 f.
Baruch, 158
berith, 40
Bildad, 168, 172

Cain and Abel, 203 f.
Canaan, Religion of, 49 ff, 75 f.
Canon, Growth of, 13 ff.
Chemosh, 32, 48
Commandments, 25, 42 ff.
Covenant, 40 ff., 58, 88 f., 101, 208 f.
  Ark of, 44, 83, 109 f.
  Book of, 61 ff., 66 f., 78
  Deuteronomic interpretation of, 45 f.,
    67 ff.
  New, 212 ff., 232
Creation, Babylonian account of, 52, 188,
  190
  Biblical account of, 52 f., 190 ff.
Cyrus, 22, 34, 96

Daniel, 225 ff.
David, 22, 74, 125, 129, 142, 218 f.
Death, 182 f., 200 f.
  in Apocalyptic thought, 228 ff.
Deborah, Song of, 50, 81 ff.
Decalogue, 42 ff., 59

Deliverance, 208
Deuteronomic Code, 67 ff.
Doubt and faith, 136 f., 147 ff., 157 ff.

Ecclesiastes, 179 ff.
Ecclesiasticus, 16, 20
Eden, Garden of, 187, 195 ff., 224
Edomites, 88, 98 f.
Egyptian deities, 55
El, 49, 55
Elephantine, 51
Elihu, 169, 176, 178 f.
Elijah, 29, 53, 74 f.
Eliphaz, 168, 171 ff.
Elisha, 85
Enuma Elish, 188, 190, 192
Esther, 99, 121
Exodus, 24 ff., 65, 115 f.
Ezekiel, 45, 97 f., 211, 216, 224
Ezra, 14 f., 98

Festivals, 113 ff.
Flood, Babylonian account of, 204 ff.
  Biblical account of, 204 ff.

Gilgamesh, Epic of, 104, 183 f., 198, 205 ff.
Gomer, 213 f.
goral, 121

haggim, 118
Hagiographa, 18 f.
Hammurabi, Code of, 61 ff.
hatta'th, 108 f., 119 f.
Henotheism, 47 f.
herem, 48, 73 f.
Herodotus, 31
hesedh, 134, 212 f.
Hezekiah, 30
  men of, 152
History, Hebrew interpretation of, 23 ff.
  35 f.
  Deuteronomic interpretation of, 27 ff.
Hittite treaty documents, 43, 64
Holiness Code, 69
Hosea, 51, 77 f., 90, 212 ff.

Immanuel, 220
Isaiah, of Jerusalem, 30, 70, 90, 111, 219 ff.
  Second, 34 f., 57, 91 ff., 96 f.

Jael, 82
Jamnia, Council of, 19
Jehoshaphat, 85
Jehovah, 17 n. 1

Jeremiah, 31 f., 60, 70, 90 f., 158 ff.,
   214 f., 221, 223
  Call of, 158 f.
  Confessions of, 158 ff.
  and Josiah's Reformation, 90, 214 f.
Jericho, 37 f., 83
Jeroboam I, 55 f.
Jewish exclusiveness, 98 f.
Job, 168 ff.
Jonah, 100 f.
Josephus, 12, 13
Joshua, 37, 58, 83
Josiah, 60, 67, 90
  Reformation of, 14, 54, 90
Judgement, 87 ff., 207
Justice, 78 f., 90

kabhodh, 57
kalil, 106
Kingship, 72
  Hebrew concept of, 74, 217 f.
  Egyptian concept of, 217 f.
  Mesopotamian concept of, 217
Koheleth, 180 ff.

Lament over the destruction of Ur, 33
Lamentations, 13, 32 f.
Law, 16 ff.
  apodictic, 64, 67
  case, 63, 67
  of Holiness, 69
  Book of the, 14 f.
  Codes in Ancient Near East, 59 f.
Lex talionis, 61, 109
Lot, 143

Maccabean revolt, 225 f.
Man, Disobedience of, 198 ff.
  Enigma of, 195 ff.
  In the image of God, 192 ff.
  Nature of, 197 f.
Manasseh, 54
Marcion, 11 f.
Marduk, 47, 52, 55, 192
mashal, 147
mashiah, 217 ff.
massoth, 116 f.
Messiah, 216 ff.
mezuzah, 80
Micah, 70, 77
Micaiah ben Imlah, 85 f.
minhah, 106
Miriam, 44
mishpat, 78, 93
Moabites, 48, 88
Moabite inscription, 29, 48
Moses, 16, 24, 44, 49, 69 f.
  Call of, 26 f.
Mot, 49
Myth, 187 ff.
  and Ritual, 189

nahhi', 84
Nathan, 74, 142
Nature, Hebrew conception of, 222 f.
  Renewal of, 222 ff.

Nehemiah, 19, 98 f.
New Year Festival, 128 f., 189
Noah, 104, 204 ff.

Obadiah, 98
'olah, 105 f.
Omri, 28 f.

Patriarchal narratives, critical assessment
  of, 36 f.
Passover, 24 n, 114 f.
Pentateuch, 15
pesah, 114 f.
Philistines, 21, 22 n, 72, 83, 109
Priest, Function of, 70 f., 102, 106
Prophet, Nature of, 29 f., 70 ff.
Prophetic call, 71
  attitude to sacrifice, 73, 110 ff.
Prophets, Former, 18
  Latter, 18
  Sons of, 84 f.
Proverbs, 145 ff.
Psalms, Headings of, 125
  as liturgical poetry, 126 ff.
  as reflecting Hebrew faith, 131 ff.
  Royal, 130 ff.
Ptah-hotep, 144
Purim, 99, 121 f.

qasir, 116, 117
qedheshoth, 77
Qumran, 231

Righteousness, 78 f.
Ritual, 103 f., 189
  Fertility, 77
ruah, 191 f., 210
Ruth, 99 f., 189

Sabbath, Origin of, 122
  Purpose of, 59, 122 ff.
Sacrifice, 103 f.
  as communion, 107 f.
  as a gift, 105 ff.
  as a means of forgiveness and restoration,
    108 f.
  prophetic attitude to, 110 ff.
saddiq, 79
Sage, 143
Samuel, 72 ff.
Sargon II, 30
Saul, 22, 72
sedhaqa, 78 f.
Seer, 72
Sennacherib, 30
Septuagint, 15, 20 f.
shabhu'oth, 117
shalom, 107, 130
Shamash, 63, 65
She'ol, 139, 229
Sisera, 82
Sodom, 143
Solomon, 22, 147
Song of Songs, 155 f.
Spirit of God, 191, 210 ff.

Suffering, problem of, 166 ff.
sukkoth, 118, 185
Syncretism, 50 ff.

Targums, 15
Tiamat, 52, 192
Torah, 16, 71, 141, 231

Ugarit, 49
Ugaritic texts, 49 ff., 60 f., 126 f., 146
Utnapishti, 198, 205 ff.

Wisdom, 142 ff., 149 f.
Worship, 103 ff., 125 ff.
Writings, 18 ff.

Yahweh, Day of, 86
    Dread of, 57 f.
    Exclusiveness of, 47 ff.
    Glory of, 56 f.
    Initiative of, 44 ff., 139 f.
    Kingship of, 44, 71, 89, 128 ff.
    Lord of History, 23 ff., 129, 228
    Meaning of name, 17, 26 f.
    Mystery of, 55 ff.
    Servant of, 91 ff., 164
    Spirit of, 84, 210 ff.
Yom Kippur, 119 ff.

zebhah, 107
Zedekiah, 221
Ziggurat, 188, 202
Ziusudra, 204
Zophar, 168, 173